Praise for the first edition of
The Trader's Guide to Key Economic Indicators
BY RICHARD YAMARONE

"Every stock and bond trader should keep this invaluable description of relevant economic indicators within easy reach."
—DAVID M. JONES, PhD

Chairman of the Board, Investors' Security Trust Company
Former Chief Economist, Aubrey G. Lanston

"Wall Street pros rely upon key economic indicators in their analysis and you should, too, if you wish to significantly increase your prospects of successful investing. Richard Yamarone has done a masterful job of describing technical economic concepts in plain English. This book will enable you to emulate the methods and successes of the pros, by instructing you as to which indicators are the most relevant and how to use them to make money in the financial markets."
—STAN RICHELSON

Coauthor, *Bonds: The Unbeaten Path to Secure Investment Growth*

"This book breaks down the often complex world of economics into an easy-to-understand guidebook for investors. Yamarone goes beyond the numbers, providing insight into what's important to financial markets and offering 'tricks from the trenches' you won't find anywhere else."
—RHONDA SCHAFFLER

Former Senior Correspondent/Anchor, CNNfn (1995–2005)

The Trader's Guide to

Key Economic Indicators

Also available from
Bloomberg Press

*Breakthroughs in Technical Analysis: New Thinking from the
World's Top Minds*
Edited by David Keller

*Flying on One Engine: The Bloomberg Book of
Master Market Economists*
Edited by Thomas R. Keene, CFA

Tom Dorsey's Trading Tips: A Playbook for Stock Market Success
by Thomas J. Dorsey and the DWA Analysts

Investing in Hedge Funds—Revised and Updated Edition
by Joseph G. Nicholas

Investing in REITs: Real Estate Investment Trusts (Third Edition)
by Ralph L. Block

*The Economist Guide to Economic Indicators:
Making Sense of Economics (Sixth Edition)*

———————————————

A complete list of our titles is available at
www.bloomberg.com/books

The Trader's Guide to Key Economic Indicators

Updated and Expanded Edition

RICHARD YAMARONE

BLOOMBERG PRESS

NEW YORK

First edition published 2004
Revised and Expanded Edition published 2007
5 7 9 10 8 6 4

Library of Congress Cataloging-in-Publication Data

Yamarone, Richard.
    The trader's guide to key economic indicators / Richard Yamarone. -- Updated and expanded ed.
        p. cm.
    Summary: "This book presents the twelve most important economic indicators, plus several others from fixed-income and commodity markets that have been added in this revised and expanded edition. These key indicators are among the most valuable of any analyst's or economist's tools for understanding and predicting what will happen in the markets"--Provided by publisher.
    Includes bibliographical references and index.
    ISBN 978-1-57660-301-7 (alk. paper)
1. Economic indicators--United States. 2. Investments--United States. I. Title.

HC106.83.Y35 2007
330.01'5195--dc22   2007036398

To Suzie,
Milton, Oskar, and Nash—felinus economicus

Contents

Acknowledgments

THIS PROJECT COULD never have been completed without the support and assistance of my wife, Suzie. She has helped in countless and immeasurable ways. Families play an integral role in dreams, aspirations, and accomplishments. My family has paved a clear path for any and every ambition that I could possibly have. They are indubitably responsible for all of my successes. My mother and father instilled in me the importance of education, hard work, freethinking, and discipline. For that I could never thank them enough. A special thanks goes to my brother, Robert, and to my in-laws, Richard and Nancy McCabe.

Educators can have a profound influence on one's life. My life, as well as this project, was no exception in the way of encouragement and wisdom disseminated by those in academia. Professors and mentors have helped, not only in the understanding of some of the roles that economic indicators and statistics assume, but as counselors to a not-so-quick-to-learn student. They include, but are not limited to, David W. Ring, William O'Dea, Robert Carson, and Thomas Gergel of the State University of New York at Oneonta. Professor Ring taught me to work hard, Professor Carson to look at each situation from alternative perspectives, and Professor Gergel to have a passion about whatever task I might take on. I practice these three lessons every day of my life.

The list of professional associates who have helped me with this project could easily take up the entire book, but some individual recognition is essential. In my eighteen-plus years of work experience on Wall Street, I have never been associated with a more professional outfit than Bloomberg News. To the scores of friends and acquaintances at the Bloomberg offices all around the world, thanks for all your help and input into this project. You are unaware of how helpful you have been. I especially wish to thank Vinny DelGiudice, Vince Golle, Yvette Fernandez, Monee Fields-White, Jackie Jozefek, and Al Yoon.

Undoubtedly the greatest gratitude with respect to the creation of this work has to go to my editors at Bloomberg Press, namely Kathleen Peterson, Chris Miles, Tracy Tait, and mostly, Betsy Ungar. Betsy's extraordinary talents transformed my muddled manuscript into a more readable and effective publication. I must extend my sincere gratitude to Sophia Efthimiatou and Dru-Ann Chuchran for ironing out the many wrinkles that I had penned in the later chapters, as well as several previously unnoticed errors in the first edition.

Many thanks to the analysts at Argus Research who help me each day with insight into their respective industries, particularly, Wendy Abramowitz, Robert Becker, Kevin Calabrese, Gary F. Hovis, Jim Kelleher, David Ritter, and Kevin Tynan—the best auto analyst on Wall Street. I must tip my hat in appreciation to John Eade, Argus Research's CEO and director of research, as well as the Dorsey family for the opportunity to work at the most prestigious research institution on Wall Street.

I would like to thank the new analysts at Argus Research that have come aboard for the writing of this updated and expanded edition: Bridget Adams, David Anthony, Suzanne Betts, Joseph Bonner, Ruth Chung, David E. Coleman, Rashid Dahodwala, Martha Freitag, Chris Graja, Paul Kleinschmidt, Maggie Liu, David Rewcastle, Bill Selesky, Erin Ashley Smith, John Staszak, Jackson Turner, Wendy Walker, and Phil Weiss.

And a very special thanks goes to Lakshman Achuthan and Anirvan Banerji from the Economic Cycle Research Institute (ECRI) in New York. They oversee some of the best economic indicators on the Street today.

Acknowledgment wouldn't be complete without special thanks to Charles Gilbert and Michele Johnson (Federal Reserve Board); Lynn Franco (the Conference Board); Richard Deitz (Federal Reserve Bank of New York); Guhan Venkatu (Federal Reserve Bank of Cleveland); Scott Scheleur (U.S. Census Bureau, Service Sector Statistics Division); Kristen Kioa (Institute for Supply Management); Jeannine Aversa and Marty Crutsinger (Associated Press); Garrett Bekker (Merrill Lynch); Steve Berman (U.S. Census Bureau); Barbara Hagenbaugh, Sue Kirchhoff (USA Today); Jason Hecht (Ramapo College); David Jozefek (UBS); Thomas Feeney (Shippensburg University); Jeffrey J. Junior (Aries Appraisal Group Inc.); and Joe Pregiato (Arbor & Ivy Photography).

Any errors or oversights that may exist in this book were not intentional and are not the fault of any of those individuals named above.

Introduction

INVESTING WITHOUT UNDERSTANDING the economy is like taking a trip without knowing anything about the climate of your destination or what season you'll be in when you get there. Just as inclement weather can wreak havoc with a vacation, putting hard-earned money into the stock or bond market when economic conditions are unfavorable or selling investments for the wrong reasons can destroy financial plans for a comfortable retirement, a new house, or a child's college education. This is as true today as it was when the first edition of this book was being written in late 2003.

No one understands this better than Wall Street investment banks, brokers, and research institutions. All have adopted a top-down approach to securities analysis that begins with a forecast of the general economic climate, including interest-rate projections, currency forecasts, and estimates of domestic and foreign economic growth. In this, they are following one of the precepts laid down by Benjamin Graham and David Dodd in their 1934 investors' bible, *Security Analysis*: "Economic forecasts provide essential underpinning for stock and bond market, industry, and company projections."

You don't need to manage millions or billions of dollars, however, to study economic conditions and plan your investment strategy accordingly. You can get much of the same information that Wall Street professionals use in their analyses from the business sections of the nation's newspapers, magazines, evening news programs, the Internet, and cable business channels.

Furthermore, you don't need a degree in economics or mathematics to interpret this information. In fact, many graduates of such programs at the nation's top universities find themselves entirely unprepared for the real world of finance.

This book attempts to bridge the wide gap between the some-times mind-numbing theories of textbook economics—the principles that are taught on college campuses—and the everyday world of Wall Street. It does so by focusing on a dozen economic indicators, plus several others from fixed-income and commodity markets that have been added in this revised and expanded edition. These key indicators are among the most valuable of any analyst's or economist's tools.

Over the past century, thousands of economic indicators have emerged, predicting everything from the demand for gasoline to the size of harvests. Some are more fun than functional, such as those claiming links between stock performance for the year and which football conference, the NFC or the AFC, wins the Super Bowl, or whether women's hemlines rise to midthigh or fall to mid-calf. Others indicators are more serious, solidly based in economic observations. These range from the arcane—such as the indicator connecting the production level of titanium dioxide, a constituent of pigments used in paints and plastics, with the demand for building materials—to the commonsensical. The price of copper, used in wiring and many other construction elements, for instance, has a clear relationship with the pace of housing activity. The same could be said of economic growth and railroad car loadings, shipping container production, wooden pallet shipments, and the manufacture of corrugated boxboard and packaging, all of which are connected with transporting freight or manufactured goods. Over time, economists have weeded out the least successful indicators, based on the most dubious relationships, to arrive at a core of about fifty consistently reliable ones that are must-haves in any analytical toolbox. The indicators covered in the first edition—and revisited in this new one—are among the most accurate at depicting economic relationships that can engender big swings in the financial markets.

After the first edition came out, I received close to a hundred inquiries about the omission of certain significant indicators. Many of my clients and other investors questioned the exclusion of the import price index, for example, or the absence of the consumer credit report. There are indeed thousands of indicators currently in use, some with exceptional track records of projecting economic conditions such as employment, inflation, manufacturing activity, and consumer spending. But including those would have taken us further from the primary goal of the book, which was to limit the list to a manageable number of key economic indicators that are most relevant to the Street.

Nonetheless, across the many inquiries one reoccurring and noteworthy theme presented itself: I had not included any market-determined indicators, which many investors felt were important components of their indicator tool sets. Most of the indicators presented in the first edition are constructed by U.S. government agencies such as the U.S. Department of Commerce's Census Bureau, the U.S. Department of Labor, and the Board of Governors of the Federal Reserve System, or are products of private organizations such as the Institute for Supply Management, the Conference Board, and the University of Michigan. Some reflect principally the current state of the economy. Others have excellent predictive powers, highlighting, for example, industries that might outperform, thus helping identify the likely path of economic activity. But many influential money managers, hedge fund participants, and proprietary traders rightfully raved about the usefulness of indicators that are determined by the markets themselves.

For this reason I felt that, in revising this book, it was important to include some of the more popular market-determined measures. They conveniently fit into two categories, fixed income and commodities, which we will examine in Chapters 13 and 14 respectively.

All the indicators brought up to date in this new edition still have one thing in common, however: In one way or another, they all relate to the business cycle. Understanding how they work will make the study of economics more palatable and can make the pursuit of investment gains more profitable.

THE BUSINESS CYCLE

The business cycle is one of the central concepts in modern economics. It was defined by celebrated economists Arthur Burns and Wesley Mitchell in their pioneering 1946 study, *Measuring Business Cycles*, written for the National Bureau of Economic Research (NBER), which today is the official arbiter of the U.S. business cycle. According to Burns and Mitchell, the business cycle is "a type of fluctuation found in the aggregate economic activity of nations that organize their work mainly in business enterprises: a cycle consists of expansions occurring at about the same time in many economic activities, followed by similarly general recessions, con-

Figure I.1   U.S. Business Cycle Durations

Business Cycle Reference Dates		Duration in Months			
Peak Quarterly dates are in parentheses	**Trough**	**Contraction** Peak to trough	**Expansion** Previous trough to this peak	**Cycle** Trough from previous trough	Peak from previous peak
	December 1854 (IV)	—	—	—	—
June 1857 (II)	December 1858 (IV)	18	30	48	—
October 1860 (III)	June 1861 (III)	8	22	30	40
April 1865 (I)	December 1867 (I)	*32*	*46*	*78*	*54*
June 1857(II)	December 1858 (IV)	18	30	48	—
October 1860(III)	June 1861 (III)	8	22	30	40
April 1865(I)	December 1867 (I)	32	46	78	54
June 1869(II)	December 1870 (IV)	18	18	36	50
October 1873(III)	March 1879 (I)	65	34	99	52
March 1882(I)	May 1885 (II)	38	36	74	101
March 1887(II)	April 1888 (I)	13	22	35	60
July 1890(III)	May 1891 (II)	10	27	37	40
January 1893(I)	June 1894 (II)	17	20	37	30
December 1895(IV)	June 1897 (II)	18	18	36	35
June 1899(III)	December 1900 (IV)	18	24	42	42
September 1902(IV)	August 1904 (III)	23	21	44	39
May 1907(II)	June 1908 (II)	13	33	46	56
January 1910(I)	January 1912 (IV)	24	19	43	32
January 1913(I)	December 1914 (IV)	23	12	35	36
August 1918(III)	March 1919 (I)	7	44	51	67
January 1920(I)	July 1921 (III)	18	10	28	17
May 1923(II)	July 1924 (III)	14	22	36	40
October 1926(III)	November 1927 (IV)	13	27	40	41
August 1929(III)	March 1933 (I)	43	21	64	34
May 1937(II)	June 1938 (II)	13	50	63	93
February 1945(I)	October 1945 (IV)	8	80	88	93
November 1948(IV)	October 1949 (IV)	11	37	48	45
July 1953(II)	May 1954 (II)	10	45	55	56
August 1957(III)	April 1958 (II)	8	39	47	49
April 1960(II)	February 1961 (I)	10	24	34	32
December 1969(IV)	November 1970 (IV)	11	106	117	116
November 1973(IV)	March 1975 (I)	16	36	52	47
January 1980(I)	July 1980 (III)	6	58	64	74
July 1981(III)	November 1982 (IV)	16	12	28	18
July 1990(III)	March 1991(I)	8	92	100	108
March 2001 (I)	November 2001 (IV)	8	120	128	128
Average, all cycles:					
1854-2001 (32 cycles)		17	38	55	56*
1854-1919 (16 cycles)		22	27	48	49**
1919-1945 (6 cycles)		18	35	53	53
1945-2001 (10 cycles)		10	57	67	67

* 31 cycles
** 15 cycles

Source: NBER

Figure I.2 GDP and Highlighted Recessions

Sources: U.S. Department of Commerce, Bureau of Economic Analysis; NBER

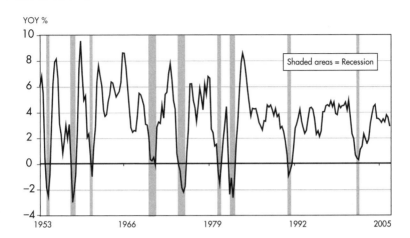

tractions, and revivals, which merge into the expansion phase of the next cycle."

No two business cycles are the same. As illustrated in **FIGURE I.1**, during the relatively short time that people have been measuring the U.S. economy, the length of expansions, from economic trough to peak, and of contractions, from peak to trough, have varied widely—although the former, especially recently, have generally been longer and steadier than the latter. Expansions have ranged from 120 months (April 1991 to March 2001) to 10 months (March 1919 to January 1920), and downturns from 43 months (September 1929 to March 1933) to 6 months (February 1980 to July 1980). The amplitude of the peaks and troughs has also differed significantly from cycle to cycle.

One way to think of the business cycle is as a graphical representation of the total economic activity of a country. Because the accepted benchmark for economic activity in the United States is currently gross domestic product (GDP), economists generally identify the business cycle with the alternating increases and declines in GDP. Rising GDP marks economic expansion; falling GDP, a contraction (see **FIGURE I.2**). That said, the business cycle, as defined by Burns and Mitchell, can't be fully captured by one indicator, not even the GDP. Rather, a compendium of indicators reflects various aspects of the economy.

Economic indicators are classified according to how they relate to the business cycle. Those that reflect the current state of the economy are *coincident*; those that predict future conditions are *leading*; and those that confirm that a turning occurred are *lagging*.

INDICATORS AND THE MARKETS

The organization responsible for an indicator generally distributes its report about an hour before the official release time to financial news outlets such as Bloomberg News, Dow Jones Newswires, Reuters, and CNBC. The reporters, who are literally locked in a room and not permitted to have contact with anyone outside, ask questions of agency officials and prepare headlines and analyses of the report contents. These stories are embargoed until the official release, at which time they are transmitted by the newswires to be dissected by the Wall Street community. Most Wall Street firms employ economists to provide live broadcasts of the numbers as they run across the newswires, together with interpretation and commentary regarding the likely market reaction. This task, known as the "hoot-and-holler" or tape reading, is among the most stressful performed by an economist. One slipup can cost a trader or an entire trading floor millions of dollars.

The more an indicator deviates from the Street's expectations, the greater its effect on the financial markets. A 0.1 percent decline in retail sales, for example, might not move the markets much if economists were looking for a flat reading or a 0.1 percent rise. But if the consensus were for an increase of 0.7 percent, and instead the 0.1 percent decline hit the tape, the markets might well be rocked. That said, it is always prudent for traders and other market participants to keep apprised of what the Street's expectations are for key economic indicators such as those covered here.

HOW TO USE THIS BOOK

You've no doubt read in a paper or heard on television or the radio forecasts of economic expansion or recession. You also probably realize that one is desirable and the other is not. But you may not know how the economists quoted came up with their predictions. Without this knowledge, how can you judge how well considered or rash they are—and whether to trust them in creating your investment strategy? This book seeks to help you form your own opinions about the possible direction of the economy and the markets and to decide how to act based on those opinions.

Each chapter corresponds to an indicator, beginning with the most comprehensive—the GDP and indexes of leading, lagging, and coincident indicators—and continuing with those tied to particular aspects or segments of the overall economy, such as consumer prices, manufacturing, housing, and retail sales. Every chapter contains four principal sections: an introduction sketching out the major attributes of the indicator and its effect on the markets; a discussion of its origins and development; a description of how the relevant data are obtained, analyzed, and presented; and an explanation of how to incorporate these data into your investment process. The last section also contains at least one "trick"—involving either a little-known subcomponent of the indicator or a combination of subcomponents—that Wall Street economists use to get a clearer or more timely picture of business activity. At the end of the book is a listing of additional reading and resources, organized by chapter, pointing those interested to references that discuss the relevant indicator in greater detail.

In putting what you learn from this book into practice, you might take some pointers from Wall Street. Just about every investment firm has a pre-market-opening meeting in which the day's events and potential trading strategies are presented. This always includes a discussion of the economic indicators scheduled for release that day. No trader wants to be caught off guard by an unexpected market-moving release. For the same reason, many traders have on their desks calendars showing which economic release is scheduled for a particular day and indicating both the value or percentage change of the previous report and the Street's estimates—highest, lowest, and consensus—for the upcoming report. That way, when the actual figure is released, they will know how it compares with expectations and can react accordingly.

Of course, no single economic indicator will tell you all you need to know about the current or future economic climate. Each has drawbacks and may send false signals because of unforeseen shocks, faulty measurements, or suspect collection processes. Piecing together the information from all the indicators discussed in this book like tiles in a mosaic will give you a dynamic representation of the economy. But if you are truly serious about understanding the macroeconomic climate and individual industry conditions, you should also take advantage of the Securities and Exchange Commission's fair-disclosure regulation, Regulation FD, which was adopted in 2000 and mandates that individual investors have the same access to companies' quarterly earnings conference calls that professional analysts have.

These calls provide a great deal of insight into corporate spending plans, manufacturing and production activity, international conditions, pricing, and the general business climate. Especially informative are the announcements of industrial behemoths such as Alcoa Inc., the Boeing Company, Caterpillar Inc., Cummins Inc., Emerson Electric Company, Ford Motor Company, General Electric Company, Illinois Tool Works Inc., Johnson Controls Inc., and United Technologies Corporation. Many companies also offer slide presentations, handouts, and supplemental data with these quarterly presentations, which often provide even greater detail on their buying intentions, prospective employment changes, and any threats to performance that they foresee. There's no cheaper and easier way to gather anecdotal evidence about business conditions. If you can't listen in, the presentations are almost always archived on company websites, from which they may be readily retrieved twenty-four hours a day.

WHO CAN BENEFIT FROM THIS BOOK?

This book was written primarily for those traders and investors lacking a formal introduction to the most popular economic indicators on Wall Street. Just because an individual is entrusted with investing millions of dollars does not guarantee a practical command of economic indicators and their meaning for investment. When newly minted MBAs arrive on the trading floors of financial firms, for example, few are equipped with a complete appreciation of these indicators—no matter from which institution that degree has come. My years of experience on a few of the largest trading floors in the world has suggested the need to fill what can be viewed as a surprisingly expansive void regarding indicators, statistics, the economic meaning of the associated figures, and the market's likely reaction.

Those new to the field of investing and economics, including students of the subject, also should benefit from the fundamental, application-oriented nature of this book. As most academics know, if students cannot see the results or directly test theories with practical data, the knowledge they hold tends to remain more theoretical than real-world and they may eventually lose interest in the field. It is here that many future economists are lost. As exercises within an imperfect "science," experiments conducted in the social discipline of economics are predominantly theorized or hypothesized and seldom tested with tangible data. In this sense, economists are not as fortunate as physicists or natural scientists, who conduct experiments in a controlled environment such as a laboratory, riverbed, or ocean. The economic indicators contained in these chapters serve as concrete guideposts within the discipline of economics, and as such make experimentation, testing, and study for investments not only possible but also understandable.

Gross Domestic Product 1

Economics has received a bad rap. In the mid-nineteenth century, the great Scottish historian Thomas Carlyle dubbed this discipline "the dismal science," and jokes about economists being more boring than accountants abound on Wall Street. But truth be told, there is nothing more exciting than watching the newswire on a trading floor of a money-center bank minutes ahead of the release of a major market-moving economic report. One of the top excitement generators is the report on gross domestic product (GDP)—an indicator that is a combination of economics and accounting.

Economists, policy makers, and politicians revere GDP above all other economic statistics because it is the broadest, most comprehensive barometer available of a country's overall economic condition. GDP is the sum of the market values of all final goods and services produced in a country (that is, domestically) during a specific period using that country's resources, regardless of the ownership of the resources. For example, all the automobiles made in the United States are included in GDP—even those manufactured in U.S. plants owned by Germany's BMW and Japan's Toyota. In contrast, gross national product (GNP) is the sum of the market values of all final goods and services produced by a country's permanent residents and firms regardless of their location—that is, whether the production occurs domestically or abroad—during a given period. Baked goods produced in Canada by U.S. conglomerate Sara Lee Corporation, for example, are included in U.S. GNP, but not U.S. GDP.

GDP is a more relevant measure of U.S. economic conditions than GNP, because the resources that are utilized in the production process are predominantly domestic. There are strong parallels between the GDP data and other U.S. economic indicators, such as industrial production and the Conference Board's index of coincident indicators (the coincident index), which will be explored in later chapters.

The GDP is calculated and reported on a quarterly basis as part of the national income and product accounts (NIPAs). The NIPAs, which were developed and are maintained today by the Commerce Department's Bureau of Economic Analysis (BEA), are the most comprehensive data available regarding U.S. national output, production, and the distribution of income. Each GDP report contains data on the following:

■ Personal income and consumption expenditures
■ Corporate profits
■ National income
■ Inflation

These data tell the story of how the economy performed—whether it expanded or contracted—during a specific period, usually the preceding quarter. By looking at changes in the GDP's components and subcomponents and comparing these with changes that have occurred in the past, economists can draw inferences about the direction the economy might take in the future.

Of all the tasks market economists perform, generating a forecast for overall economic performance as measured by the GDP data is the one to which they dedicate the most time. In fact, the latest report on GDP is within arm's reach of most Wall Street economists. Because several departments in a trading institution rely on the economist's forecasts, this indicator has emerged as the foundation for all research and trading activity and usually sets the tone of all of Wall Street's financial prognostications.

EVOLUTION OF AN INDICATOR

Measuring a nation's output and performance is known formally as national income accounting. This process was pioneered largely by Simon Kuznets, an economist hired by the U.S. Department of Commerce in the 1930s—with additional funding from the National Bureau of Economic Research—to create an accurate representation of how much the U.S. economy was producing. Up until that time, there was no government agency calculating this most critical of economic statistics.

The initial national income estimates produced by Kuznets in 1934 were representations of income produced, measures of the national economy's net product, and the national income "paid out," or the total compensation for the work performed in the production of net product. At that time, no in-depth breakdown of components existed. In fact, Kuznets didn't even have a detailed representation of national consumption expenditures. This was the first step of several in the creation of a formal method of national income accounting, and yet was still a far cry from today's highly detailed representation of the macroeconomy.

The result was the national income and product accounts. In addition to this immense task, Kuznets reconstructed the national income accounts of the United States back to 1869. (He was awarded a Nobel Prize in Economics in 1971 in part for this accomplishment.) Kuznets's first research report, presented to Congress in 1937, covered national income and output from 1929 through 1935.

In 1947, the first formal presentation of the national income accounts appeared as a supplement to the July issue of the *Survey of Current Business*. This supplement contained annual data from 1929 to 1946 disseminated in thirty-seven tables. These data were separated into six accounts:

1. National income and product account
2. Income and product account for the business sector
3. Government receipt/expenditure account
4. Foreign account

5. Personal income/expenditure account
6. Gross savings and investment account

Before the creation of the NIPAs, households, investors, government policy makers, corporations, and economists had little or no information about the complete macroeconomic picture. There were indexes regarding production of raw materials and commodities. There were statistics on prices and government spending. But a comprehensive representation of total economic activity wasn't available. In fact, the term *macroeconomy* didn't appear in print until 1939. Policy making without knowing the past performance of the economy, how it operated under different conditions and scenarios, or which sectors were weak and which were strong was a daunting task. This may have been the reason for many of the economic-policy failures of the early twentieth century.

Many economists have laid the blame for the Great Depression of the 1930s on the Federal Reserve Board's failure to respond to the ebullient activity during the Roaring Twenties (sound familiar?). The Fed may bear much of the responsibility; but very few, if any, have defended the Federal Reserve's failures on the grounds of insufficient information. The Great Depression forced the government to develop some sort of national accounting method. World War II furthered the government's need to understand the nation's capacity, the composition of its output, and the general economic state of affairs. How could the government possibly plan for war without an accurate appreciation of its resources? The NIPAs permit policy makers to formulate reasonable objectives such as higher economic growth rates or lower inflation rates, as well as to formulate policies to attain these objectives and steer the economy around any roadblocks that might impede the attainment of these goals.

DIGGING FOR THE DATA

Tracking the developments in an economy as large and dynamic as that of the United States is not easy. But through constant revision and upgrading, a relatively small group of dedicated economists at the BEA accomplishes this huge task every quarter. Each quarterly report of economic activity goes through three versions, all available on the BEA website, www.bea.gov. The first, the advance report, comes one month after the end of the quarter covered, hitting the newswires at 8:30 a.m. (ET). So, the GDP report pertaining to the first three months of the year is released sometime during the last week of April, the second quarter's advance report during the last week of July, the third quarter's in October, and the fourth quarter's during the last week of January of the following year. Because not all the data are available during this initial release, the BEA must estimate some series, particularly those involving inventories and foreign trade.

As new data become available, the BEA makes the necessary refinements, deriving a more accurate estimate for GDP. The second release, called the preliminary report, comes two months after the quarter covered—one month after the advance report—and reflects the refinements made to date. The last revision to the data is contained in the final report, which is released three months after the relevant quarter and a month after the preliminary report. The release dates for 2007 are shown in **FIGURE 1.1**.

Annual revisions are calculated during July of every year, based on data that become available to the BEA only on an annual basis, such as state and local government consumption expenditures. The BEA estimates these data on a quarterly basis via a judgmental trend based on annual surveys of state and local governments. Judgmental trends are quarterly interpolations of source data that are available only on an annual basis. Because the surveys are available on an annual basis, estimates can only be made during the annual revision.

Figure 1.1   2007 Release Schedule for GDP Reports

	2006: QIV	2007: QI	2007: QII	2007: QIII
Advance report	January 31	April 27	July 27	October 31
Preliminary report (1st revision)	February 28	May 31	August 30	November 29
Final report (2nd revision)	March 29	June 28	September 27	December 20

Source: U.S. Department of Commerce, Bureau of Economic Analysis

As source data for the components of the accounts are continuously updated and revised, the components of the NIPAs must be updated to reflect these revisions. That's the primary function of the annual revision. Each of the three years' (twelve quarters') worth of data is subject to revision during this annual updating. Every five years the BEA issues a so-called benchmark revision of all of the data in the NIPAs. This has typically resulted in considerable changes to the five years of quarterly figures.

Benchmark revisions are different from annual revisions in that they generally contain major overhauls to the structure of the report, definitional reclassifications, and new presentations of data. New tables need to be created to account for products that are developed. As the economy evolves, new goods and services come to market and therefore need to be accounted for. Obviously, there were times when CDs, microwave ovens, MP3 players, and DVDs didn't exist. Because the U.S. economy develops and produces these goods, there must be a place for this production to be recorded. All of the data—quarterly and annual—are revised during benchmark revisions.

SOME DEFINITIONS

As noted previously, GDP is the sum of the market values of all final goods and services produced by the resources (labor and property) of a country residing in that country. This definition contains two particularly important terms: *final* and *produced*. When economists refer to final goods, they mean those goods produced for their final intended use, that is, as end products, not as component or intermediate parts in another stage of manufacture. As an example, consider that each year, the Goodyear Tire & Rubber Company produces some hundred million tires. Most are produced for use on new vehicles. But there are still quite a number created for distribution in retail and wholesale stores as replacements and spares. Those tires produced and delivered to automakers intended for use on new automobiles are not counted as production, because we do not calculate the value of automobiles in the national accounts by summing the value of its components. In other words, we don't add the cost of the radio, the seats, the heating elements, the spark plugs, and so on. We count only the value of the final product, the automobile.

Obviously, the economists at the BEA would make a serious miscalculation if they counted all the tires sold by the manufacturer to Wal-Mart and Sears, as well as those sold by the automakers as part of their automobiles. The same holds true for the production of wool. BEA economists count only the wool purchased for final use. Because countless final uses exist for wool—sweaters, hats, blankets, and so on—the BEA would make the same double-counting error by adding the production of raw wool as well as the wool used in sweaters, blankets, and the like.

Let's consider the other important term, *produced*. Resales are not included in the accounts. Rightfully so, the BEA has determined that because the pace of reselling is not indicative of the current pace of production, it shouldn't be included in the output figures.

Another segment of the economy that the BEA excludes from the GDP release is the activity that goes on "off the books." This seems an obvious exclusion, but it's a big one. Believe it or not, some of the most conservative studies have set the size of the U.S. underground economy at around 10 percent of the official U.S. GDP, or what was roughly $1.3 trillion in the first quarter of 2007. The BEA doesn't count or make any adjustments for non-state-sanctioned gambling, prostitution, trade in illegal drugs, fraud, the production and sale of counterfeit merchandise, and the like, because, officially, they don't exist—wink, wink, nudge, nudge. These activities aren't reported, so how can they be measured? Clandestine activity like this can understandably alter the estimate of several economic indicators, but none more than GDP.

GDP VERSUS GNP

The NIPAs contain figures for both gross domestic product and gross national product. Before 1991, GNP was the benchmark for all economic activity in commentaries, reports, articles, and texts. GDP became the official barometer when the BEA decided

Figure 1.2   GNP Derived from GDP (QII 2006 Final Report)

U.S. GDP	$13,197.3 billion
plus income receipts from the rest of the world+	661.4 billion
minus income payments to the rest of the world–	638.6 billion
equals U.S. GNP=	$13,220.1 billion

Source: U.S. Department of Commerce, Bureau of Economic Analysis

that the measure was a better fit with the United Nations system of national accounts used by other nations, and so made international comparisons of economic growth easier.

GDP differs from GNP in what economists call "net factor income from foreign sources": the difference between the value of receipts from foreign sources and the payments made to foreign sources. The table in **FIGURE 1.2**, based on data from the final GDP report of the second quarter of 2006, illustrates how the BEA quantifies this relationship in its GDP report.

The difference between the value of GDP and GNP is typically minuscule, usually less than 0.5 percent. In **FIGURE 1.2**, for example, GDP is approximately $13.197 trillion and GNP $13.220 trillion, a difference of about $23 billion, or 0.17 percent of GNP.

CALCULATING GDP: THE AGGREGATE-EXPENDITURE APPROACH

Every transaction in an economy involves two parties, a buyer and a seller. To calculate total economic activity, economists can focus either on the buyers' actions, adding together all the expenditures on goods and services, or on the sellers' actions, tallying the total income received by those employed in the production process. These two approaches correspond to the two methods of calculating the GDP: the aggregate-expenditure method, which is the more popular and the one used on most Wall Street trading floors, and the income approach. The totals reached by both measures should theoretically be the same. In practice, however, there are small differences.

To calculate GDP, the BEA uses the aggregate-expenditure equation:

$$GDP = C + I + G + (X - M),$$

where C is personal consumption expenditures, I is gross private domestic investment, G is government consumption expenditures and gross investment, and $(X - M)$ is the net export value of goods and services (exports minus imports). The identity expressed in this equation is probably the most widely cited of all economic relationships and appears in virtually all introductory macroeconomic texts.

Because the U.S. economy is extremely dynamic and susceptible to sudden and unforeseen influences like inclement weather and war, the percentage of GDP contributed by each of the equation's components varies over time, even from quarter to quarter. For the most part, though, the proportions don't deviate significantly from those represented in **FIGURE** 1.3, which depicts the composition of second quarter 2006 GDP.

Personal consumption expenditures (also referred to as **consumer spending** or simply **spending**) are the largest component of GDP, accounting for roughly two-thirds of total economic output. During the second quarter of 2006, consumer spending climbed to approximately 70 percent of GDP ($9.228 trillion divided by $13.197 trillion).

Consumer spending is the total market value of household

Figure 1.3 Composition of GDP

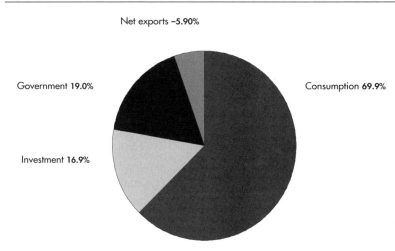

Source: U.S. Department of Commerce, Bureau of Economic Analysis

purchases during the accounting term, including items such as beer, telephone service, golf clubs, CDs, gasoline, musical instruments, and taxicab rides. As shown in the table in **FIGURE 1.4**, these items fall into three categories: durable goods, nondurable goods, and services. Durable goods are those with shelf lives of three or more years. Examples include automobiles, refrigerators, washing machines, televisions, and other big-ticket items such as jewelry, sporting equipment, and guns. Nondurable goods are food, clothing and shoes, energy products such as gasoline and fuel oil, and other items such as tobacco, cosmetics, prescription drugs, magazines, and sundries. Services include housing, household operation, transportation, medical care, and recreation, as well as hairstyling, dry cleaning, funeral services, legal services, and education.

Services constitute by far the largest category of consumer purchases. They account today for roughly 59 percent of all con-

Figure 1.4   Consumer Spending Breakdown

	2006: QII ($ in billions)	Percent of Total Spending
Consumer spending	$9,228.1	100.0%
Durable goods	1,061.8	11.5
Motor vehicles and parts	441.7	4.8
Furniture and household equipment	401.3	4.3
Other	218.8	2.4
		0.0
Nondurable goods	2,721.4	29.5
Food	1,274.0	13.8
Clothing and shoes	355.1	3.8
Gasoline, fuel oil, and other energy goods	359.1	3.9
Other	733.3	7.9
		0.0
Services	5,444.9	59.0
Housing	1,370.1	14.8
Household operation	499.1	5.4
Transportation	335.9	3.6
Medical care	1,578.2	17.1
Recreation	377.2	4.1
Other	1,284.3	13.9

Source: U.S. Department of Commerce, Bureau of Economic Analysis

sumer spending, up from a mere third in 1950. No wonder the United States is said to have a service-based economy. Spending on nondurable goods is the second-largest category of expenditures, representing about 29 percent of the total. Durable goods expenditures, the most volatile component, account for the remaining 12 percent.

A more detailed summary of personal consumption expenditures is available on a monthly basis in the BEA's Personal Income and Outlays report, which is the direct source of data for this component of the GDP report. Personal income and outlays are discussed in Chapter 11.

Gross private domestic investment encompasses spending by businesses (on equipment such as computers, on the construction of factories and production plants, and in mining operations); expenditures on residential housing and apartments; and inventories. Inventories, which consist of the goods businesses produce that remain unsold at the end of a period, are valued by the BEA at the prevailing market price. This value fluctuates greatly from quarter to quarter, making the level of gross private domestic investment quite volatile. Accordingly, economists often look at **fixed investment**—gross private domestic investment minus inventories. This, in turn, has two major components, **residential** and **nonresidential**. The latter, which is also referred to as **capital spending**, includes expenditures on computers and peripheral equipment, industrial equipment, software, and nonresidential buildings such as plants and factories. The former comprises spending on the construction of new houses and apartment buildings and on related equipment.

Even without the volatile influence of inventories, investment spending is prone to extreme movements, because most of this activity is linked to the ever-changing interest-rate environment. Gross private domestic investment usually accounts for 15 percent of GDP. During the second quarter of 2006, it represented 16.9 percent ($2.237 trillion divided by $13.197 trillion) of GDP.

Government consumption expenditures and gross investment covers all the money laid out by federal, state, and local governments for goods (both durable and nondurable) and services, for both military and nonmilitary purposes. The category includes spending on building and maintaining toll bridges, libraries, parks, highways, and federal office buildings; on compensation for government employees; on research and development, spare parts, food, clothing, ammunition; and on travel, rents, and utilities. Government expenditures and investment usually account for 20 percent of total GDP. During the second quarter of 2006, government consumption expenditures and gross investment accounted for about 19 percent of total economic activity ($2.514 trillion divided by $13.197 trillion).

Net exports of goods and services, the last component in the equation, is simply the difference between the dollar value of the goods and services the United States sends abroad (exports) and the dollar value of those it takes in across its borders (imports). Because the country generally imports more than it exports, this figure is usually negative, thus acting as a drag on economic growth. During the second quarter of 2006, net exports subtracted 5.9 percent from total economic activity (–$781.8 billion divided by $13.197 trillion).

NOMINAL AND REAL NUMBERS

The data reported in the GDP release are presented in two forms, nominal and real. **Nominal**, also known as **current-dollar**, GDP is the total value, at current prices, of all final goods and services produced during the reporting period. **Real**, or **constant-dollar**, GDP is the value of these goods and services using the prices in effect in a specified base year. Economists tend to prefer the real to the nominal measure. To understand why, consider a country that produces only two goods, pencils and vodka—a very interesting economy. If during Year 1, it sells two thousand pencils at $0.10 each and one thousand bottles of vodka at $5.00 a bottle (cheap vodka), its nominal GDP will be $5,200:

Pencils	2,000 × $0.10	=	$ 200
Vodka	1,000 × $5.00	=	$5,000
Nominal GDP			**$5,200**

Next year, the same country produces only a thousand pencils and five hundred bottles of vodka but doubles its selling prices, to $0.20 a pencil and $10.00 a bottle. Its nominal GDP is again $5,200:

Pencils	1,000 × $ 0.20	=	$ 200
Vodka	500 × $10.00	=	$5,000
Nominal GDP			**$5,200**

Is the economy larger during the second year? Did it produce the same amount? The difficulty in answering these questions illustrates the problem with nominal values. Economists have no way of telling whether it was the price or the quantity produced that increased, or by what magnitude. As more goods and services are considered, the problem gets bigger.

Real GDP is a more accurate indicator of changes in production. Referring to a base year eliminates the uncertainty of whether an increase in the value of the goods and services produced was the result of increased prices or of higher production. The table below shows how real GDP would be calculated in another country with two products—in this case, telescopes and hockey sticks.

To calculate Year 1 GDP, the quantities of the goods produced that year are multiplied by the prices at which they were sold and the results summed, to yield $6,000. For Year 2, instead of multiplying the quantities of goods produced by that year's prices—which would yield the nominal value—they are multiplied by their prices in the base year, Year 1. This yields a real, or inflation-adjusted, GDP of $7,650. According to this calculation, Year 2 GDP rose a real $1,650 over Year 1 GDP:

	Year 1	Year 2
Telescopes	10 × $100 = $1,000	14 × $125 = $1,400
Hockey sticks	200 × $25 = $5,000	250 × $27 = $6,250
Nominal GDP	**$6,000**	**$7,650**

Until 1996, the BEA used 1982 as the base year for calculating all real GDP estimates. Settling on one base year in this manner has the effect of imposing that year's price structure on subsequent periods and fixing the relative weights given the goods associated with these prices in the GDP calculation. The BEA found, however, that this **fixed-weight** approach introduced distortions: the farther away a period under study was from the chosen base year, the more inflated its real GDP growth rate tended to be. For example, Karl Whelan, an economist at the Federal Reserve Board, has observed in a working paper that the growth rate of fixed-weight real GDP in 1998 was 4.5 percent when calculated using a base year of 1995, 6.5 percent using 1990 prices, 18.8 percent using 1980 prices, and an incredible 37.4 percent when 1970 is the base year.

The BEA constantly refines its measures. (That's part of the reason the economic statistics in the United States are better and more accurate than those in any other developed nation.) In the mid-1990s, the bureau decided it was time to refine its weighting method and in late 1995, adopted chain weighting. The chain-weighting process is far too complex for this introduction, but in essence, rather than hold constant a basket of goods and services, as in the fixed-weight system, it holds the "utility" of the basket constant, allowing substitution of cheaper for more expensive items. Moreover, the base year is moved forward as the estimate progresses through time. The result is a series of links, or a "chain" of estimates that minimizes deviations.

The primary drawback of using chain-weighted (chained) data is the loss of additivity. In the fixed-weight calculation, total real GDP measured in 1996 dollars was equal to the sum of its components valued in 1996 dollars, and the value of each component was equal to the sum of the values of its subcomponents. As illustrated in **FIGURE 1.5**, this is not the case when chain weighting is used. Note that when the real chained components are summed, they do not add up to the actual real chained-dollar total consumption figure of $9,228.1 billion.

Figure 1.5   Second Quarter 2006 Consumption Expenditures ($ in billions)

	Nominal (current dollar)	Real chained dollar
Nondurable goods	$2,721.4	$2,351.1
Durable goods	1,061.8	1,190.3
Services	5,444.9	4,535.4
Total consumption	**$9,228.1**	**$8,055.0**

Source: U.S. Department of Commerce, Bureau of Economic Analysis

DEFLATORS

The difference between nominal GDP and real GDP is essentially inflation. It is thus possible to compute an economy's inflation rate from this difference. The result of the computation is called an implicit price deflator.

Every GDP report contains implicit price deflators for the headline GDP number and also for many of its subcomponents, such as consumption expenditures, government spending, and gross private domestic investment. Economists at the BEA calculate the GDP implicit price deflator using the formula

$$\text{implicit deflator} = (\text{nominal value}) \, / \, (\text{real value}) \times 100.$$

For example, using data from the 2003 first quarter GDP report, the GDP deflator for that period would be

$$\frac{\$10.698}{\$9.556} \times 100 = 111.95$$

The annualized inflation rate for a period can be derived using the formula

$$\frac{\text{annualized}}{\text{inflation}} = (\text{current-period deflator}/\text{previous-period deflator})^4 - 1.$$

To compute the annualized inflation rate for first quarter 2003, for example, the first quarter 2003 GDP deflator computed above and the fourth quarter 2002 deflator of 111.25 would be plugged into the formula, to give

$$\text{annualized inflation rate} = (111.95 / 111.25)^4 - 1$$
$$= (1.00629)^4 - 1$$
$$= 1.025398 - 1$$
$$= 0.025398, \text{ or approximately } 2.54\%.$$

A similar formula is used to calculate the annualized quarterly growth rate of GDP as a whole, as well as each of its components and subcomponents:

$$\text{annualized quarterly growth rate} = (\text{current quarter} / \text{previous quarter})^4 - 1$$

For example, to compute the fourth quarter 2002 growth rate, the third and fourth quarter 2002 GDP figures would be plugged into the formula, giving

$$\text{quarterly annualized growth rate} = (\text{QIV 2002 GDP} / \text{QIII 2002 GDP})^4 - 1$$
$$= (9{,}518.2 / 9{,}485.6)^4 - 1$$
$$= (1.00344)^4 - 1$$
$$= 1.013831165 - 1$$
$$= 0.013831165, \text{ or approximately } 1.38\%$$

NATIONAL INCOME

As noted earlier, economic activity has two sides—expenditures and income—which correspond to two different ways of calculating GDP. The discussion so far has involved expenditures. The income side of the GDP calculation is not as sexy as the expenditure approach because it doesn't identify the industries or products that are being created. Traders tend to pay less attention to the factors involved in national income, but it is equally important. Investors, particularly equity traders, like to see the quarterly performance of their respective investment industries. For example, those traders heavily invested in software stocks want to know how software investment fared during the particular quarter. The income-determined approach of GDP calculations does not provide this perspective.

The sum of the incomes generated in the course of production is termed **national income**. Its components fall into the following five categories:

1. Compensation of employees (wages and salaries, plus supplements)
2. Net interest
3. Proprietors' income
4. Rental income of persons
5. Corporate profits

FIGURE 1.6, from the BEA's second quarter 2006 report on GDP, identifies these components together with the percentage each contributes to total national income. Unlike expenditure-based GDP and its components, the income data are reported only in nominal terms—that is, they are valued only in current prices. They are also subjected to valuation adjustments.

Figure 1.6   National Income ($ in billions)

	2006:QII		Percent of Total Income
Compensation of employees	$7,533.2		64.28%
Wage and salary accruals		*6,081.2*	*51.89*
Supplements to wages and salaries		*1,452.0*	*12.39*
Proprietors' income with inventory valuation and capital consumption adjustments	1,011.9		8.63
Rental income of persons with capital consumption adjustment	71.4		0.61
Corporate profits with inventory valuation and capital consumption adjustments	1,591.8		13.58
Net interest and miscellaneous payments	513.2		4.38
Taxes on production and imports less subsidies	914.0		7.80
Business current transfer payments	93.1		0.79
Current surplus of government enterprises	−9.4		−0.08
National income	$11,719.3		100.00%

Source: U.S. Department of Commerce, Bureau of Economic Analysis

EMPLOYEE COMPENSATION

Employee compensation accounts for roughly 65 percent of national income. It comprises two parts. The largest is composed of wages and salaries, including commissions, tips, bonuses, and employee contributions to deferred-compensation plans such as 401(k)s. For the most part, the BEA estimates this component by multiplying employment in the Bureau of Labor Statistics' monthly Employment Situation report (described in Chapter 3) by earnings and the number of hours worked. The second component of compensation, accounting for approximately 12 percent of the total, is composed of "supplements," such as employer contributions for social and unemployment insurance.

Net interest is the interest that businesses, foreign corporations operating in the United States, life insurance companies, and several other related interest-disseminating sources pay out as part of the expense of operating, less the interest they receive. Interest payments on mortgages and on home-improvement and equity loans are considered business costs because the NIPAs treat home ownership as a business. The BEA gathers most of the data for the net-interest calculation from Internal Revenue Service (IRS) tax returns, the Federal Reserve Board, regulatory agency annual reports, and the Department of Agriculture.

OTHER INCOME CATEGORIES

Three other categories—proprietors' income, rental income, and corporate profits—are usually tweaked through the application of an inventory valuation adjustment (IVA) and a capital consumption adjustment (CCAdj). The IVA adjusts for the data discrepancies that occur because some businesses value their inventories at their historical cost (that is, the cost at the time of initial acquisition) rather than at their current replacement cost, which is the BEA's method. The CCAdj deals with the fact that the method businesses use to account for depreciation—the reduction in value throughout the measurement period of income, profits, inventories, and goods—differs from that of national income accountants (the BEA). Because businesses have several methods of inventory accounting, including the BEA's CCAdj, the BEA has adopted the CCAdj as a more consistent and uniform inventory and capital consumption adjustment system. The IVA and CCAdj are two reasons that the income and the expenditure computations of GDP aren't the same.

Proprietors' income comprises the earnings of nonincorporated businesses (sole proprietorships and partnerships). The dollar amount of this income is calculated using IRS business tax returns, with inventory valuation and capital consumption adjustments. The category accounts for about 9 percent of total income.

Rental income is composed of the rents earned from residential and nonresidential property by people not primarily engaged in the real estate business, plus royalties received from copyrights and patents.

The GDP report refers to several types of corporate profits. **Pretax profits**, also known as book profits, are what companies earn before paying taxes and distributing dividends to shareholders. Applying the IVA and CCAdj to this total results in **profits from current production**, termed **operating profits** in the business community. This is the corporate profits figure used in computing national income. Subtracting companies' tax liabilities from book profit gives **after-tax profits**. FIGURE 1.7, taken from the final GDP report of first quarter 2006, illustrates how the various corporate profit measures are related.

The corporate profits data are obtained from IRS tabulations, as well as from the Census Bureau's quarterly survey of corporate profits and publicly available corporate financial statements. Corporate profits account for approximately 10 percent of total national income.

Not every GDP report depicts corporate profits in the same detail as the table shown in Figure 1.7. Because corporate earnings reports are scattered throughout the quarter and IRS processing of corporate tax returns is rather lengthy, accurate tallies are only possible months after the end of the quarter. The most complete

Figure 1.7 Corporate Profits ($ in billions)

	2005:QII	2005:QIII	2005:QIV	2006:QI
Corporate profits with inventory valuation and capital consumption adjustments	$1,342.9	$1,266.3	$1,393.5	$1,569.1
Less: Taxes on corporate income	392.8	378.9	424.6	456.9
Equals: Profits after tax with inventory valuation and capital consumption adjustments	950.1	887.5	968.9	1,112.1
Net dividends	568.2	584.0	601.0	615.7
Undistributed profits with inventory valuation and capital consumption adjustments	381.9	303.5	367.9	496.4
Cash flow:				
Net cash flow with inventory valuation and capital consumption adjustments	1,209.8	1,230.7	1,223.9	1,349.2
Undistributed profits with inventory valuation and capital consumption adjustments	381.9	303.5	367.9	496.4
Consumption of fixed capital	827.9	927.2	856.0	852.8
Less: Inventory valuation adjustment	−21.0	−30.9	−39.2	−22.9
Equals: Net cash flow	$1,230.8	$1,261.5	$1,263.2	$1,372.1

Source: U.S. Department of Commerce, Bureau of Economic Analysis

presentation of corporate profits is usually provided in a year's final report of GDP.

GNP, GDP, AND NATIONAL INCOME

National income, as noted above, is the sum of all the incomes generated by the factors involved in production. This total does not equal the expenditure-determined GDP. To reach equality, several adjustments must be made. These adjustments are shown in **FIGURE 1.8**, which reproduces Table 9 of the second quarter 2006 GDP report.

One of the largest adjustments concerns the consumption of fixed capital. This is essentially the depreciation charge taken by private and government owners of fixed capital located in the United States, to account for the assets used up in the course of

Figure 1.8   Relation of GDP, GNP, and National Income ($ in billions)

	QII: 2006
Gross Domestic Product	**$13,197.3**
Plus: Income receipts from the rest of the world	661.4
Less: Income payments to the rest of the world	638.6
Equals: Gross national product	**13,220.1**
Less Consumption of fixed capital	1,572.8
Less: Statistical discrepancy	35.8
Equals: National income	**11,611.5**
Compensation of employees	7,425.5
Wage and salary accruals	5,980.9
Supplements to wages and salaries	1,444.5
Proprietors' income with inventory valuation and capital consumption adjustments	1,011.9
Rental income of persons with capital consumption adjustment	71.4
Corporate profits with inventory valuation and capital consumption adjustments	1,591.8
Net interest and miscellaneous payments	513.2
Taxes on production and imports less subsidies	914.0
Business current transfer payments	93.1
Current surplus of government enterprises	−9.4
Addendum: **Gross domestic income**	**$13,161.6**

Source: U.S. Department of Commerce, Bureau of Economic Analysis

production. The amount of the charge is estimated by the BEA from IRS business tax returns and studies of resale prices of used equipment and structures.

The next group of adjustments involves various income measures like proprietors' income with inventory valuation and capital consumption adjustments, rental income of persons with capital consumption adjustment, and corporate profits with inventory valuation and capital consumption adjustments. The BEA also adds taxes on production and imports less subsidies.

Another category consists of business current transfer payments—distributions that private (that is, nongovernmental) businesses make to individuals without any products changing hands or services being rendered. Two examples are charitable donations and liability payments made for personal injury. The BEA gets these data from IRS business tax returns, government agency reports, and other trade sources.

All these figures—for income, profits, taxes, and transfers—are added to national income. In contrast, the last category of adjustments, the current surplus of government enterprises, is subtracted. The subsidies referred to are the distributions that government agencies make to private businesses as well as to other levels of government, such as to the U.S. Postal Service.

After all these adjustments are made, gross domestic income should equal the gross domestic product. However, a difference, termed the **statistical discrepancy**, still remains—second quarter 2006 GDP, for instance, was $13.197 trillion and gross domestic income $13.162 trillion by the income-based calculation, a difference of $35.7 billion. This discrepancy reflects differences in the sources for data used in the two calculations. Those used in deriving national income are less directly observable, and so less reliable. As mentioned earlier, moreover, illicit expenditures are not reported or estimated.

This section of the chapter has described the multitude of figures included in the GDP report, how they are related to one another, and how they are derived. Next comes the nuts and bolts: how economists and traders use the report numbers in analyzing both big-picture issues, such as the future course of the business cycle, and smaller issues, such as when to put their money where.

WHAT DOES IT ALL MEAN?

The GDP report contains a wealth of information about the nation's economy. Each of its components tells a different story about a particular group, sector, industry, or activity. Not surprisingly, then, different market participants look at different sections and draw different inferences. Retail analysts, for instance, focus mostly on consumer spending. Those covering housing, construction, or real estate investment trusts (REITs) concentrate on the residential activity in investment spending. Defense-industry analysts focus on the national defense spending component of government consumption expenditures and gross investment. Fixed-income analysts and investors, ever wary of the eroding effects of inflation, concern themselves with the GDP deflators and GDP growth rate. Traders, who are always on the lookout for possible market movers, watch for numbers that contradict expectations, which they track carefully, often jotting them down in notebooks kept at their desks, for quick reference when the real figures are announced.

GDP GROWTH

The annualized quarterly growth rate of real GDP is the headline number of the GDP report. As with most economic figures, strong positive postings are generally good news for the economy, corporate profits, and stock valuations. Not so for bonds, however. Inflation erodes the value of fixed-income securities, and more torrid economic growth is usually associated with higher rates of inflation.

Market reactions—both positive and negative—are more pronounced when the announced numbers differ from the expected ones. The larger the difference, the greater the market move. Say the Street consensus for the third quarter was for an annualized GDP growth rate of 4.2 percent. On the one hand, a weak posting of between 1 and 2 percent would probably spark a sell-off in the stock market and boost the price of fixed-income securities, lowering yields. Stronger-than-expected growth of 5.5 to 6.5 percent, on the other hand, would be well received by equity traders and frowned upon by fixed-income dealers.

Although the annualized quarterly figure is important, many economists prefer to look at the year-over-year change in GDP. The longer perspective makes it easier to spot turning points in the economy, such as an approaching recession or an acceleration of activity. **FIGURE 1.9** illustrates this predictive effect.

Figure 1.9   Year-Over-Year Percent Change in Real and Nominal GDP

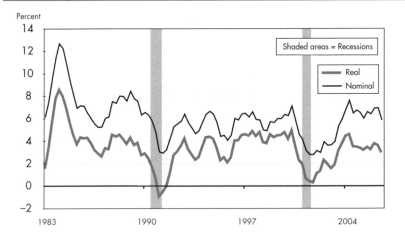

Sources: U.S. Department of Commerce, Bureau of Economic Analysis; National Bureau of Economic Research

As the chart shows, in the past twenty years the U.S. economy has experienced two recessions—in 1990–1991 and 2001—both of which were preceded by significant declines in the growth rates of real and nominal GDP. Note that although the real GDP growth rate falls below zero, the nominal rate declines but stays out of negative territory. This is because the nominal figure incorporates the effects of inflation, which is almost always rising. For the growth rate of nominal GDP to become negative, the inflation rate would have to be negative (reflecting a decline in prices)—a condition known as deflation—at the same time that the economy was contracting. Deflation is extremely rare in the United States and indeed has been recorded only a couple of times anywhere.

On average, the year-over-year growth rate in GDP starts declining four to five quarters before a recession. Not all slowdowns, however, result in recession. By the time the warning signals appear, government policy makers have usually put in place measures to avert an economic downturn. Still, watching changes in year-over-year GDP growth can be useful for short-term forecasts: very rarely do trends reverse immediately. It takes a great deal to knock a $13 trillion economy like that of the United States off kilter. Luckily for those in the financial markets, several "leading" indicators usually send alerts when the behemoth is running out of energy.

To form a clearer picture of the economy, economists like to look at several indicators at once. This helps reduce the transmission of false signals. There are times when some individual indicators trend lower, suggesting a potential decline in activity. If several indicators are observed, and a majority point to positive activity, then it is possible to dismiss the weaker performing indicators as outliers, and draw the conclusion that the economy isn't in trouble.

DEFLATORS

If GDP growth is the most important number in the release, the GDP deflators run a close second. As indicators of inflation, these deflators are preferred to the consumer price index (CPI), the producer price index (PPI), and other commodity price gauges by many traders and economists, including those at the Federal Reserve. Special favorites are the headline deflator, or implicit GDP deflator, the personal consumption expenditure deflator, and the personal consumption expenditures less food and energy deflator, also known as the core PCED deflator. The Street has adopted the last deflator as an unofficial benchmark for the core rate of inflation. Bond traders in particular watch the deflators, knowing that greater-than-expected increases in these numbers usually depress fixed-income prices.

Why have the deflators superseded the other inflation measures? For starters, policy makers, traders, and investors in general want to see overarching economic trends, not smaller, more targeted ones. GDP deflators reflect price activity in the broader economy. The consumer price index, in contrast, is merely a "basket" of a few hundred goods and services, chosen by the Bureau of Labor Statistics. (For a fuller explanation of price activity and the core rate of inflation, see Chapter 12.)

Traders focus on movements in the personal consumption expenditure excluding food and energy deflator, commonly referred to as the core PCED. This inflation measure is preferred to most of the others as it measures the core, excluding food and energy, rate of inflation that consumers face. Because prices of food and energy can fluctuate greatly during the month, economists like to view price trends without these noisy readings. Also, because private individuals are doing the overwhelming majority of the economy's consumption and this indicator contains all of the goods and services consumed, as opposed to a couple of hundred as in the case with the consumer price index, the core PCED has risen to the top of the list of most watched inflation gauges.

CONSUMPTION EXPENDITURES

As the consumer goes, so goes the U.S. economy. And this old saw may be more truthful than ever before. It is believed that the consumer's utter resilience to recent disruptions such as war, attacks against the United States on U.S. soil, widespread corporate malfeasance, eight of the top ten corporate bankruptcies in U.S. history, and presidential impeachment proceedings is the reason for the underlying strength of the economy. In previous decades, any single one of these disruptions likely would have upended the U.S. economy. Now it seems as though the consumer is capable of keeping the economy humming. It is the consumer that has prolonged expansion and made recessions shorter and milder.

Generally, a drop in the growth rate of consumer spending is a surefire sign that the economy is on the verge of petering out. When people are feeling uneasy about the economic climate—perhaps unemployment is on the rise, or inflation is eroding the dollar's purchasing power, or individuals are just feeling tapped out—it shows in their spending habits. As the chart in **FIGURE 1.10** shows, pronounced declines in the year-over-year growth in consumer expenditures have preceded each of the six recessions in the United States since 1963. Traditionally, the first retrenchment occurs in purchases of big-ticket items, such as durable goods. So it is in that portion of consumer spending where you'll find early warnings of economic downturns. (For a more detailed discussion of consumer spending and its trends, see Chapter 11.)

Figure 1.10   Personal Consumption Expenditures

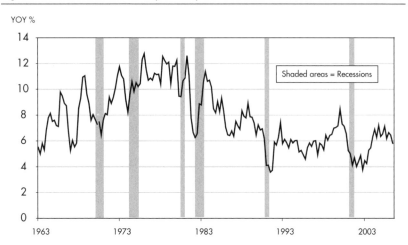

Sources: U.S. Department of Commerce, Bureau of Economic Analysis; National Bureau of Economic Research

INVESTMENT SPENDING

Capital equipment comprises all the industrial and technological items used to produce other goods and services for sale. The amount of money companies invest in this equipment is thus a good predictor of future economic activity. It indicates whether corporate profitability is accelerating or decelerating, how managers view future economic conditions, and how strong or weak the economy is.

As explained earlier, the Street tends to focus on fixed investment—gross domestic investment minus inventories. Of the two categories of fixed investment, residential and nonresidential (or capital spending), the former is by far the smaller, accounting for just 25 to 30 percent of the total. One shouldn't underestimate the influence of residential business investment, however. It represents roughly 5 percent of total economic output, and housing construction has a tremendous multiplier effect on the economy: once a house or apartment building has been built, personal consumption expenditures usually receive a big boost as owners head out to paint, decorate, and furnish their homes.

That said, analysts and economists tend to pay more attention to nonresidential investment. In part, this is because of the component's size—it accounts for almost three-quarters of total fixed investment. It also provides a great deal of insight into how the corporate sector views economic conditions. Finally, many equity traders, especially those active in the Nasdaq and on the lookout for the next Microsoft or Intel, are particularly interested in technology investment, which falls into the nonresidential category.

A certain amount of nonresidential fixed investment is always required, regardless of the overall state of the economy. Equipment and machinery, for example, constantly need to be refurbished, updated, and repaired. Every year the auto industry shuts down its plants for about two weeks to allow engineers to retool machinery for upcoming new car models. Weather, overuse, and just plain wear and tear cause capital equipment to break down. During booming periods of technological advances, some capital equipment becomes obsolete. Upgrades often help a business raise its level of productivity, which in turn helps the company's bottom line.

Rising capital spending is generally associated with periods of solid corporate profitability and economic prosperity. For businesses to invest in new capital equipment, they need sufficient profit growth. After all, they can't spend what they don't have. (Actually businesses can spend or invest by borrowing via issuance of bonds. But if the company doesn't have respected profit growth, then the ability to obtain the financing is hampered. With a poor financial history, companies are saddled with low credit ratings and are forced to pay higher returns for borrowing those needed funds.)

Management also needs to be positive about the economic outlook. If conditions are soft and consumer demand unpromising, they will be less inclined to purchase new machinery and equipment. If, however, the economy is expanding at a respectable pace, economic fundamentals are conducive to continuing growth (low interest rates, low inflation, firm labor market growth), and consumers are spending, then businesses will be more likely to pick up the pace of their investment.

Capital equipment is generally very costly—think of the specialized machinery on automakers' assembly lines, the ovens and packaging systems in food-processing plants, the industrial-size kilns of cement manufacturers. Companies thus usually need to borrow to purchase such equipment. So the amount of business investment is closely related to the level of interest rates: lower rates ease spending; higher rates make it more difficult. Accordingly, the Federal Reserve can influence capital spending by altering its target for the federal funds rate, the rate banks charge each other for overnight loans used to meet reserve requirements. If the Fed wants to spark capital spending, it lowers the overnight rate. Over time, yields on the entire maturity spectrum, from 3-month Treasury bills to the 10-year Treasury note, decline as well, making it less expensive for businesses to finance costly investments such as new plants, factories, and equipment.

When investors realize that interest rates may be headed lower, whether as a result of slower inflation rates or the Federal Reserve's influence, they know that businesses are likely to pick up the pace of investment, because the financing of those products and services is going to be cheaper. To capitalize on such developments, traders might bid up the prices of those stocks that have their primary business in investment-related concerns like technology, machinery, tools, or capital equipment. Some of the more common companies that are involved in capital equipment include Cummins Inc., Deere & Company, Paccar Inc., Briggs & Stratton Corporation, Danaher Corporation, Dover Corporation, Eaton Corporation, Illinois Tool Works Inc., Ingersoll-Rand Company Limited, Parker-Hannifin Corporation, the Timken Co., and Wolverine Tube Inc.

GOVERNMENT SPENDING

Wall Street doesn't generally pay much attention to government consumption expenditures and gross investment. One reason is that number's stability. Since 1947, government spending and investment has accounted for about 15 percent of total economic output. Only during periods of profound economic weakness or military conflict does the percentage rise, as the government picks up the pace of spending to boost economic growth or to support the war effort. In the post–World War II era, a peak of 24 percent was registered in 1953, at the end of the Korean War.

Within the government data, however, is one item to which some economists do pay attention, especially in recent times. That item is national defense spending. The long-term trend in national defense spending as a percentage of total government spending since the end of World War II has been consistently downward. Still, increases (in some instances, slight) have occurred when the government has ramped up purchases for military conflicts such as the Korean War in the early 1950s; Vietnam, in the mid-1960s to early 1970s; Desert Storm, in 1990; and most recently, the wars in Afghanistan and Iraq. Keep in mind that government spending on national defense isn't limited to the increased output of aircraft, electronic tracking devices, and missiles. Greater defense spending raises the level of employment—everything from engineering positions to manufacturing positions. And because of security reasons, those jobs tend to stay here in the United States and are not shipped abroad as so many of the other manufacturing positions have been in recent years.

Stock analysts responsible for the defense contractors and aerospace companies, such as Northrop Grumman Corporation, Raytheon Company, Lockheed Martin Corporation, General Dynamics Corporation, Curtiss-Wright Corporation, and the Boeing Company, find the detail on national defense expenditures in the report a treasure trove. The category is broken down into spending on aircraft, missiles, ships, vehicles, electronics and software, ammunition, petroleum, and compensation. If the government bought it, it will be recorded here.

NET EXPORTS

When the United States imports more than it exports—as has been the case for the better part of the past three decades—the net export balance is said to be in deficit. This reduces the level of GDP produced in a given period. Conversely, when exports outweigh imports, the trade balance is said to be in surplus. This results in an addition to economic activity. Such an outcome stands to reason, as U.S. export goods are produced by plants located in the United

Figure 1.11   Net Exports as a Percentage of GDP

Source: U.S. Department of Commerce, Bureau of Economic Analysis

States, whereas imports are produced by foreign workers and sent to the United States. **FIGURE 1.11** represents the value of net exports as a percentage of GDP. This percentage has been negative for a majority of the last thirty years, implying that the pace of imports is greater than that of exports, which reduces the level of domestic economic activity.

Imports needn't have a negative connotation, however. A number of resources are not as abundant in the United States as they are outside its borders. One obvious example is crude oil. The United States has domestic sources of oil but not enough to fuel its consumption. For that reason, it has to import about half its crude oil from foreign countries. Should we consider these imports disapprovingly? Probably not. The mere fact that the United States consumes so much crude is testament to its economic vitality. Its plants and factories need a great deal of oil to produce what is the largest output in the world, employing millions of people and creating an economic climate that permits its citizens to prosper like no others on Earth. Spending on imports to heat our homes, run our transportation system, and conduct business should not be considered a drag on prosperity but an enhancement.

As with government expenditures, the trading community has little reason to get excited about the net export balance. It's true that the business community frowns on widening trade deficits because increasing imports slow U.S. GDP growth. But rising imports also mean that U.S. businesses and households are consuming more goods and services that they deem attractive. Nobody forces consumers to purchase Italian wine, Japanese cars, or Canadian lumber. U.S. businesses and households purchase foreign-made goods for any number of reasons including, price, quality, size, and taste. The primary force behind demand for foreign-produced goods is simply desirability.

Furthermore, several foreign-produced goods tend to be cheaper. Because many countries in the world, particularly China, India, and several Asian-Pacific nations, have relatively low-cost labor, they are capable of producing goods at lower costs. These low-priced products are usually sent to the United States, which influences the prices of similar U.S.-produced goods. This globalization has led to a lower inflation rate here in the United States—especially since the mid 1990s.

Perhaps the major reason investors ignore the trade data is the data's minor influence on total economic activity. Over the past fifty-five years, the net export position has averaged a mere half a percentage point of total economic output.

FINAL SALES

Included in the addenda to Table 1 in the GDP report are three measures little noted by the financial media but closely scrutinized by the trading community because of the insights they provide into the underlying spending patterns in the GDP numbers. These three indicators are the final sales of domestic product, gross domestic purchases, and final sales to domestic purchasers.

Final sales of domestic product is a measure of the dollar value of goods produced in the United States in a particular period that are actually sold, rather than put into inventory. To calculate this figure, the BEA first computes "the change in private inventories" by comparing the current level of inventories with that of the previous period. This indicates how many goods have been added to businesses storage and thus how much of current production has remained unsold. This change in private inventories is then subtracted from GDP to give final sales. This is an important number, because it paints a more accurate picture than GDP of the current pace of spending in the economy. Economists say *current* pace because the quarterly figure excludes inventories that have been produced in previous quarters. Many times economists will compare the growth rates of GDP with those of final sales to determine whether economic growth is being driven by new production or by the consumption of goods that were previously produced and stored as inventories.

Gross domestic purchases measures all the goods U.S. residents have bought, no matter where the goods were produced. This figure is obtained by subtracting net exports from GDP. There is indeed a difference between GDP and gross domestic purchases. GDP is a measure of domestically produced goods and services, whereas gross domestic purchases is a measure of all the goods domestically purchased. Strong quarterly increases in gross domestic purchases generally imply solid demand by U.S. consumers, as only those purchases of domestic goods are calculated.

Final sales to domestic purchasers is the level of gross domestic purchases less the change in private inventories. It depicts the desire of Americans, both households and businesses, to spend, no matter where the goods or services are produced. Some economists consider it a good indicator of overall economic well-being. Slumping final sales to domestic purchasers suggests that U.S. consumers are tapped out.

Economists keep track of the year-over-year percentage change in final sales to domestic purchasers because of this measure's excellent record of foretelling periods of softer economic growth. As the chart in **FIGURE 1.12** illustrates, each of the four recessions since 1980 was preceded by about a three-quarter-long decline in the year-over-year growth rate of final sales to domestic purchasers.

Figure 1.12   Final Sales to Domestic Purchasers

Sources: U.S. Department of Commerce, Bureau of Economic Analysis; National Bureau of Economic Research

CORPORATE PROFITS

Market participants don't generally pay as much attention to the income side as to the expenditure side of GDP. That isn't to say the trends in wages and salaries aren't important to economists or to analysts who cover retail issues. What could be more telling about the future pace of spending, after all, than the amount of income earned by would-be consumers? It's just that the trends of the expenditure side are accepted as being more accurate, because they aren't subject to inventory and capital consumption value adjustments, as the income-determined data are. Still, some income-side components can give valuable insights into economic trends. Among the most important of these are the measures of corporate profits.

As with most of the other measures discussed, a rise in corporate profits indicates a healthy business climate. The economy's growth cycle really starts with a lift in corporate profits. When businesses are successful, their incomes exceed costs, and they make profits. This permits them to invest in new capital equipment or employees.

Even more significant than pretax earnings are after-tax profits. From this figure, economists and analysts can judge how much money companies actually have to spend on new equipment or additional staff. As the chart in **FIGURE 1.13** shows, businesses have generally shed workers when corporate profit growth contracts (below zero in the chart). The same holds true for business investment. After-tax corporate profits have generally declined approximately three quarters prior to periods of slowing economic growth or recessions.

The best measure of the funds that companies have available for spending and hiring, however, is the level of undistributed profits. Undistributed profits are a company's earnings after tax payments and dividend distributions. One striking feature of the chart in **FIGURE 1.14**, which shows the amount of undistributed profits in the last third of the twentieth century, is the paltry level of undistributed profits during the early 1970s, 1987, and 2002. All three periods were associated with tumbling stock prices, high unemployment rates, and lackluster business investment.

The economic signals associated with corporate profits might not be as telling as they once were. As was noted earlier, in recent years the U.S. economy has become practically impervious to a whole host of negative influences that, if they had occurred in previous periods, would have resulted in recession and in some

Figure 1.13   After-Tax Corporate Profits and Payroll Growth

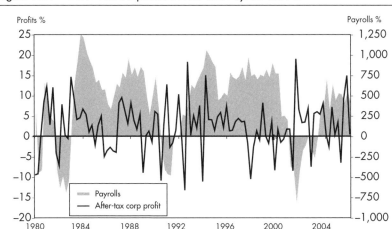

Sources: U.S. Department of Commerce, Bureau of Economic Analysis; U.S. Department of Labor, Bureau of Labor Statistics

Figure 1.14   Undistributed Profits

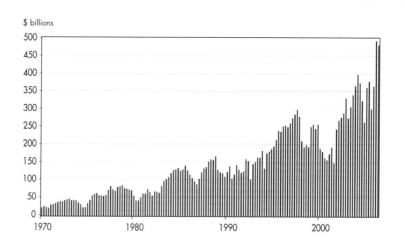

Source: U.S. Department of Commerce, Bureau of Economic Analysis

instances, quite possibly depression. Beginning in early 2001, the stock market bubble of the late 1990s burst, wiping out trillions of dollars in personal wealth. Widespread accounting scandals and egregious corporate impropriety also hammered investors' confidence, stalling the financial markets. For the first time in more than fifty years, the United States was attacked on its own soil, virtually paralyzing the economy. Hundreds of thousands of businesses closed for weeks, and the borders were sealed. Fear of anthrax attacks was widespread. As if all of this weren't enough, U.S. armed forces became engaged in military conflicts in Afghanistan and Iraq. Yet despite all these profoundly negative influences in a relatively short period, the economy managed to avoid a deep or prolonged recession. Perhaps the ultimate sign of resiliency is that consumer spending never fell.

HOW TO USE WHAT YOU SEE

There aren't as many tricks associated with the national income and product accounts as with other economic series. One reason may be that these accounts are the benchmark of economic activity, and traders use other indicators to anticipate movements in GDP. In other words, the level of GDP is usually the variable that other indicators attempt to forecast or emulate. GDP is also released on a quarterly basis, and the economic associations and relationships it points to aren't as predictive as those expressed on a monthly or weekly basis. That said, Wall Street economists and policy makers do have one particularly useful strategy that employs data from the GDP report: calculating the output gap.

TRICKS FROM THE TRENCHES

The output gap is the difference between the economy's actual and potential levels of production. This difference yields insight into important economic conditions, such as employment and inflation.

The economy's potential output is the amount of goods and services it would produce if it utilized all its resources. To determine this figure—the trend level—economists estimate the rate at which the economy can expand without sparking a rise in inflation. It is not an easy calculation, and it yields as many different answers as there are economists with different definitions for the maximum level of output, productivity, hours worked, and so on. Luckily, a widely accepted estimate of potential output is reported relatively frequently, about once a quarter, by the Congressional Budget Office (CBO). The CBO's website, www.cbo.gov, contains information about its methodology and underlying assumptions in computing the trend level, as well as a detailed historical data set.

A negative output gap exists when actual GDP growth is below its estimated potential. This suggests that the economy isn't utilizing all its labor and capital resources. Such periods of underutilization are usually characterized by high unemployment and low inflation, with plants and factories closing down, workers furloughed, and machinery idled. The chart in **FIGURE 1.15** shows that in 1990–1991 and 2001–2002, periods of profound economic weakness, the actual growth rate of real GDP was considerably below its potential.

When GDP growth exceeds its calculated potential, creating a positive gap, the economy is pushed to its limit. All plants and factories are running at capacity, the labor force is fully employed, and

Figure 1.15   GDP Versus Potential GDP

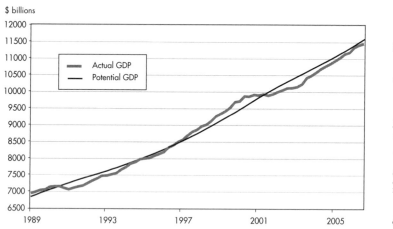

Sources: U.S. Department of Commerce, Bureau of Economic Analysis; Congressional Budget Office

economic output is skyrocketing. The chart in **FIGURE 1.16** illustrates the relationship between a positive gap and falling unemployment. In periods of overutilization, such as 1997–2001, strains on the system develop, usually sparking inflation.

Economists sometimes express the output gap in the form of a ratio derived by dividing the difference between actual output and potential output by potential output. When this ratio falls below zero, conditions are said to be soft, or sluggish; when it rises above zero, conditions are expansionary.

Because the output gap provides such telling economic insight into a whole host of economic relationships, it is a favorite of policy makers. The Federal Reserve, for example, considers it in determining where to set the federal funds rate. If the gap is negative, indicating that the economy is growing below its potential, the Fed may try to spark activity by lowering the overnight rate. This results in a decline all along the maturity spectrum, making it easier for companies to fund capital projects. It also spurs individuals' spending by rendering loans to purchase items such as automobiles and homes more affordable. Conversely, when the gap is positive, indicating that the economic party is getting a bit out of hand, the Fed may take away the punch bowl by increasing its overnight target

Figure 1.16   Output Gap and Unemployment (inverted scale)

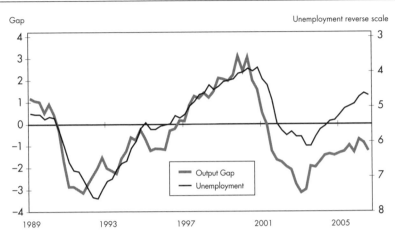

Sources: U.S. Department of Commerce, Bureau of Economic Analysis; Congressional Budget Office; U.S. Department of Labor, Bureau of Labor Statistics

Figure 1.17   Output Gap and Federal Funds Rate

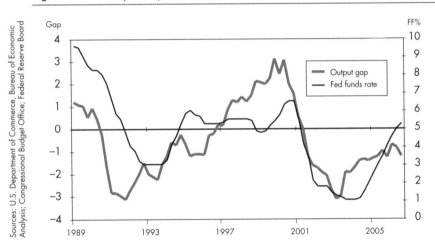

Sources: U.S. Department of Commerce, Bureau of Economic Analysis; Congressional Budget Office; Federal Reserve Board

rate, thus discouraging consumers and businesses from spending and investing. The chart in **FIGURE 1.17** illustrates the tendency of the federal funds rate to follow the output gap.

Indexes of Leading, Lagging, and Coincident Indicators 2

I F A MARKET ECONOMIST were given one wish, it might be for a single indicator that would consistently predict both the direction and the pace of the economy. Unfortunately, none has so far been discovered that fits the entire bill. Some indicators are wonderful at pinpointing levels of activity but fail to depict trends. Others excel at identifying particular areas of economic strength and weakness but can't measure broad-based performance.

Unable to find a single omnipotent indicator, economists have taken an assortment of those showing the most predictive accuracy and combined them into the index of leading economic indicators (LEI), or the leading index. This index is one of three composite indexes—along with the indexes of lagging and coincident indicators—that the Conference Board compiles and publishes in its monthly Business Cycle Indicators report. This report is usually released to the public at 10:00 a.m. (ET) four to five weeks after the end of the record month. It is available, together with historical data and explanations of the methodology behind the indexes, on the Conference Board's website, www.conference-board.org/economics/bci/, or by subscription for a small annual fee.

Wall Streeters often refer to the entire Business Cycle Indicators report as the index of leading indicators, because that's the part to which they pay the most attention. In actuality, the charts, commentary, and data provided on all three indexes are extremely useful in identifying and explaining the different phases of the business cycle. Whereas the leading economic index points to future trends and turning points, the coincident index identifies those that are

Figure 2.1 Timing of the Composite Indexes Relative to Cyclical Turning Points*

	Composite Leading Index	Composite Coincident Index	Composite Lagging Index
Leads (-) or lags (+) at business cycle peaks (months)			
Apr 1960	−11	0	3
Dec 1969	−8	−2	3
Nov 1973	−9	0	13
Jan 1980	−15	0	3
Jul 1981	−8	0	2
Jul 1990	−18	−1	−12
Mar 2001	−11	−6	−4
Leads (-) or Lags (+) at business cycle troughs (months)			
Feb 1961	−11	0	9
Nov 1970	−7	0	15
Mar 1975	−2	1	17
Jul 1980	−2	0	3
Nov 1982	−10	1	6
Mar 1991	−2	0	21
Nov 2001	−7	17	28

* Business cycle peaks and troughs are determined by the NBER.

Source: The Conference Board

in the process of developing, and the lagging index confirms that these events have indeed occurred. The table in **FIGURE 2.1** shows the number of months by which the three composite indicators led or lagged business cycle peaks or troughs, as defined by the National Bureau of Economic Research (NBER), from 1960 through 2001.

Because the components of the indexes are released earlier than the indexes themselves, the markets generally don't react strongly to the indicators report. Market participants, however, can still glean a great deal of information from the movements of the indexes and their components, not to mention the commentary and interpretation that the Conference Board's staff economists supply each month.

EVOLUTION OF AN INDICATOR

The concept of composite economic indicators is not new, nor did it originate with the Conference Board. In the early 1930s, economists Arthur Burns and Wesley Mitchell at the NBER were already combining economic data series to identify trends and turning points in the economy. NBER first published the results of these efforts in 1938. By the 1960s, the U.S. Department of Commerce was releasing monthly reports containing the NBER's leading, lagging, and coincident indicators. The Commerce Department–NBER collaboration lasted until 1995, when the Conference Board—a private, not-for-profit, nonadvocacy research and business-membership group—assumed the responsibilities of calculating, reporting, and maintaining the composite indexes.

The leading, lagging, and coincident indexes have all undergone considerable revision in the course of their history. As the structure of the U.S. economy has changed, newer indicators have periodically replaced older ones that no longer accurately reflect the business cycle or simply aren't calculated any more. As recently as November 1996, the Conference Board dropped two indicators— the price of sensitive materials and the volume of unfilled orders for manufactured durable goods—from the leading index and added a new one: the yield spread. This fine-tuning has kept the report an accurate tool for Wall Street economists and market participants.

DIGGING FOR THE DATA

The three indexes in the Conference Board's report are constructed from series of cyclical indicators, most of which are seasonally adjusted. Some of the components must be estimated; all are subject to later revision. The indexes themselves thus also need to be revised. The monthly release contains both initial values for the record month and revisions for the previous six months.

In constructing an index, the Conference Board calculates each component's month-over-month percentage change and then "standardizes" it—that is, adjusts it for volatility so that indicators with more dramatic month-to-month movements won't dominate the index. The standardized percentage changes for all the index's components are then added together. The sums derived for the leading and lagging indexes are adjusted again, so that their standard deviations equal that of the coincident index. Finally, the results for all three indexes are translated into levels representing changes from a base date, currently 1996, whose level is set at 100.

Because the composition of the three indexes is modified as the structure of the economy evolves, to remain in or be added to one of the indexes, a component must demonstrate consistency as a leading, coincident, or lagging indicator. It must also be the end product of a reliable data-collection process, adhere to a timely publication schedule, and be subject to only minor—or no—revisions.

COINCIDENT INDEX

The four components of the Conference Board's coincident index are the number of employees on nonagricultural (that is, nonfarm) payrolls (in thousands), personal income less transfer payments (nominal rate in billions of chained 2000 dollars), the industrial production index (2002 = 100), and manufacturing and retail trade sales (in millions of chained 2000 dollars).

The **number of employees on nonagricultural payrolls** is obtained from a survey of about 160,000 businesses conducted by the Bureau of Labor Statistics (BLS). The change in this number is one of the headline figures in the BLS's monthly Employment Situation report (see Chapter 3). The path followed by nonfarm payrolls has, in the main, paralleled that of growth in gross domestic product (GDP).

Personal income less transfer payments is derived from the Personal Income and Outlays report produced by the Bureau of Economic Analysis (BEA) (see Chapter 11). The largest income source is wages and salaries, which account for about 55 percent of the total; transfer payments—government disbursements such as

Social Security payments, veterans' benefits, and food stamps—usually constitute about 15 percent. Transfer payments are generally spent immediately on basic necessities, such as food or rent, not on durable goods and services. They thus have relatively little influence on macroeconomic activity. So income less transfer payments is generally considered a stronger, more representative economic indicator.

The **total industrial production index** is the headliner of the monthly Industrial Production and Capacity Utilization report published by the Federal Reserve Board (see Chapter 4). It is constructed of 295 components—representing the manufacturing, mining, and utilities industries—that are weighted according to the value they add during the production process. The index mirrors the general economy so closely that it is often used as a more timely proxy for the quarterly GDP report.

Manufacturing and retail trade sales data are collected as part of the national income and product accounts calculations. These data may be found in the Manufacturing and Trade Inventories and Sales (MTIS) report published by the Department of Commerce. (For additional information, see the discussion of the sales portion of the MTIS report in Chapter 7.)

LEADING INDEX

The ten components of the leading index are the following:
1. Average weekly hours worked in manufacturing
2. Average weekly initial claims for unemployment insurance
3. Manufacturers' new orders for consumer goods and materials
4. The slower deliveries diffusion index of vendor performance
5. Manufacturers' new orders for nondefense capital goods
6. Monthly building permits for new private housing
7. Stock prices
8. The M2 money supply (in chained 2000 dollars)
9. The interest-rate spread between the 10-year Treasury bond and the federal funds rate
10. The index of consumer expectations

The rationale behind including some of these indicators is clear from their names: new "orders" and "expectations," for instance, are obviously forward looking. The inclusion of others is less self-evident. All the components, however, were chosen because of their potency as *predictors* of economic activity.

The **average weekly hours worked in manufacturing** is derived from the same survey as the nonagricultural payroll figure described above and is also published in the BLS's Employment Situation report. Average weekly manufacturing hours constitute a good measure of future production levels and economic strength. Assuming workers maintain the same level of productivity, the more hours they put in on the job, the greater their output. When manufacturers foresee a softening in demand for their products, they tend to reduce workers' hours before cutting staff, which is more time consuming and expensive to implement. It is also easier and cheaper to extend hours, should business seem poised to pick up, than to hire new employees. Substantial changes in the average hours worked thus reflect companies' pessimism or optimism about future economic conditions.

The **average number of weekly initial claims for unemployment** reflects the condition of the labor market (see Chapter 3). A rise in claims, as businesses lay off more and more employees, usually occurs in the early stages of economic downturns and can thus point to a coming recession. The correlation between jobless claims and the economy is not precise, however, in part because unemployment statistics are distorted by the differing eligibility requirements imposed by different states.

Manufacturers' new orders for consumer goods and materials and for nondefense capital goods are excellent signs of how businesses regard the coming economic climate (see Chapter 6). Given the expenses involved in financing large purchases and in carrying inventory, wholesalers and retailers don't place orders for consumer goods unless they foresee a demand for these products. Similarly, companies don't invest in costly capital goods unless they believe they'll need the additional production capacity or efficiency created by such investments. Capital goods orders constitute a particularly powerful leading indicator, because business investment makes up approximately 15 percent of total GDP.

The **vendor performance diffusion index** is one of the five seasonally adjusted diffusion indexes that the Institute for Supply Management uses to construct the purchasing managers' index (PMI), the headline index of its monthly Manufacturing ISM Report on Business (see Chapter 5). The vendor index—which the ISM creates from responses to its survey of approximately four hundred purchasing managers across the United States—measures how long it takes suppliers to deliver parts and materials that are integral to the production process. Readings above 50 percent indicate slowing deliveries, usually a sign of increased demand and robust economic activity; readings below 50 percent indicate faster deliveries and economic stagnation.

Statistics concerning **building permits for new private housing** are contained in the New Residential Construction report, released jointly by the U.S. Department of Housing and Urban Development and the U.S. Department of Commerce's Census Bureau (see Chapter 8). These data present insights into an element of the U.S. economy that both is crucial to its growth and signals its general well-being. Although new housing construction accounts directly for only a small percentage of GDP, it drives other activity, such as purchases of paint, home furnishings, and countless other consumer durables. Moreover, because buying a house is a huge undertaking for most individuals, it implies confidence in the stability of employment and earnings, as well as sound economic fundamentals.

The **stock price** component of the leading index is the monthly average for the Standard & Poor's 500 index, published in the S&P publication *The Outlook*. Inclusion of this has been questioned by some economists, who argue that stock prices are determined by speculation rather than by economic fundamentals and so should not be considered accurate gauges of future economic activity. The rationale for including stock prices is that they reflect the informed expectations of sophisticated traders and investors. To get ahead of the curve, these knowledgeable market participants make their trades before earnings are actually announced. Rising equity prices thus indicate expectations of greater corporate profitability, which in turn implies an expanding economy: When businesses are more profitable, they are better able to invest in new projects, plants, and factories, and to hire additional workers. Falling prices, conversely, indicate that investors expect lower profitability, which in turn means a slower economy.

Money supply is simply the amount of money in the economy. The Federal Reserve recognizes three types of monetary aggregates, which it labels M1, M2, and M3. The leading economic index uses M2, which in addition to currency in circulation and deposits in savings and checking accounts includes money market fund shares and other liquid assets, such as overnight repurchase agreements issued by commercial banks.

Economists commonly refer to money as the oil in the engine of economic activity. So it makes sense that the growth rate of the money supply is related to the growth rate of the economy. The relationship that associates money with economic activity is called the "quantity theory of money," which may be summarized by the following expression:

$$M \times V = \text{nominal GDP},$$

where M is the money supply and V is the velocity of money—how often a dollar changes hands in a given period. Economists have assumed that velocity changes slowly, if at all, over time. Given this assumption, any increase in the money supply would be mirrored by an increase in nominal GDP. Conversely, a contraction in money supply would be reflected in a contracting economy. This relationship is illustrated in the chart in **FIGURE 2.2**.

Economists have discovered, however, that the velocity of money has not been constant. Without V as a constant, the equation of exchange breaks down. Historically, velocity levels have varied for a number of reasons, including new regulations and innovations in banking such as the advent of ATM machines, direct-deposit banking, and e-banking. Still, the relationship between money and economic activity enjoys a long, successful association, as evidenced in the associated chart, and is therefore included in the index of leading economic indicators.

Figure 2.2   Changes in Money Supply and in Real GDP

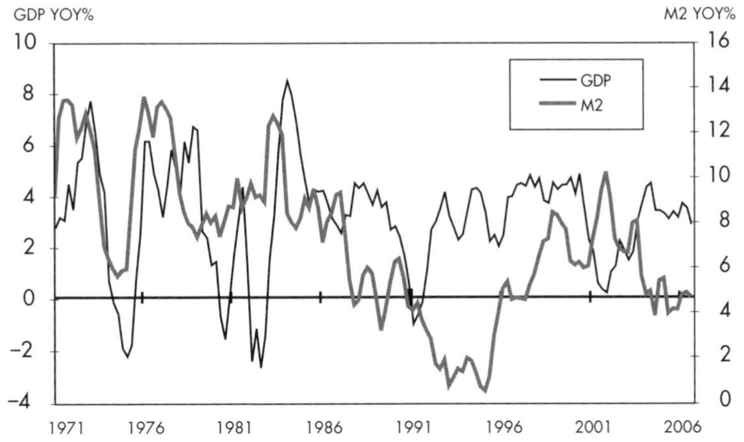

Sources: Federal Reserve Board; U.S. Department of Commerce, Bureau of Economic Analysis

GDP YOY%   M2 YOY%

| | GDP |
| | M2 |

1971   1976   1981   1986   1991   1996   2001   2006

The **interest-rate spread** component of the leading index is the difference between the yield on the 10-year Treasury note and the federal funds rate—the rate banks charge one another on overnight loans needed to meet reserve requirements set by the Federal Reserve. For instance, if the federal funds rate is 3.25 percent and the 10-year Treasury is yielding 5.35 percent, the spread is 2.10 percent, or 210 basis points (a basis point is one-hundredth of a percent). The interest-rate spread is included among the leading indicators because interest-rate spreads determine the shape of the yield curve and the shape of the yield curve embodies fixed-income traders' expectations about the economy.

The yield curve shows the relationship between the yield on U.S. Treasury securities and their maturities. Longer-term rates are usually higher than shorter-term rates, because more things can affect the value of the bond in ten years than in two and lenders require greater rewards for undertaking these greater risks. Thus, under "normal" economically favorable conditions, interest-rate spreads are positive, and the shape of the yield curve is gently convex—rising somewhat more steeply at the short end and leveling off a bit at the longer maturities.

Steep curves—large spreads—may temporarily be the result of current economic weakness. The Federal Reserve seeks to counter such weakness by reducing the overnight rate, thus lowering borrowing costs and encouraging business investment and consumer spending on interest rate–sensitive goods and services like housing and automobiles. This move stimulates the economy but can spark inflationary fears among the fixed-income community. Inflation erodes the value of future interest and principal payments. In anticipation, fixed-income investors sell off longer-term (more inflation-sensitive) bonds, depressing their prices and raising their yields. This, combined with the Fed's lowering of the short-term rate, steepens the yield curve. Conversely, when the economy seems to be running too hot, the Fed may seek to forestall a rise in inflation by raising its target overnight rate, discouraging spending and so slowing growth. The result is a flatter yield curve (smaller spreads).

The curve may also be inverted, with short-term rates higher than long-term rates and spreads below zero. This situation is generally associated with economic downturns, even recessions, as illustrated in **FIGURE 2.3**. The coincident index—which, because it reflects current economic conditions, may serve as a proxy for the

Figure 2.3　The Interest Rate Spread and the Coincident Index

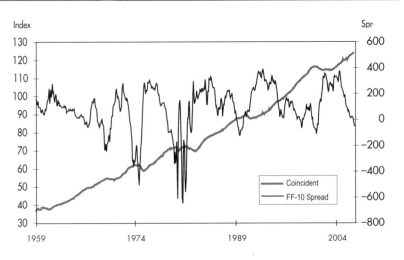

Sources: Federal Reserve Board; The Conference Board

business cycle—declines every time the spread between the federal funds rate and the 10-year Treasury becomes negative. This close correlation is one reason the Conference Board decided to include this gauge in its index of leading economic indicators.

Why does an inverted yield curve predict recessions? There is no definitive answer. Actually, one answer sometimes put forward is that an inverted curve may result from the Fed's overdoing it—raising rates so high they not only cool but stifle growth (as well as any fears of inflation). What is clear is that expectations of weak economic conditions may encourage expectations of lower interest rates. This in turn leads to more purchases of longer-term bonds, pushing up their prices and lowering their yields. The result is an inverted curve.

The **index of consumer expectations** is compiled monthly, along with the indexes of consumer sentiment and current economic conditions, by the University of Michigan's Survey Research Center, using responses to the university's Survey of Consumers. The survey asks consumers about their personal financial situations, overall economic conditions, and their buying attitudes, as well as various current issues and concerns. The index of consumer expectations summarizes the economic trends the respondents foresee.

Including this index among the leading indicators is a no-brainer. Consumer expectations about the economy are shaped mainly by consumers' experiences in the workplace. High confidence springs from expanding employment, increased production schedules, and rising wages, and thus points to a positive economic climate. It also helps foster that climate by encouraging spending, one of the major contributors to GDP. On the other hand, consumers are among the first to sense worsening economic conditions, reflected in slowdowns at their workplaces, and to retrench. This generally depresses the economy further. Not surprisingly, then, the index of consumer expectations has a good record of predicting turning points in both consumer spending and total economic activity.

LAGGING INDEX

The lagging index has the following seven components:
1. Average duration of unemployment
2. Ratio of manufacturing and trade inventories to sales
3. Manufacturing labor cost per unit of output
4. Average prime rate
5. Commercial and industrial loans outstanding
6. Ratio of consumer installment credit to personal income
7. Change in the consumer price index for services

The **average duration of unemployment** is the average number of weeks that people are out of work (see Chapter 3). As this number rises, so does consumer frustration, which depresses spending and holds back economic growth. Decreases in the length of unemployment traditionally occur after a recovery is already under way. This is generally a function of businesses' reluctance to take on new workers until they are absolutely assured of recovery. Similarly, the steepest increases in the average duration of unemployment generally take place after a downturn has begun. That is why this is a lagging indicator.

The **ratio of manufacturing and trade inventories to sales** is calculated by the U.S. Department of Commerce's Census Bureau, using data from its Manufacturers' Shipments, Inventories, and Orders (M3) survey (see Chapter 6) and its Monthly Wholesale Trade Survey. The results are published in the Commerce Department's Manufacturing and Trade Inventories and Sales (MTIS) report (see Chapter 7). The ratio indicates how many months, given the current pace of sales, it will take for inventories to be entirely liquidated. A rising ratio means that businesses are unable to effect a steady reduction in their back stock, either because sales are too weak or because their inventories are accumulating too fast. In either case, this is a sign of economic weakness. A falling ratio, conversely, indicates that companies' shelves are emptying and that manufacturers may soon have to increase production to replenish their disappearing stocks—a bullish economic signal. Although economists watch the

ratio for insight into future production activity, it is a lagging economic indicator. That's because, historically, inventories rise long
after sales growth has halted. So the ratio reaches its peak in the
middle of a recession.

The percentage change in **manufacturing labor cost per unit
of output** is measured by an index constructed by the Conference
Board from sources including the BEA's seasonally adjusted data on
manufacturing employees' compensation and the Federal Reserve
Board's data on manufacturing production. The index rises when
manufacturers' labor costs increase faster than their output. Because
monthly index movements are erratic, the percentage change used
is measured over a six-month period. Peaks in the six-month rate of
change are typically reached during recessions.

Data on the average monthly **prime rate** are compiled by the
Fed. As the interest rate that banks charge their most creditworthy customers, such as blue-chip companies, the prime rate
serves as a benchmark for loans to lesser credits. For instance,
a smaller, younger company might have to pay two percentage
points over prime. Because the prime rate moves with respect
to changes in the federal funds overnight rate, periods of rising prime rates are usually the result of rate hikes instituted by
the Federal Reserve in response to a potential overheating in the
economy and possible mounting inflationary pressures. Falling
prime rates are usually the result of the Fed's reductions in the
overnight target rate, which are designed to stimulate economic
activity. Banks tend to change the prime rate only after movements occur in the general economy.

The value of **outstanding commercial and industrial loans** is
computed by the Fed and adjusted for inflation by the Conference
Board. High commercial and industrial loan levels indicate that businesses have a favorable economic outlook and that they are willing
to build and expand their operations and finance such growth with
borrowed monies. Conversely, when the outlook is less encouraging
and businesses are skeptical, loan growth is weaker. It tends to reach
a peak after an expansion reaches its high-water mark and to bottom
out more than a year after the end of a recession.

The **ratio of consumer installment credit to personal income** is computed using data from the Fed's monthly release detailing the amount of currently outstanding consumer credit as well as from the BEA's monthly Personal Income and Outlays report (see Chapter 11). Consumer credit is not included in the BEA income figure, but for many Americans it is a critical income supplement. In times of financial insecurity, such as those that occur during downturns and recessions, people tend to reduce their personal borrowing and don't pick up the pace again until a trend of increasing income is firmly established. Accordingly, this ratio generally reaches its nadir a year or more after the end of a recession.

The **change in the consumer price index for services** measures the movement in the services component of the consumer price index, which is calculated monthly by the BLS (see Chapter 12). The month-to-month change in the consumer price index is the most popular measure of inflation. Service-sector inflation tends to increase after a recession has already begun and decrease even after it has ended. These tendencies result from what has been termed "recognition lags" and other such rigidities in the market.

WHAT DOES IT ALL MEAN?

The Conference Board's function in creating, refining, and maintaining the leading, lagging, and coincident indexes, which are presented monthly in its Business Cycle Indicators report, shouldn't be confused with what the National Bureau of Economic Research does. The NBER is the official arbiter of peaks and troughs in the business cycle. In pinpointing the dates of these crucial turning points, the bureau's economists consider many factors and consult several indicators, including, but not limited to, components of the coincident index. The Conference Board's Business Cycle Indicators report does not determine the official peaks and troughs of the U.S. economy. However, the turning points these indicators signal are remarkably similar to those the NBER designates.

COINCIDENT INDEX

The coincident index is rarely mentioned in the business press. Still, it is very useful for assessing the current pace of economic activity. As the table in Figure 2.1 demonstrates, the coincident index closely tracks the turning points in the business cycles. It can thus serve as a benchmark in assessing the relationship of any economic statistic to the business cycle. One of the most commonly used representatives of this cycle is the GDP. A simple linear regression between the growth rates of real GDP and the coincident index yields an impressive correlation of around 86 percent. This close correlation, illustrated in **FIGURE 2.4**, makes the coincident index a useful and more timely proxy for the quarterly GDP.

The individual indicators composing the leading index differ considerably in their abilities to predict economic turning points. Some are very farsighted, others relatively nearsighted. The composite index combines these components in such a way that the whole outperforms any of its parts. The predictive accuracy of the composite is illustrated in **FIGURE 2.5**, which charts the quarterly year-over-year percentage change in the leading index against real GDP.

The chart clearly shows that hikes and dips in the leading index precede those in the economy by significant periods. According

Figure 2.4   Index of Coincident Economic Indicators and Real GDP

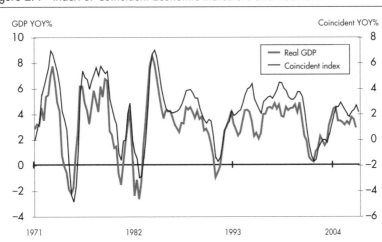

Sources: U.S. Department of Commerce, Bureau of Economic Analysis; The Conference Board

Figure 2.5   Index of Leading Economic Indicators and Real GDP

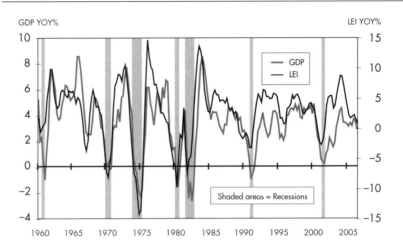

Sources: The Conference Board; U.S. Department of Commerce, Bureau of Economic Analysis; National Bureau of Economic Research

to the latest research, the index's average lead time is roughly nine months. The individual periods composing this average, however, vary considerably. This is in part because of the revisions that the index's components undergo, necessitating commensurate revisions in the composite. It also reflects the fact that every recession and every recovery is caused by different sets of circumstances. The ability of the leading index to foresee these turning points therefore also varies.

LAGGING INDEX

The lagging index follows downturns in the business cycle (as represented by the coincident index) by about three months and expansions by about fifteen. At first blush, this may seem to be pretty useless information—like driving a car by looking through the rearview mirror. Economists, however, argue that you can't know where you're going if you don't know where you've been. The index of lagging economic indicators confirms that turning points in economic activity that were identified by the leading and coincident indexes actually have occurred. It thus helps prevent the transmission of false signals.

HOW TO USE WHAT YOU SEE

Market participants don't generally pay a great deal of attention to the Conference Board's Business Cycle Indicators report because they've already had a chance to view and process for themselves the underlying data. Nevertheless, economists and businesses have traditionally looked for longer-term trends in the leading index to predict turning points in the economy.

The old rule of thumb was that three consecutive monthly declines in the index signaled a recession within a year, whereas three consecutive increases signaled a recovery. This rule was roughly accurate. It did predict several recessions that failed to materialize, however, and in the case of some correct calls, the lead times were negative—that is, the predictions came after the recession was already established. A reason for false recession predictions could be that although the index contains components representing the manufacturing, consumer, financial, employment, and business investment sectors, it has none that reflect demand for, or investment and employment in, the services industries that now dominate the economy. Moreover, the financial sectors that are represented often move in ways that don't parallel movement in the broader economy, generating both volatility and some of the false signals mentioned.

The leading index's record of predicting, as a popular quip has it, "seven of the last five recessions" has led some cynics to term it the index of misleading indicators. That's not really fair. Still, to improve its predictive accuracy, economists often consider the index's moves in three dimensions—duration, depth, and diffusion—instead of just one, duration, as the three-month rule did. That is, in addition to requiring that changes extend over three months, the refined method looks at how large changes are and how many components are involved. For example, if nine of the index's ten components show increases, but one—say average weekly hours worked in manufacturing—falls, an expansion is more certain than if only four components increase, three decrease, and three are unchanged.

TRICKS FROM THE TRENCHES

Wall Streeters, being innovators, have sought ways to improve even on the three-dimensional analysis. Their trick, with respect to the Business Cycle Indicators report, is to compute the ratio of the coincident index to the lagging index. The theory behind this ratio, informally referred to as the coincident-to-lagging ratio, is this: In the early stages of a recovery, coincident indicators are rising while lagging indicators, reflecting the conditions of earlier months, remain unchanged, resulting in a rising ratio. When an expansion is peaking, both sets of indicators will be rising, but the rate of increase for the coincident indicators will be slower, so the ratio will fall. Similarly, near the nadir of a recession, all the component indicators will again be moving in the same direction—this time, down—but the coincident indicators will fall more slowly, so the ratio will rise.

As you can see from the chart in **FIGURE 2.6**, the coincident-to-lagging ratio, like the leading index, has declined before every recession since 1959. But it has transmitted fewer false signals. One explanation for this relative success is that the coincident and lagging indexes do a better job of representing current and past economic performance, respectively, than the leading index does of assessing future activity.

Figure 2.6   Coincident-to-Lagging Ratio and Recessions*

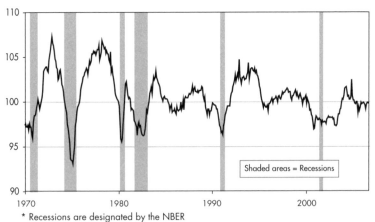

Sources: The Conference Board, National Bureau of Economic Research

* Recessions are designated by the NBER

The Employment Situation   3

THE MOST IMPORTANT economic indicator by far is the monthly Employment Situation report published by the Bureau of Labor Statistics (BLS). No economic release can move stocks and bonds like employment data, and no indicator is more revealing of general economic conditions than labor-market data. This is why the first Friday of every month, when the Employment Situation report is released, is the most important trading session of the month.

The fixed-income market often moves violently, in a matter of seconds, after the employment report is released. The Dow Jones Industrial Average has on occasion opened up or down from the previous day's close by a couple hundred points (stocks begin trading an hour after the report's release). The employment report is so crucial to financial-market participants that dealers, brokers, and economists plan their vacations around its release. Many traders can "make their month" (that is, earn a month's salary in a single trading session) on the day the report is released. People have actually been fired for missing the 8:30 a.m. (ET) release.

Employment data are important because they reveal how businesses and others responsible for hiring decisions view the current and upcoming economic environment. Companies will not shoulder the expenses involved in adding to their payrolls if they believe they won't need the extra workers in the near future. Similarly, they will be reluctant to dismiss workers if they foresee increasing demand for their wares. From the household perspective, nothing is more important than employment status. It is said that consumers can be expected to cut spending when faced with higher prices or declining wealth. Truth be told, consumers will indeed continue to spend despite higher prices and lower portfolio values. But nothing erodes consumer confidence and subsequently stops a consumer from spending like the loss of a job. Because consumer expenditures account for about 70 percent of economic activity, every economist, trader, and investor should know the current condition of the labor market.

The monthly employment report is based on two separate surveys: the Current Population Survey (CPS), also known as the household survey, and the Current Employment Statistics survey (CES), referred to as the establishment, or payrolls, survey. The household data are aggregated and disseminated in the "A" tables found in the first half of the report; the establishment survey information is presented in the "B" tables. Wall Street tends to pay more attention to the B tables than to the A tables.

The commissioner of the Bureau of Labor Statistics also provides a statement to the Joint Economic Committee of the U.S. Congress, as a supplement to each release. The statement, generally three pages long, highlights significant strengths and weaknesses in the month's employment statistics.

The employment report contains several headliners, but top billing is generally shared by two figures: the unemployment rate and the monthly change in nonfarm payrolls. Average hourly earnings, hours worked, overtime hours worked, and the monthly change in manufacturing jobs also command a great deal of Wall Street's attention. Unlike many other economic releases, the Employment Situation report takes a great deal of time to digest.

When unexpected increases in the unemployment rate occur, equity investors generally sell off stocks. The same occurs when nonfarm payrolls decline by a particularly large amount—usually in the vicinity of 150,000 or more. Because employment determines income and spending, and consumer spending accounts for the largest portion of economic activity, traders like to see solid employment growth. When the unemployment rate declines and jobs are being created, stock prices tend to rise.

Things are different in the fixed-income market, which is sensitive to inflation threats. Increasing nonfarm payrolls and a falling unemployment rate spark inflation fears, which can cause a sell-off in bonds, depressing prices and raising yields.

EVOLUTION OF AN INDICATOR

Like many of the most respected economic indicators, the Employment Situation report was born in the 1930s, during the Great Depression. The BLS had conducted the first monthly studies of employment and payrolls in 1915, but these covered only four manufacturing industries. By 1932, ninety-one manufacturing and fifteen nonmanufacturing industries were participating in the surveys. The deepening economic crisis of the early 1930s led the Hoover administration to expand the BLS program to include working hours and earnings series. Statistics on average weekly hours and hourly earnings were published for the first time in 1933. At the same time that this program was proceeding nationally, another was being rolled out on the state level. In 1915, New York and Wisconsin entered into agreements with the BLS to provide the agency with state employment data. This pact grew to embrace all the states in the union plus the District of Columbia and today, Puerto Rico and the Virgin Islands. The state and national efforts evolved into the Current Employment Statistics Survey, the source for Table B data in the employment report.

The Current Population Survey, the source for Table A, started as a program of the Work Projects Administration (WPA), which in 1940 initiated a national survey of households called the Monthly Report of Unemployment. Responsibility for the survey was transferred to the Census Bureau in late 1942, and a few years later its name was changed to the Current Population Survey. In 1959, the Bureau of Labor Statistics, within the Census Bureau, took over the job.

Both surveys have undergone refinements in sampling and reporting techniques, incorporating advances in computer-aided data-gathering and voice-recognition technologies. The result is that today we have a timely, accurate, and comprehensive indicator of labor-market conditions, reported from both the employees' and the employers' perspective.

DIGGING FOR THE DATA

In its employment surveys, the BLS includes only persons older than sixteen. That seems logical, because most U.S. states have compulsory education for youths through sixteen years of age, and several states prohibit the employment of minors in many jobs. Also excluded from surveys are people in mental or penal institutions and members of the armed forces.

The monthly employment report includes figures for one-month, three-month, six-month, and twelve-month periods. To understand the significance of these figures, you need to know what is denoted by terms such as *employed* and *unemployed*. The meanings may seem obvious, but the BLS uses these and related words in quite precise senses, developed through years of debate and experience.

People qualify as employed in two ways. First are those who, during a given period, have worked as paid employees in someone else's company or in their own businesses or on their own farms, or have done fifteen hours or more of unpaid labor in a family-operated enterprise. Second are those with jobs or in businesses from which they have taken temporary leave, paid or unpaid, because of illness, bad weather, vacation, child care problems, labor disputes, maternity or paternity leave, or other family or personal obligations.

Unemployed people are those not working during the period in question, whether because they voluntarily terminated their employment, in which case they are classified as *job leavers*, or because they were involuntarily laid off, making them *job losers*. Although the report doesn't make this distinction, economists identify several types of unemployment. *Seasonal unemployment* results from short-term cyclical changes in the labor market; examples include the January layoffs of retail staff who were added to take care of the Christmas shopping rush, and the winter furloughs of construction and landscaping workers in regions where harsh weather makes such activity virtually impossible. *Frictional unemployment* refers to the situation of workers in the process of changing occupations who are temporarily between jobs. *Structural unemployment* is the result of economic restructuring caused by new technologies or other innovations, such as when the invention of the automobile put buggy-whip makers out of a job. Finally, *cyclical unemployment*, the most relevant type for Wall Street economists, occurs when jobs are eliminated as part of the business cycle because of declining demand and the consequent drop in production.

To be included among the unemployed, a person must have made an effort to find work. Those who have given up looking, believing their skills, qualifications, or geographic area preclude finding a job, are regarded as *discouraged workers*. Increasing numbers of discouraged workers usually signal a weak economy.

Discouraged workers and others who don't fit into either the employed or unemployed groups are classified as "not in the labor force." The percentage of the employable population that *is* in the labor force is known as the **labor force participation rate**. This rate is generally in the mid-60 percent range. The **employment-population ratio** is the percentage of employed persons in the total population. It is usually lower than the participation rate.

HOUSEHOLD SURVEY (A TABLES)

Officially called the Current Population Survey, the household survey contains the responses of a sample of about 60,000 households to questions about work and job searches. It is generally conducted during the week containing the nineteenth day of the month. This is known as the **survey week**. It addresses employment conditions during the week containing the twelfth of the month, which is known as the **reference week**. The statistics gathered are compiled and presented in the following tables:

- ■ **Table A.** Major indicators of labor market activity, seasonally adjusted
- ■ **Table A-1.** Employment status of the civilian population by sex and age

- **Table A-2.** Employment status of the civilian population by race, sex, and age
- **Table A-3.** Employment status of the Hispanic or Latino population by sex and age
- **Table A-4.** Employment status of the civilian population twenty-five years and over by educational attainment
- **Table A-5.** Employed persons by class of worker and part-time status
- **Table A-6.** Selected employment indicators
- **Table A-7.** Selected unemployment indicators, seasonally adjusted
- **Table A-8.** Unemployed persons by reason for unemployment
- **Table A-9.** Unemployed persons by duration of unemployment
- **Table A-10.** Employed and unemployed persons by occupation, not seasonally adjusted
- **Table A-11.** Unemployed persons by industry and class of worker, not seasonally adjusted
- **Table A-12.** Alternative measures of labor underutilization
- **Table A-13.** Persons not in the labor force and multiple jobholders by sex, not seasonally adjusted

The nation's civilian unemployment rate is calculated by dividing the number of unemployed workers by the civilian labor force, the figures for which are listed in the household survey. In November 2006, for example, the unemployment rate was computed to be 4.5 percent: 6.817 million unemployed divided by the 152.381 million-person labor force.

ESTABLISHMENT SURVEY (B TABLES)

The establishment survey is based on a sample of about 160,000 businesses comprising some 400,000 individual work sites. Like the household survey, it is conducted with respect to a reference week, in this case the pay period containing the twelfth day of the month. The data are organized in the following tables:

- **Table B-1.** Employees on nonfarm payrolls by industry sector and selected industry detail
- **Table B-2.** Average weekly hours of production or nonsupervisory workers on private nonfarm payrolls by industry sector and selected industry detail
- **Table B-3.** Average hourly and weekly earnings of production or nonsupervisory workers on private nonfarm payrolls by industry sector and selected industry detail
- **Table B-4.** Average hourly earnings of production or nonsupervisory workers on private nonfarm payrolls by industry sector and selected industry detail, seasonally adjusted
- **Table B-5.** Indexes of aggregate weekly hours of production or nonsupervisory workers on private nonfarm payrolls by industry sector and selected industry detail
- **Table B-6.** Indexes of aggregate weekly payrolls of production or nonsupervisory workers on private nonfarm payrolls by industry sector and selected industry detail
- **Table B-7.** Diffusion indexes of employment change

Nonfarm payrolls fall into two categories: goods-producing and goods-providing. The goods-producing category includes manufacturing jobs, which account for 64 percent of the category total; construction jobs, accounting for 33 percent; and jobs in natural resources and mining, accounting for 3 percent. The majority of manufacturing positions are in the production of transportation equipment, mostly motor vehicles. Other big manufacturing sectors are food, fabricated metal products, computer and electronic products, machinery, and chemicals. The majority of construction jobs are with specialty trade contractors, such as tradesmen engaged in practices like drywall and insulation, framing, roofing, siding, electrical, masonry, and painting.

Over the past six decades, the U.S. economy has changed from one based on manufacturing, with a heavily unionized labor force, to one dominated by service industries. Service jobs, which fall in the goods-providing category, currently make up about 81 percent of total nonfarm payrolls, compared with 56 percent during World War II. Service payrolls are grouped into the following categories:

■ Government
■ Education and health services
■ Professional and business services
■ Retail trade
■ Leisure and hospitality
■ Finance, insurance, and real estate (FIRE)
■ Transportation and warehousing
■ Information
■ Other

Economists pay particular attention to the growth rate of total private payrolls, that is, the number of employees on nonfarm and nongovernmental payrolls. During periods of subpar economic growth, economists ideally wish to see widespread growth in payrolls across several industries. If job creation is limited to the government sector, it may be a signal that private industry does not have much confidence in the economic environment and may not be willing to hire new workers.

As shown by the chart in **FIGURE 3.1**, the level of employment deduced from the household survey is different from, and generally higher than, that gleaned from the establishment survey. This is largely because of the differences between their methodologies, pools of respondents, sample sizes, and reference periods. That said, the trends in employment revealed by the two surveys are largely the same.

The data obtained in the establishment survey are used in constructing the Personal Income and Outlays report (aggregate earnings), the Industrial Production and Capacity Utilization report (aggregate hours in manufacturing, mining, and public utilities), the Conference Board's indexes of leading and coincident economic indicators (average weekly hours in manufacturing and employment, respectively), and the quarterly productivity measures (aggregate hours). This survey attracts considerable attention from the investment community and the business media. Because the data come directly from corporations and firms, economists tend

Figure 3.1   Employment Levels per Household Survey Versus Establishment Survey

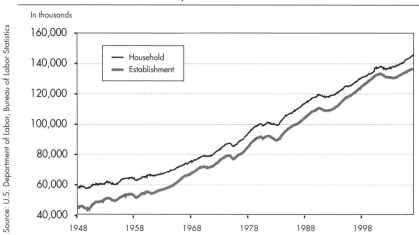

Source: U.S. Department of Labor, Bureau of Labor Statistics

to trust these figures more than the household statistics that are gathered via subjective, and less scientific, telephone interviews.

WHAT DOES IT ALL MEAN?

No indicator is as telling about the economic state of affairs, on as timely a basis, as the BLS's monthly Employment Situation report. It is the first comprehensive report of the month that presents both business and household perspectives on the most important of all economic measures: employment.

Strong relationships exist between the employment data and virtually every other economic indicator. The growth rate of nonfarm payrolls, for instance, is strongly correlated with the growth rate of GDP, industrial production and capacity utilization, consumer confidence, spending, income—even with Federal Reserve activity. If it's relevant to economic activity, it will have links with the payrolls data.

EMPLOYMENT, UNEMPLOYMENT, AND THE BUSINESS CYCLE

The ties between employment and the business cycle are extremely close. As **FIGURE 3.2** illustrates, the quarterly change in

Figure 3.2   Nonfarm Payroll Growth and Real GDP

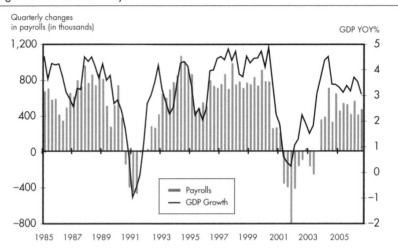

nonfarm payrolls has, in the main, hewed closely to the path of quarterly GDP growth. This association is very useful for those monitoring economic growth. The GDP report is released quarterly, with a one-month delay. The employment report is monthly. So those needing a timely read on the economy can infer its growth rate from the payrolls data.

One corollary of employment's intimate relationship with GDP growth is the coincidence of declining payrolls and recession. **FIGURE 3.3** shows that since 1960, there has never been an instance when three consecutive monthly reductions in nonfarm payrolls haven't been accompanied by an economic downturn. Conversely, each of the last ten post–World War II recessions was characterized by at least three consecutive months—and most by three consecutive quarters—of falling nonfarm payrolls.

In recoveries, unemployment is a lagging indicator—that is, it continues to rise for several months after the economy has reached a definitive bottom. The lag has become more marked in recent years. A look at **FIGURES 3.3** and **3.4** reveals that the last two U.S. recessions (1990–1991 and 2001) were both followed by protracted periods of joblessness.

Figure 3.3   Growth Rate in Nonfarm Payrolls and Recessions

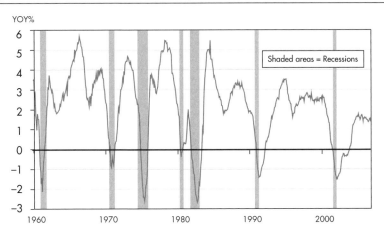

Sources: U.S. Department of Labor, Bureau of Labor Statistics; National Bureau of Economic Research

Figure 3.4   Unemployment Rate and Recessions

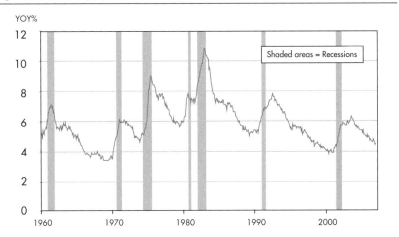

Sources: U.S. Department of Labor, Bureau of Labor Statistics; National Bureau of Economic Research

INFLATION INDICATORS

Average hourly earnings are considered a proxy for inflation and as such, are closely watched by fixed-income traders. When monthly earnings are increasing at a torrential rate, the bond market usually sells off, because inflation erodes the value of fixed-income holdings.

Inflation is inversely related to unemployment. That insight grew out of a 1958 study by New Zealand–born economist A. W. Phillips. The study demonstrated that when annual wage growth and unemployment rates were plotted against each other, the result was a shallow convex curve. Known as the Phillips curve, it served to represent the fact that during the period studied, years of low unemployment coincided with rapid wage increases, whereas years with high rates of unemployment saw inflation slow or even reverse. This suggested a trade-off between inflation and unemployment that could be exploited by economic policy makers: the central bank could keep inflation low by accepting higher unemployment levels or vice versa. This relationship soon became one of the most disputed in economics.

The Phillips curve and its policy implications led to the notion of a non-accelerating-inflation rate of unemployment. The NAIRU, as it is called, is the lowest level to which unemployment may fall without increasing the inflation rate. For decades economists believed that the NAIRU, sometimes referred to as the natural unemployment rate, was around 6 percent. As the chart in **FIGURE 3.5** graphically illustrates, particularly in the 1960s and 1970s, higher unemployment rates—above 6 percent—were soon followed by periods of falling inflation. Conversely, especially in the late 1980s, as employment fell below 6 percent, inflation gathered steam. The hypothesis pretty much lost its luster in the late 1990s, when the unemployment rate tumbled to 3.9 percent and inflation didn't move higher. In fact, inflation actually fell during the period, sparking fears of deflation at the Federal Reserve Board and in the investment community.

Economists seeking another link between unemployment and inflation latched on to the notion of "available labor pool." This is the number of unemployed who are actually available for work, calculated by adding the number of unemployed (the traditional measure defined as in the labor force, unemployed, and still looking for employment) to the number of workers not in the labor force who currently want a job. The reasoning is that when the pool of available workers begins to evaporate, employers have to increase wages

Figure 3.5   Unemployment Rate and Inflation

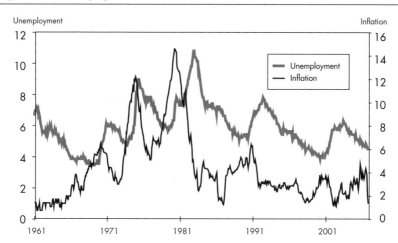

Source: U.S. Department of Labor, Bureau of Labor Statistics

to attract the employees they want, often having to outbid other employers, and that this sparks widespread inflation. The theory hasn't been borne out, however. The available labor pool shrank in the mid- to late 1990s to one of the lowest levels in history, yet harmful rates of inflation never developed.

SENTIMENT AND UNEMPLOYMENT

President Truman once remarked: "It's a recession when your neighbor loses his job. It's a depression when you lose yours." The barometer that best measures the downbeat sentiment associated with job loss is the median duration of unemployment— that is, the median number of weeks that people are out of work. FIGURE 3.6 suggests that as the median number of weeks of unemployment rises, workers become more and more frustrated, evidenced by declines in the University of Michigan's consumer sentiment index. Notice how the two spikes in the duration of unemployment during 2002 and 2003 were quickly followed by some of the lowest levels of consumer sentiment in the decade. Keep in mind that this measure is the median—the center point—not the average number of weeks.

Figure 3.6   Median Weeks of Unemployment Versus University of Michigan's Consumer Sentiment Index

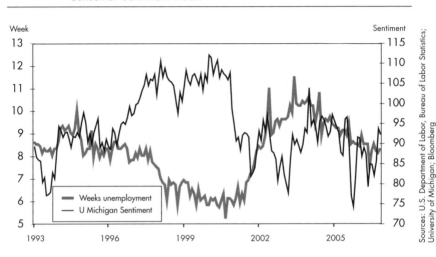

Sources: U.S. Department of Labor, Bureau of Labor Statistics; University of Michigan; Bloomberg

During extended periods of unemployment, marriages may be strained and families disrupted. Depression is common. As underlying labor-market conditions worsen, consumers become increasingly aware of how difficult it is to find a job. They hear of friends, neighbors, and immediate family members losing their jobs. Then distant relatives call asking about any available positions. Daily reminders in the newspapers and evening news only increase the gloom. These conditions aren't exactly conducive to greater consumer spending and positive economic growth.

AVERAGE HOURS WORKED AND TEMPORARY WORKERS

The BLS calculates the aggregate weekly hours worked index, formed by dividing the current month's estimates of aggregate hours by the corresponding annual average levels. This index, as well as several subindexes, are found in Table B-5 of the monthly Employment Situation report.

Because economic activity is basically a function of the number of people employed and the amount of time they are working, economists have discovered the ability to arrive at a "synthetic" forecast for

Figure 3.7   Average Weekly Hours Worked Index and Recessions

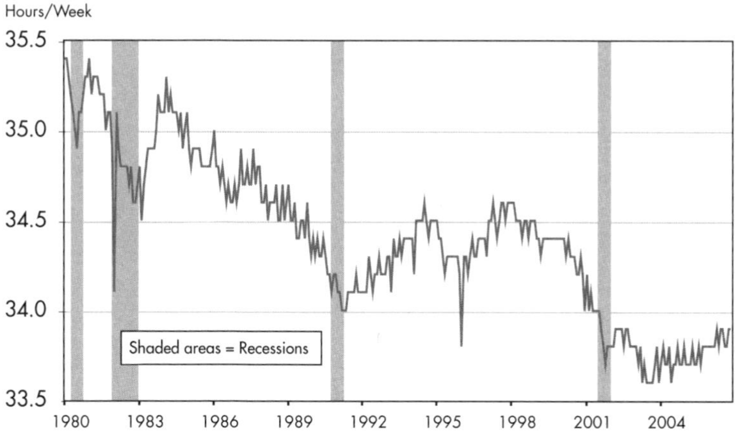

Hours/Week

Shaded areas = Recessions

economic growth, by charting the year-over-year percentage change in the quarterly average of the aggregate hours index. Clearly, there is an extremely tight correlation between these two indicators.

When economic conditions begin to sour, employers reduce the number of hours worked before they eliminate staff. That way, if economic activity recovers, they can ramp up production quickly by merely adding hours, rather than having to spend time and money finding and training new hires. This makes the aggregate hours worked index and the average hours worked, in some instances, a leading indicator of economic growth. **FIGURE 3.7** charts the average hours worked index over the past two decades.

If economic conditions—and profits—continue to deteriorate, management's next step is to reduce the number of workers on the payroll. Among the first people to get pink slips are temporary, or contingent, workers. The tasks they perform are not critical to the day-to-day performance of the company—otherwise, they would be employed full-time. Furthermore, temporary workers usually aren't unionized, so they can be cut most easily and cheaply during downturns. Temporary workers aren't usually entitled to severance or unemployment insurance. Conversely, in the initial stages of recovery, companies are not sure of future demand, so rather than go through the costly process of hiring full-time workers, they add temporary ones.

Sources: U.S. Department of Labor, Bureau of Labor Statistics; National Bureau of Economic Research

Figure 3.8   Temporary Employment and Recessions

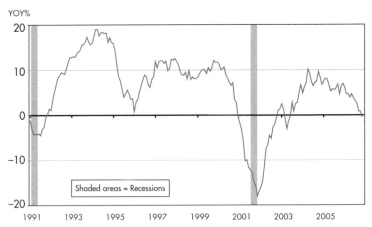

FIGURE 3.8 shows that a decline in temporary-help payrolls preceded the 2001 economic recession by a considerable degree, approximately six months. In general, increases in the growth rate of temporary workers precede the upturn in the business cycle.

Knowing that businesses operate in this fashion, traders like to keep a close eye on the trends in employment at temporary-help service establishments. An alternative manner at appreciating the goings-on in the temporary-services sector may be identified by watching the quarterly earnings announcements of the temporary staffing and recruiting agencies. Many companies, such as Adecco, Kelly Services Inc., Manpower Inc., and Robert Half International Inc. provide a great deal of information regarding industry trends, statistics, and forecasts. Trade organizations such as the American Staffing Association provide timely outlooks and related publications on temporary help and flexible staffing.

How to Use What You See

As always, the main strategy is to find ways to predict what a potentially market-moving number will be before it is released. Because the payrolls figure is such an accurate indicator of economic activity, for instance, economists and traders try to get ahead of the curve by forecasting it. Many keep a journal by their desks, recording events they come across in their daily reading that could influence employment. Unexpected disruptions such as labor strikes, mass layoffs, and natural disasters like hurricanes, tornadoes, floods, and blizzards can greatly alter the number of workers in a given month.

Economists also watch a number of alternative indicators for evidence to support or refute the developments suggested by data in the employment report. One of these alternative indicators is the index of monthly layoff announcements made by companies. The index, compiled by the employment consulting firm Challenger, Gray and Christmas, measures intended dismissals rather than actual firings. It is thus something of a leading indicator. It gives economists an insight into industries that may be experiencing difficulties. Movements in the index are also helpful in gauging the bigger picture contained in the BLS employment report. That is, increases in the number of layoff announcements usually portend a softer payroll picture, whereas a decline in the number of announced layoffs generally results in stronger payroll growth.

Another resource is the help-wanted advertising index. Created and maintained by the Conference Board, it tracks the monthly volume of help-wanted advertisements in the top fifty-one newspapers across the nation, thus identifying regional demand for labor. Since the advent of the Internet, however, businesses have had other ways to advertise available positions, so the popularity of the index has faded. Still, it can be helpful in determining general trends in demand for workers.

Probably the most helpful resource for predicting movements in monthly payrolls is the weekly claims for unemployment insurance. Rising jobless claims usually portend a deteriorating labor market. Many economists argue that when the four-week moving average of claims tops 400,000, job creation is stagnant. Of course, the correlation between claims for jobless benefits and the employment data is not precise. Employment conditions can change at any time, and short-lived changes are more likely to show up in the weekly jobless-claims report than in the monthly BLS employment report. Also, although unemployment-insurance benefits generally last only thirteen weeks, bear in mind that people can be out of work for months at a time. Finally, some unemployed workers are not entitled to jobless benefits.

TRICKS FROM THE TRENCHES

This chapter's trick is simply to call your attention to a little-known, but very useful, section of the employment report: the diffusion indexes. The BLS provides diffusion indexes for one-, three-, six-, and twelve-month periods, both for private nonfarm payrolls, which comprise 278 industries, and for manufacturing payrolls, which represent 84 industries. Economists tend to gravitate to the one-month indexes, as they are not as noisy as the others.

The diffusion indexes are derived from establishments' responses to questions about whether they intend to add or eliminate workers or leave payrolls unchanged. To calculate the indexes, the percentage of responses indicating an intention to add workers is added to half the percentage of the unchanged responses. When the indexes are above 50, indicating that a greater percentage of industries intend to add workers than to lay off workers or keep employment levels stable, employment conditions are strong. High readings are usually accompanied by economic expansions. When the indexes fall below 50, industries are leaning toward cutting their payrolls. That situation is typical of recession. As shown by **FIGURE 3.9**, most of the recessions designated by the National Bureau of Economic Research coincide with sub-50 postings in the BLS diffusion indexes.

Figure 3.9   Employment Diffusion Index and Recessions

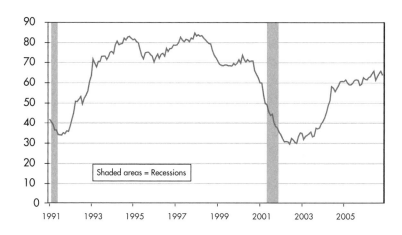

Shaded areas = Recessions

Sources: U.S. Department of Labor, Bureau of Labor Statistics; National Bureau of Economic Research

Industrial Production and Capacity Utilization

4

T HE INDUSTRIAL PRODUCTION and Capacity Utilization report, assembled and released around the fifteenth of each month by the Federal Reserve Board, presents data on the output of the nation's manufacturing, mining, and utility sectors. The Federal Reserve's G.17 report, as it is also known, organizes these data into industrial production and capacity utilization indexes. The industrial production indexes measure the physical volume of the output of various industries and markets; the capacity utilization indexes show what portion of the nation's production capacity was involved in creating that output. The total industrial production index is usually the headline grabber. Investors may react strongly to the monthly percentage change in this index, especially when it deviates from Wall Street's consensus estimates. But market participants also value the report's individual industry, aggregate industry, and market indexes.

Equity analysts scan the Industrial Production and Capacity Utilization report for telling details about the condition of the chemical, home electronics, paper, textile, fabricated metals, lumber, or industrial machinery sectors. Economists scrutinize the data for early insights into what the quarterly national income and product accounts (NIPAs) (see Chapter 1), will say about the health of the economy. Policy makers search the numbers for inflationary trends. And the National Bureau of Economic Research (NBER), the official arbiter of U.S. business cycles, incorporates the industrial production index—which it finds a good marker of the start and end of recessions—in its statement on the status of the economy. The Industrial Production and Capacity Utilization release, together with historical data, is available on the Federal Reserve's website, www.federalreserve.gov.

EVOLUTION OF AN INDICATOR

The industrial production index is among the oldest measures of U.S. manufacturing and macroeconomic activity, predating even the venerable national income and product accounts. It is as old, in fact, as the Federal Reserve Board. Soon after the central bank was created with the passage of the Federal Reserve Act on December 23, 1913, Federal Reserve officials realized that they needed a pool of accurate economic data and measurements if they were to steer the nation through the widespread bank failures, frequent recessions, and bouts of joblessness that characterized the late nineteenth and early twentieth centuries. No formal measurement of economic activity existed, however, in 1913. The National Bureau of Economic Research, now the primary agency responsible for maintaining the national accounts, didn't begin estimating income until 1920. So the Fed created its own Physical Volume of Trade report. This consisted of unaggregated indexes tracking the production of commodities such as coal, coke, crude oil, steel, textiles, metals, and paper, measured in tons, feet, barrels, and other relevant physical units. By 1919, these indexes represented seven sectors of the economy: agriculture, forestry, mining, manufacturing, trade and transportation, banking and finance, and labor.

In 1922, the Fed introduced the monthly Indexes of Domestic Business report, which combined fifty-five gauges of commodity production into indexes representing three facets of production: agriculture, mining, and manufacturing. Later that year, it created the more detailed index of production in selected basic industries. This was composed of twenty-two commodities weighted according to the level of employment in the manufacturing process of each respective commodity industry, which was obtained in the 1919 census, and the value added by each industry—that is, the portion of a good's final value that is contributed by the industry in the course of production. The two largest components in the index were pig iron and cotton, with weights of 18 and 15 percent, respectively. In structure it was similar to the industrial production index of today.

The industrial production index was used to estimate industrial capacity utilization for about two decades after World War II. In the 1960s, the Federal Reserve developed a process for estimating industrial capacity and capacity utilization rates, releasing these estimates in a separate statistical report called Capacity Utilization: Manufacturing, Mining, Utilities and Industrial Materials. This monthly report, known as statistical release G.3, was released one business day after the industrial production report. Capacity indexes were estimated using data obtained from the McGraw-Hill Companies and the U.S. Census Bureau surveys of plant capacity, in addition to surveys of industry businessmen.

Most of the meaningful changes to the capacity utilization measures occurred in the 1970s, particularly in 1974 with the revision of the materials measures, and then again in 1976 with the augmentation of total materials data in the industrial production index.

In December 2002, the Federal Reserve revised the industrial-production and capacity-utilization measures, switching from the Standard Industrial Classification (SIC) system to the new North American Industry Classification System (NAICS). It also introduced more reliable methods of calculating manufacturing activity in the communications equipment, semiconductor, light vehicle, and newspaper industries, and regrouped the major market classes according to stage of processing, very much like the system used for the producer price index (PPI).

DIGGING FOR THE DATA

The Industrial Production and Capacity Utilization report is an assemblage of fifteen tables arranged over nineteen or twenty pages. The tables display the current month's values for the various industrial production and capacity utilization indexes, revisions to previous months' values, month-to-month percentage changes in the indexes, and their quarterly and annual rates of growth. The front page of the release contains a summary of the most important indicators—the monthly percentage changes in the total industrial production index and the capacity utilization rate—as well as revisions to the three previous months. The Federal Reserve also provides a number of detailed charts—a trader's best friend—before the meat of the report is presented.

INDUSTRIAL PRODUCTION

The industrial production indexes measure the quantity of output (that is, in terms of production units like tons, cubic feet, or kilowatt hours), not the dollar volume, relative to a base year, currently 1997, whose value is set at 100. An index value of 109, for instance, denotes that output for that month was 9 percent higher than the average for 1997.

The Federal Reserve obtains the production data it uses to construct these indexes both directly and indirectly. Direct sources include trade associations such as the American Forest and Paper Association (for pulp, wood, and paper and paperboard output), the U.S. Geological Survey (for copper, lead, zinc, gold, and silver ore numbers), the Bureau of Alcohol, Tobacco, Firearms, and Explosives of the U.S. Department of the Treasury (for beer, wine, and brandy), and the Leather Industries of America (formerly the Tanners Council of America) (for leather and belting figures). Actual production data, however, are available at different times for different industries. When hard figures aren't available, the Federal Reserve estimates output based on the number of production-worker hours in the Bureau of Labor Statistics' monthly Employment Situation report or on electric power use by industry. Only a few sectors—usually motor vehicles, steel and other metals, lumber, and paper—have hard figures ready for the initial release. By the third monthly revision, actual physical production accounts for 46 percent of the data by value added, production-worker hours for 31 percent, electric power use for 19 percent, and Federal Reserve judgments based on anecdotal evidence for 4 percent.

Figure 4.1   Industry Groups

	2005 Proportion
Total Industrial Production	**100.00**
Manufacturing	80.94
Durable	40.23
Nondurable	36.37
Other manufacturing (non-NAICS)	4.34
Mining	9.20
Utilities	9.86

Source: Federal Reserve Board

Figure 4.2   Market Groups

	2005 Proportion
Total Industrial Production	**100.00**
Final product and nonindustrial supplies	57.48
Consumer goods	30.27
Durable	7.46
Nondurable	22.8
Business equipment	9.36
Defense and space equipment	1.73
Construction supplies	4.38
Business supplies	11.08
Materials	42.52

Source: Federal Reserve Board

The total industrial production index is constructed from 295 components or individual series such as copper, instruments, computers, and lumber, each of which is weighted according to the value of the associated sector added during the production process in the base year. Each individual series is expressed in its own respective quantity (that is, steel in tons, automobiles in units) so that month-to-month changes in production are measured without respect to price movements. The report presents these components according to two different classification schemes: by industry, representing the supplier perspective; and by market, representing the demand perspective.

The industry schema is based on the North American Industry Classification system (NAICS). The three primary industry groups are manufacturing, mining, and utilities. Manufacturing is subdivided into durable and nondurable goods. The table in **FIGURE 4.1** shows the major groupings together with the percentage each contributed to production growth in 2005.

In the classification by market groups, shown in **FIGURE 4.2**, the total index is divided into two major groups: final products/nonindustrial supplies, and materials. Final products/nonindustrial supplies is itself divided into consumer goods (further subdivided into durable and nondurable), business equipment, defense and space equipment, construction supplies, and business supplies.

CAPACITY UTILIZATION

Capacity utilization is a measure of how close the nation's manufacturing sector is to running at full capacity. Formally, it is the ratio of the industrial production index to an index of full capacity. But what is meant by full capacity? The Fed defines it as sustainable practical capacity, or "the greatest level of output that a plant can maintain within the framework of a realistic work schedule, taking account of normal downtime and assuming sufficient availability of inputs to operate the machinery and equipment in place."

The annual full capacity number is derived through a complex process that involves both hard data—obtained from industry surveys such as the U.S. Census Bureau's annual Survey of Plant Capacity, which all businesses (with a class D SIC code classification, manufacturing) with five employees or more must complete, and by inference, using the ratio given above. The Fed assumes that month-to-month growth is smooth and so derives the monthly capacity figure by straight-line interpolation from the annual number.

The monthly capacity utilization rate is derived by dividing the monthly industrial production number by the monthly capacity figure. For example, during November 2006 the index of industrial production was 112.3 and the capacity index was 137.3, resulting in a capacity utilization rate of 81.8 percent. In layman's terms, this suggests that factories were running at 81.8 percent of full capacity.

Figure 4.3 Capacity Utilization Percentage of Capacity, Seasonally Adjusted

	2005 Proportion
Total Industry	**100.00**
Manufacturing	82.51
Manufacturing (non-NAICS)	78.44
Durable	42.53
Nondurable	35.91
Other manufacturing (non-NAICS)	4.08
Mining	8.41
Utilities	9.08

Source: Federal Reserve Board

The report contains capacity and capacity utilization rates for eighty-five industries, including the following major categories:
- Semiconductors and related electronic components
- Motor vehicles and parts
- Apparel and leather
- Paper
- Chemicals
- Wood products
- Electric utilities

The total capacity utilization rate is compiled from these components, weighted as shown in **FIGURE 4.3**.

WHAT DOES IT ALL MEAN?

Economists, analysts, and investors look to the Industrial Production and Capacity Utilization report for timely indications of overall economic health as well as manufacturing and inflationary trends. The two main sections of the report provide different types of information and signals.

INDUSTRIAL PRODUCTION

The index of industrial production is *procyclical*—that is, it moves in unison with the business cycle. As the chart in **FIGURE 4.4** illus-

Figure 4.4 Industrial Production and Real GDP

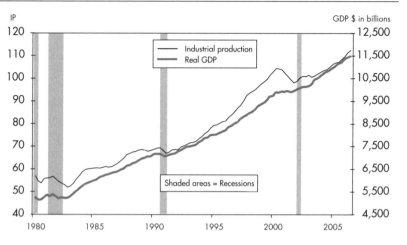

Sources: Federal Reserve Board; U.S. Department of Commerce, Bureau of Economic Analysis; National Bureau of Economic Research

Figure 4.5 Industrial Production and Recessions

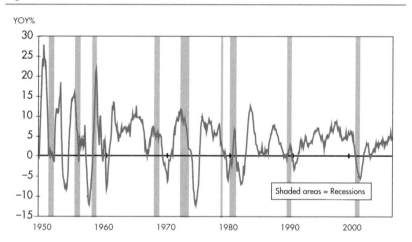

Sources: Federal Reserve Board; National Bureau of Economic Research

trates, the correlation between the index and economic activity is quite tight—so tight, in fact, that the monthly index is used as a more timely proxy for the quarterly GDP report.

The National Bureau of Economic Research uses the index to discern turning points in the business cycle. As the chart in **FIGURE 4.5** shows, each of the NBER-designated recessions since 1950 has co-incided with a precipitous drop in the twelve-month growth rate of industrial production. The converse, however, is not necessarily true: the manufacturing sector can be in recession while the broader economy continues to prosper.

At first blush, the close relationship between the industrial production index and the overall economy seems odd. Manufacturing, after all, accounts for only 20 percent of total economic activity. The United States has evolved from a smokestack to a services-dominant economy, and mammoth service industries, such as health care, software, telecommunications, travel and entertainment, pharmaceuticals, and banking and finance, are not directly represented in the industrial production index. Nor does the index contain any measure of construction-related activity, although it does represent industries that manufacture construction machinery such as wheel loaders and wheel tractors.

On closer examination, however, the close relationship between the index and the broad economy makes sense. For starters, one-fifth of total activity isn't altogether small. The U.S. manufacturing sector moves very much in line with aggregate demand, just as retail sales, another small and equally cyclical statistic, moves with consumer spending. Moreover, manufacturing and production activity have a large "multiplier effect." Manufactured goods, especially durable goods—those with expected shelf lives of three or more years—generally come with service contracts that cover the cost of repairs, damages, and maintenance. Obviously, the value and level of such services are driven by the demand for the products themselves.

Finally, and most crucially, many service industries are large consumers of manufactured goods. Taxi companies require automobiles; airlines need jets and electronic security systems; bars and restaurants use refrigerators, dishwashers, ovens, and foodstuffs. Financial institutions and law firms are big customers of computers and peripherals, and the health-care industry is one of the largest consumers of industrial products, including operating tables, beds, lamps, imaging machines, and surgical supplies.

The industrial production index shows another strong correlation—with the purchasing managers' index (PMI), published by the Institute for Supply Management. The relationship between the two indexes is illustrated in the scatter chart in **FIGURE 4.6**. The points in the upper-right quadrant represent periods of extremely strong manufacturing output, such as recoveries from recession and the 1991–2001 economic expansion, the longest in U.S. history. The points in the lower-left quadrant represent periods of severe manufacturing weakness, generally recessions. A simple econometric analysis suggests that when the purchasing managers' index is at 50, a level generally consistent with an expansion in manufacturing, the industrial production index is advancing at an annual rate of approximately 2 percent.

At a more detailed level, the industrial production subindexes can depict, and in some instances explain, what is happening in specific industries. Take the spectacular expansion and equally spectacular collapse in the technology sector that occurred during the late 1990s and early 2000s. The chart in **FIGURE 4.7** shows that while high tech was soaring, the production of nontechnology goods was plodding along, posting average annual gains of around 2 percent.

It was during this period that then Federal Reserve chairman Alan Greenspan uttered his famous "irrational exuberance" comment at the annual Francis Boyer Lecture of The American Enterprise Institute for Public Policy Research. Although he was referring to asset prices, Chairman Greenspan was doubtless aware that production of high-tech goods such as computers, communications equipment, and semiconductors was growing at more than 40 percent annually, dwarfing the 15 percent or so registered a mere year and a half earlier.

That pace was not sustainable. Beginning in late 2000, the chart shows, there was a precipitous decline in the high-tech industry growth rate. Manufacturers, afraid to miss out on the hot market for their goods, had overproduced. When demand, inevitably, slackened, these companies—particularly telecommunications equipment providers—were left with record inventories. In reaction, they slashed production and consequently, staff until consumers could draw down existing stock. Inventory depletion took the better part

Figure 4.6   Correlation of Purchasing Managers' Index and Industrial Production Index

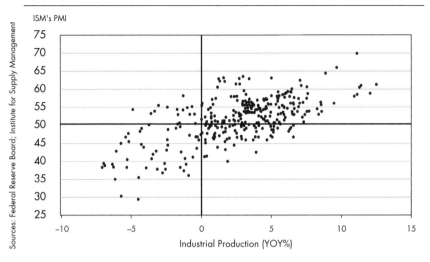

Industrial Production (YOY%)

Figure 4.7   Industrial Production Index: High-Tech and Excluding High-Tech

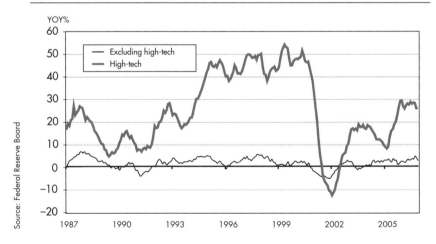

of three years. This situation, exacerbated by fraudulent accounting practices, misstated earnings, and countless corporate improprieties, forced Global Crossing Limited, WorldCom, and Qwest Corporation, among other companies, into bankruptcy. Not surprisingly, the stock market plunged between 2000 and 2002. This

Figure 4.8 Capacity Utilization and Recessions

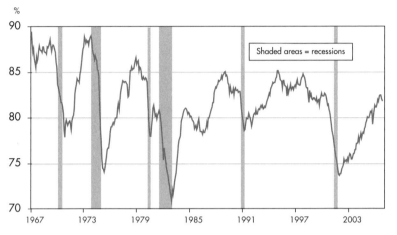

Sources: Federal Reserve Board; National Bureau of Economic Research

entire story can be traced in the contrasting paths of the high-tech and ex-tech indexes shown in the figure.

CAPACITY UTILIZATION

Economists, particularly central bankers, look at the total capacity utilization rate to discern trends in production, general economic activity, manufacturing conditions, and inflation. In addition, the rates for particular industries can pinpoint areas of overcapacitization (production that pushes capacity to its limit) that could become manufacturing bottlenecks, constraining production farther down the line and possibly pushing up prices. Such information is useful not only to economists but also to company managers trying to forecast costs and plan production schedules.

Low levels of capacity utilization—78 percent or below—indicate that the economy is headed to, or already in, recession. In fact, as the chart in **FIGURE 4.8** illustrates, each of the last six economic recessions was characterized by utilization rates in that range. This relationship is logical: subpar economic conditions simply don't warrant strong production.

When demand and commerce are booming, on the other hand, factories tend to ramp up and produce at rates closer to their capacity. The downside to this is that the higher production rates tend to stoke inflation.

When factories approach their maximum production potential, machinery and other goods-producing capital are strained. As a result, electronic components may short, pumps overheat, lubricants dry up, or core parts crack. If the overworked equipment cannot be repaired in a reasonable, profitable period of time, mass layoffs could ensue. Complicating matters is the fact that all this occurs just when demand is greatest and increased production most necessary. To understand how this cycle can spark inflation, consider the case of a company that produces about 50,000 tons of cement a week.

During normal conditions the company's plants operate at 80 percent of capacity. At that rate, market conditions dictate a price of $50 a ton for the cement. Over time, though, a housing boom develops, and demand for cement surges. To capture more of the increased market, the company begins operating its plants at 92 percent of their full capacity. At this rate, the rotating kiln breaks down because it is not accustomed to so much pressure. The damage may take weeks, even months to repair. Beyond laying off the workers that operated the broken machinery, what can the company do to offset the lost revenue?

Answer: raise prices. Rather than charge the normal market rate of $50 a ton, the cement manufacturer tells wholesalers that it expects $55, $60, or even $65 a ton. Because demand has skyrocketed, the wholesalers will gladly fork over the additional money, knowing that they too will be able to pass along the increase to contractors and retailers. These price hikes are transferred to new homes, driveways, sidewalks, and highways, and eventually into the general economy.

As this example illustrates, during periods of high capacity utilization, inflationary pressures mount. The economic consequences can be serious. Inflation erodes the purchasing power of bonds' coupon and principal payments, depressing their prices and raising yields. Higher interest rates, in turn, impede future investment.

Concerned over this vicious cycle, economists have sought to quantify the relationship between the capacity utilization rate and inflation, just as they did for the unemployment rate (see Chapter 3). And just as they identified a minimum level of unemployment that could be sustained without sparking inflation—the non-accelerating-inflation rate of unemployment (NAIRU)—they have identified a maximum non-accelerating-inflation rate of capacity utilization (NAICU).

The NAICU for the manufacturing sector as a whole has long been accepted to be 84 percent. Individual businesses differ, however, in their susceptibility to technical innovations, legal barriers, work stoppages, and cyclical abandonment rates, all of which can drastically affect total capacity. Each industry thus has its own NAICU. Some rates are higher than 84 percent, like the paper industry's 87 percent; some are lower, like the mining sector's 80 percent. Of course, none of these is set in stone. Changing business conditions can alter particular NAICUs. It is thus best to regard individual industry numbers as shorthands for ranges, rather than as precise rates.

Even with this looser definition, the applicability of NAICUs in today's economy has been called into question, much as the applicability of the NAIRU has been. The chart in **FIGURE 4.9** shows why. The expected relationship between the general manufacturing NAICU and inflation appears to exist through the late 1980s, but then disappears. A sustained period of capacity utilization above 84 percent that occurred in the late 1970s was indeed followed by an acceleration in the growth of the producer price index for intermediate materials; likewise, depressed capacity utilization rates during the early 1980s did precede a period of disinflation—positive but slowing price growth—and even deflation, or falling prices. In the 1990s and early 2000s, however, a disconnect occurred, with capacity utilization rising to fairly high rates without spawning inflation.

Does this mean that the theory no longer holds and that high capacity utilization rates do not increase inflationary pressures? Probably not. It is more likely that the breakdown in the relationship illustrated in the chart occurred because of the heavy business investment in productivity-enhancing technologies that took place in the latter half of the 1990s, increasing manufacturing capacity. The

Figure 4.9 Manufacturing Capacity Utilization and PPI for Intermediate Goods

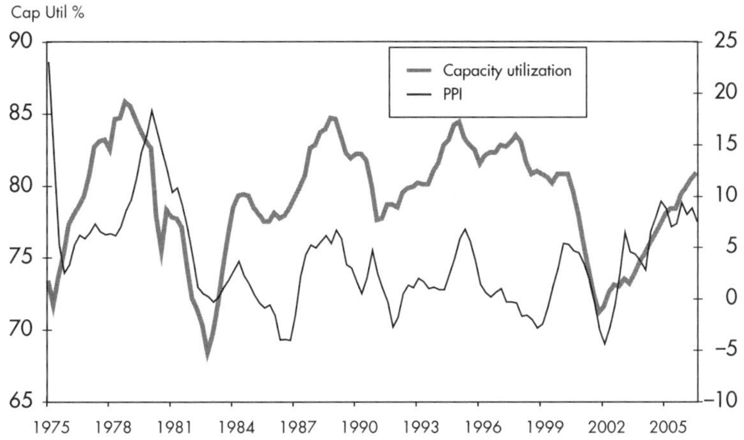

Sources: Federal Reserve Board; U.S. Department of Labor, Bureau of Labor Statistics

substitution of low-priced imports for domestic products played an important role as well, by keeping manufacturing costs low and inflation in check. That said, it is also possible that the true capacity utilization threshold may be a tick or two higher than 84 percent, say 85 or 86 percent.

One indication that the Fed bellieves the general reasoning behind NAICUs still holds is the reaction of the Federal Reserve to high capacity utilization readings. The Fed is concerned with keeping a lid on inflation and adjusts its monetary policy accordingly. At the first signs of an overheating economy, it generally raises its target for the federal funds rate (the interest rate banks charge each other for overnight loans used to meet reserve requirements; see Chapter 1). This increase eventually extends throughout the maturity spectrum, discouraging borrowing and so slowing the pace of investment and production.

If the Fed governors are still using NAICU as an inflation indicator, you'd expect hikes in the federal funds rate to correspond to high rates of capacity utilization. And that does seem to be the case. The chart in **FIGURE 4.10** shows that from 1989 through 2003, whenever the capacity utilization rate rose into the high 80s, the federal funds rate rose as well.

Figure 4.10   Capacity Utilization and the Federal Funds Rate

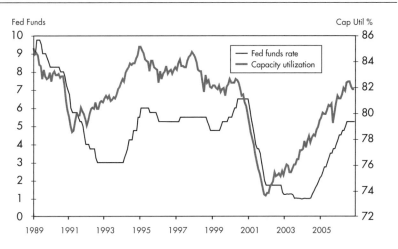

The conclusion: although the relationship has loosened in recent years, the Federal Reserve clearly believes that capacity utilization is still a powerful inflation marker and watches the reported rate carefully. That's a good enough reason for traders, especially those in the fixed-income market, to keep a close eye on capacity utilization too.

HOW TO USE WHAT YOU SEE

As is the case with most indicators, Wall Streeters want to get a preview of what's inside the Industrial Production and Capacity Utilization report: the earlier they can approximate the industrial production index readings, the earlier they can capitalize on any anomalies in the numbers. Useful tools in this project are the number of worker hours in the Department of Labor's monthly employment report. This chapter's "tricks" describe how market participants use the Labor Department's data in forecasting the industrial production indexes.

TRICKS FROM THE TRENCHES

As noted above, when the actual data are not available, the Federal Reserve may estimate industrial production based on the number of production-worker hours. Wall Street economists use the same statistics in a simple back-of-the-envelope calculation to predict the industrial production index reading up to two weeks before it is released. Here's what the computation would look like using the data in the Bureau of Labor Statistics' March 2002 Employment Situation report, released on April 5 of that year. The report stated that in February 2002, 16.869 million people were employed in manufacturing, working an average of 40.7 hours a week, whereas in March, 16.831 people worked 41.1 hours a week on average. The first step in the computation is to calculate the total number of manpower hours (mh) worked in each month:

February: 16.869 million workers × 40.7 hours = 686.5683 mh
March: 16.831 million workers × 41.1 hours = 691.7541 mh

The next step is to determine how many more or fewer manpower hours were worked in March:

691.7541 – 686.5683 = 5.1858

The last step is to derive the month-over-month percentage change:

(5.1858 ÷ 691.7541) × 100 = 0.7496 percent.

So the predicted change in the March industrial production index, based on the number of manufacturing workers and the hours they worked, is 0.75 percent. The actual industrial production index reading in the report released on April 16 was 138.8, a 0.65 percent increase over the revised February reading of 137.9. Of course, the result of the calculation is not always that close to the actual reading. But the method is certainly simple, and it is helpful in determining the direction, if not always the magnitude, of change in the index—an extremely important statistic.

Institute for Supply Management Indexes 5

T HE PURCHASING MANAGERS' INDEX (PMI) garners more attention than any other economic release except the monthly Employment Situation report (see Chapter 3). Markets move considerably on its readings, and rumor has it that the index is former Federal Reserve chairman Alan Greenspan's "desert island statistic"—that is, if he were stranded on an island and needed to conduct policy with respect to only one economic indicator, this would be it.

The purchasing managers' index is the headline index of the Manufacturing ISM Report on Business. This report is created by the Tempe, Arizona–based Institute for Supply Management (ISM), a not-for-profit professional association, and is made available on ISM's website (www.ism.ws) on the first business day of every month, after 10:00 a.m. (ET). In addition to providing a comprehensive introduction of the various indexes contained in the report, the website houses a complete historical data set subject to timely revisions and updates.

The ISM Report on Business describes and discusses the current readings of ten seasonally adjusted diffusion indexes constructed by the ISM from the responses to a survey of approximately three hundred purchasing managers across the United States. Conducted around the middle of the previous month, the survey polls participants about their opinions on prices paid for materials used in the production process, production levels, new orders, order backlogs, the speed of supplier deliveries, inventories, customer inventories, employment, new export orders, and imports. The purchasing managers' index is a weighted composite of the following five indexes:

- ▪ new orders
- ▪ production
- ▪ employment
- ▪ vendor performance
- ▪ inventories

Economists look at the purchasing managers' index primarily to determine the health of the manufacturing sector, but the index provides an accurate picture of the broader economy as well. Its movements closely parallel those of the index of leading economic indicators (see Chapter 2), and it has shown an uncanny ability to predict recessions months before the National Bureau of Economic Research (NBER) declares them. This may not be so surprising: what better way is there to find out about manufacturing activity and associated spending than from those business people who are responsible for making the purchasing decisions for the nation's manufacturers?

According to research conducted by the Federal Reserve Bank of New York, the financial markets, in particular the fixed-income market, react very strongly to the monthly postings of the ISM's purchasing managers' index. On several occasions, the purchasing managers' index has been identified as the biggest market mover in the monthly reporting cycle of indicators.

EVOLUTION OF AN INDICATOR

The Manufacturing ISM Report on Business has its origins in the 1920s, when the ISM's predecessor association (first called the National Association of Purchasing Agents, then the National Association of Purchasing Management) began polling members periodically—at first, only about commodity availability across the country, but soon about other types of information, as well. In 1930, the association was part of a committee formed by the U.S. Chamber of Commerce under President Herbert Hoover in response to the stock market collapse and the Great Depression. The committee was charged with collecting business data from members of the Chamber of Commerce. Although the committee was disbanded in 1931, the association decided to carry on the project and with encouragement from the government, started conducting surveys and publishing the results on a regular basis.

This project has continued ever since, except for a four-year hiatus during World War II, when the spotty availability of data disrupted publication. The purchasing managers' index—also known as the ISM index, or among old-timers, the NAPM index (in reference to the association's name until May 2001)—has been part of the association's monthly report since 1948.

DIGGING FOR THE DATA

As noted above, the ten diffusion indexes contained in the Report on Business reflect the survey responses of purchasing managers from various regions of the United States. The participants are drawn from about eighteen manufacturing industries, based on the North American Industry Classification System (NAICS), with each industry represented according to its contribution to gross domestic product (GDP). The eighteen industries include the following:

- Apparel, leather, and allied
- Chemicals
- Computers and electronics
- Electrical equipment, appliances, and components
- Fabricated metals
- Food, tobacco, and beverages
- Furniture
- Machinery
- Miscellaneous (for example, jewelry, toys, sporting equipment, and musical instruments)
- Nonmetallic minerals
- Paper

The Institute for Supply Management™ 2003 Survey Questions

1. GENERAL REMARKS: Comment regarding any business condition (local, national, or international) that affects your purchasing operation or the outlook for your company or industry. Your opinion and comments are very important.

2. PRODUCTION:

Check the ONE box that best expresses the current month's level (units, not dollars) compared to the previous month.

❏ Better than a month ago ❏ Same as a month ago ❏ Worse than a month ago

3. NEW ORDERS:

Check the ONE box that best expresses the current month's new orders (units, not dollars) compared to the previous month.

❏ Better than a month ago ❏ Same as a month ago ❏ Worse than a month ago

4. BACKLOG OF ORDERS:

Check the ONE box that best expresses the current month's backlog of orders (unfilled sales orders) (units, not dollars) compared to the previous month.

❏ Do not measure backlog of orders   ❏ Greater than a month ago
❏ Same as a month ago   ❏ Less than a month ago

5. NEW EXPORT ORDERS:

Check the ONE box that best expresses the current month's new export orders (units, not dollars) compared to the previous month.

❏ Do not export   ❏ Better than a month ago
❏ Same as a month ago   ❏ Worse than a month ago

6. COMMODITY PRICES:

Check the ONE box that indicates the current month's level of change in approximate net weighted average prices of the commodities you buy compared to the previous month.

❏ Higher than a month ago ❏ Same as a month ago ❏ Lower than a month ago

List specific commodities (use generic terms, not proprietary) which are up or down in price since the last report.

UP IN PRICE:_____   DOWN IN PRICE:_____

7. INVENTORIES OF PURCHASED MATERIALS:

Check the OVERALL inventory level (units, not dollars) including raw, MRO

(Maintenance, Repair, Operating Supplies), intermediates, etc. (not finished goods, unless purchased) compared to the previous month.

❑ Higher than a month ago ❑ Same as a month ago ❑ Lower than a month ago

Do you perceive THIS MONTH, your customers' inventories of products they order from you, as being: ❑ Too High ❑ About Right ❑ Too Low

8. IMPORTS:
Check the ONE box that best expresses the current month's OVERALL imports (units, not dollars) including raw, MRO (Maintenance, Repair, Operating Supplies), components, intermediates, etc. (not finished goods unless purchased) compared to the previous month.

❑ Do not import   ❑ Higher than a month ago
❑ Same as a month ago   ❑ Lower than a month ago

9. EMPLOYMENT:
Check the OVERALL level of employment compared to the previous month.

❑ Greater than a month ago ❑ Same as a month ago ❑ Less than a month ago

10. SUPPLIER DELIVERIES:
Check the ONE box that best expresses the current month's OVERALL delivery performance compared to the previous month.

❑ Faster than a month ago ❑ Same as a month ago ❑ Slower than a month ago

11. ITEMS IN SHORT SUPPLY:
Report specific commodities (use generic names, not proprietary) you purchase that are in short supply, even if mentioned in previous reports.

12: BUYING POLICY:
Indicate by checking ONE appropriate box for each category of purchases and the approximate weighted number of days ahead for which you are committed. Do not report hedging or speculative purchases.

Production Materials
❑ Hand to Mouth ❑ 30 Days ❑ 60 Days ❑ 90 Days ❑ 6 Months ❑ Year

MRO Supplies
❑ Hand to Mouth ❑ 30 Days ❑ 60 Days ❑ 90 Days ❑ 6 Months ❑ Year

Capital Expenditures
❑ Hand to Mouth ❑ 30 Days ❑ 60 Days ❑ 90 Days ❑ 6 Months ❑ Year

■ Petroleum and coal
■ Primary metals
■ Printing
■ Rubber and plastics
■ Textiles
■ Transportation equipment
■ Wood

Each month, the ISM asks its member companies in the above industries twelve questions (reprinted on the preceding pages with permission from the Institute for Supply Management). The responses are then aggregated by around the twentieth or twenty-first of the month.

In addition to direct responses, which are used in the calculation of the diffusion indexes, the ISM asks for remarks after each question regarding the reasons for higher or lower commodity prices, or greater or less employment. The ISM also asks its participants to report specific commodities (using generic, not proprietary, names) they purchase that are in short supply, even if mentioned in previous reports. These remarks are used in the text prepared for the monthly report, as well as the summary provided in the beginning of the report that precedes the presentation of the individual components.

The ISM separates the responses to each question into positive, neutral, and negative groups and calculates the percentage of the whole that each represents. It then plugs the appropriate percentages for each question into the following formula:

Percentage of Positive Responses + ½ (Percentage of
Neutral Responses)

The result is a diffusion index. Suppose the question regarding the level of employment received 350 responses, of which 20 are negative, or "lower than a month ago"; 275 neutral, or "same as a month ago"; and 55 positive, or "higher than a month ago." Plugging those numbers into the formula would give a value for the ISM employment index as follows:

employment index = [(55 ÷ 350) × 100] + ½ [(275 ÷ 350) × 100]
$$= 15.7 + ½ (78.57)$$
$$= 15.7 + 39.28$$
$$= 55.0$$

Indexes calculated in this manner have values between 0 and 100. Values above 50 are interpreted as predicting expansion; those under 50, contraction. Thus, the expansion-contraction cutoff level is 50, not 0. Historically, the individual ISM indexes have tended to fluctuate between 35 and 70, depending on the current phase of the business cycle and the individual index. For example, the price index has fluctuated between 30 and 90, whereas the export index has maintained a range of 40 to 70.

Five of these indexes, as was noted earlier, are weighted and summed to create the purchasing managers' index. The indexes and their associated weightings are new orders (30 percent), production (25 percent), employment (20 percent), supplier deliveries (15 percent), and inventories (10 percent). The November 2006 purchasing managers' index, for instance, was calculated as follows:

PMI (November 2006) = new orders (0.30 × 48.7)
+ production (0.25 × 48.5)
+ employment (0.20 × 49.2)
+ supplier deliveries (0.15 × 52.8)
+ inventories (0.10 × 49.7)
= 14.61 + 12.125 + 9.84 + 7.92 + 4.97
= 49.5

The heaviest weighting is given to new orders and reflects the fact that it has the greatest predictive value of the five components. This makes economic sense because orders are, by definition, a representation of intended purchases. This weighting, in turn, contributes to the accuracy of the composite purchasing managers' index in forecasting turning points in the business cycle.

WHAT DOES IT ALL MEAN?

The ISM manufacturing report is valued not only for the diffusion indexes but also for the accompanying discussion and comments made by the purchasing and supply executives participating in the survey. Together, the indexes and executives' anecdotal insights paint a detailed picture of the state of the manufacturing sector. The information is also timely, because the report is released on the first business day of the month, thus unofficially kicking off the monthly cycle of economic indicators.

All these features make the report a valued tool for Wall Street economists, government forecasters, and business planners. Because these professionals' concerns, actions, and pronouncements all affect the stock and bond markets, investors too need to pay close attention to the report.

When strong postings are registered in the purchasing managers' index, production, new orders, and employment indexes, it is generally a safe bet that many of the nation's manufacturers are experiencing some positive growth. Granted that countless factors and risks influence the value of a particular company and industry, but when economic fundamentals are strong (that is, low inflation, low interest rates, solid employment growth, and increased global demand for U.S. manufactured goods), and the ISM's indexes are on the rise, industrial companies like Caterpillar Inc., Ingersoll-Rand Company Limited, International Paper Company, United Technologies Corporation, Eaton Corporation, and Leggett & Platt Inc. tend to prosper.

The following sections discuss the economic significance of the purchasing managers' index and a few of the subindexes contained in the Report on Business, as well as some of the relationships between these indexes and other economic indicators. There are countless relationships between each of the subindexes and various other economic indicators, far too many, in fact, for inclusion in this introductory book. It is highly recommended that readers attempt to discover some of these relationships by charting the data from the ISM's website against other economic indicators. Let's examine a handful of the more popular relationships studied by Wall Streeters.

PURCHASING MANAGERS' INDEX

A few characteristics that set the purchasing managers' index apart from most other economic indicators discussed in this book, and that contribute greatly to its appeal for analysts, economists, and investors, are its relative simplicity, its strong correlation with macroeconomic trends, and its unique perspective. The fact that it is more of an anecdotal representation of the goings-on in the economy, from the perspective of those responsible for the actual purchasing of manufactured goods, than a calculated measure of output or volume of production is indeed a distinctive quality of this index. Perhaps the most attractive feature of the purchasing managers' index and its subindexes, however, is its ease of interpretation, permitting the trader to interpret month-to-month changes almost instantly.

The purchasing managers' index is not solely an indicator of manufacturing activity. **FIGURE 5.1** shows that monthly movements in the index closely mirror the year-over-year percentage change in real GDP. This makes the purchasing managers' index extremely valuable as a predictor of total macroeconomic activity.

The chart depicts the relationship between the purchasing managers' index and GDP as a concurrent or coincident association. That's because the purchasing managers' index in Figure 5.1 is charted on a quarterly basis, with the quarterly calculation of the purchasing managers' index derived by averaging the individual months' data for each respective quarter. But because the ISM's purchasing managers' index is released on a monthly basis and the GDP report is on a delayed, quarterly basis, the purchasing managers' index in fact assumes a leading, or predictive, tenor.

As discussed previously, a level of 50 is considered the cutoff between expansion and contraction for manufacturing conditions. But when it comes to movements in the broader macroeconomy, different levels are associated with expansion and contraction. For example, a reading of about 42.0 in the purchasing managers' index serves to identify turning points in the overall business cycle.

Figure 5.1   Real GDP Versus ISM's Purchasing Managers' Index

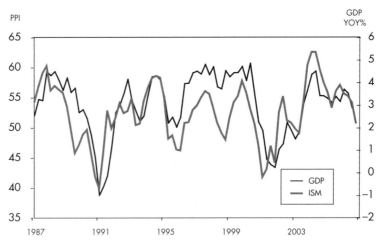

The reason for the lower level is due to the underlying composition of the economy. From the 1940s through the 1970s, manufacturing activity was a much greater influence on the total U.S. economy than during the 1980s, when the economy became less industrialized and more services oriented. So, in earlier times when manufacturing fell into a slump, it dragged the entire economy into recession. Today, manufacturing accounts for only 20 percent or so of total economic output. As a result, declines in manufacturing activity don't always result in macroeconomic recessions. This is the reason, in the case of the purchasing managers' index, lower index levels equate to macroeconomic recessions.

FIGURE 5.2 shows that post–World War II recessions in the United States have been associated with steep declines in the purchasing managers' index, which have sometimes preceded the downturn and always continued through them. Before the 1980s, virtually every time the purchasing managers' index fell below 50, the economy slipped into recession. After the 1980s, however, sub-50 readings were associated with only two—very short and mild—recessions. If you were to go back and review press clippings about the sub-50 postings that occurred in 1995–1996 and in late 1998, for example, you'd find many an economist predicting recession.

Figure 5.2   Recessions and ISM's Purchasing Managers' Index

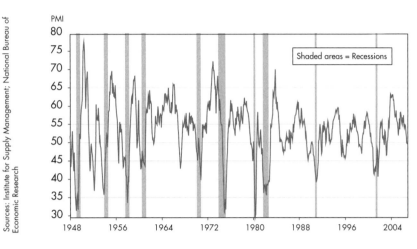

Sources: Institute for Supply Management; National Bureau of Economic Research

Those recessions never developed—again, underlining the fact that manufacturing slumps no longer designate overall recession. That is, the manufacturing sector can experience a recession without the broader economy falling into recession.

ISM EMPLOYMENT INDEX

The purchasing managers' index by itself depicts the general state of the manufacturing sector and of the larger economy. It does so in broad strokes, however. For a more detailed view, economists and traders look at the subindexes, each of which possesses a considerable amount of predictive power with respect to the particular aspect of manufacturing condition and activity that it portrays.

The ISM's employment index, which is compiled from the answers to how the current level of employment compares with last month's, shows the employment trends at U.S. manufacturers. For instance, **FIGURE 5.3** charts the employment index against the year-over-year percentage change in manufacturing payrolls as reported by the Bureau of Labor Statistics and gives more evidence of the movement in the U.S. economy away from manufacturing and toward service industries: from 1980 through 2002, the index was

Figure 5.3 ISM's Employment Index Versus Manufacturing Payrolls

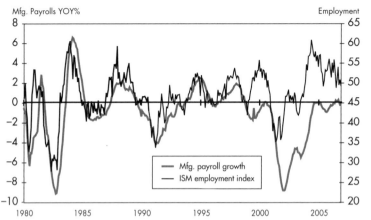

below 50 for a staggering 190 of the 276 months. In other words, for roughly 69 percent of the last quarter century, manufacturing employment has been contracting, rather than expanding.

The relationship between manufacturing payroll growth and the ISM's employment index is indeed close. Figure 5.3 also shows that the employment index is good at predicting declines in the growth rate of manufacturing payrolls but not so good at signaling upturns. During the period covered, whenever the index fell below 50 and stayed there for at least five months, manufacturing payroll growth turned negative about six months after the first sub-50 posting. In contrast, since 1980, the employment index rarely, if ever, has predicted positive manufacturing payroll growth. The reason behind this inability probably lies in the fact that manufacturers shed an overwhelming proportion of workers during the 1980–2003 period—with many manufacturing positions sent abroad.

Economists have recently begun to conclude that there has been a structural change in the U.S. economy, particularly in the employment of manufacturing workers. With soaring productivity rates beginning in the latter half of the 1990s—economists define productivity as the amount of output produced per hour worked—businesses could get away with employing fewer workers. What's more, multinational manufacturers had looked overseas to nations

Figure 5.4   ISM's Price Index Versus Intermediate PPI

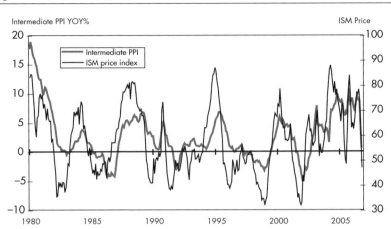

Sources: Institute for Supply Management; U.S. Department of Labor, Bureau of Labor Statistics

like China, India, the Czech Republic, and Mexico for lower-cost labor. It has been argued that these job eliminations are permanent and the jobs are never coming back. This trend is supported by the extended sub-50 postings in the ISM's employment index from the mid-1990s to early 2007.

ISM PRICE INDEX

The ISM's price index, which is compiled from the answers to the question about current prices paid by manufacturers of commodities used in the production process compared with last month's prices, provides an indication of possible inflationary pressures faced by manufacturers. The index receives a considerable amount of attention from the Street, especially the credit markets, because inflation erodes the value of fixed-income securities. And because the Federal Reserve is so concerned with the possibility of rising inflation, it is atop the Fed's economic-indicator watch list as well.

Of course, the index *directly* indicates only how prices are moving in the manufacturing industry. How accurate a reflection it is of inflation in this sector is shown in **FIGURE 5.4**, which charts the ISM's price index against the year-over-year rate of growth in the intermediate goods producer price index. The intermediate goods index is one of the wholesale price measures calculated by the Bureau of Labor Statistics (BLS) as part of the producer price index (PPI). It is a representation of price activity of goods that are one stage after raw materials—in other words, intermediate goods that have received some processing—and includes products such as flooring, newsprint, rubber tires and inner tubes, steel wire, and refined sugar. These are the types of materials that manufacturing companies are most likely to buy. Once again, who better to know about price developments in this area than the purchasing managers who buy these goods? That's why the ISM's price index is so closely respected and watched by the financial markets, as well as by the Federal Reserve.

One question that might reasonably arise is, If these two indexes are so closely related, why not just watch the intermediate goods producer price index? Because the ISM's Report on Business is released on the first business day of the month, it precedes the release of the BLS's producer price index report by about two weeks. To a bond trader, two weeks is an eternity. Decisions regarding the purchase and sale of fixed-income securities are made in a matter of seconds. The faster a bond trader can get the skinny on developing inflation trends, the more money he stands to make.

Investors and economists watch the price index to glean information beyond the cost of intermediate goods. The greatest concern for policy makers is that manufacturers may pass any higher costs on to the final user of the goods being produced. If any such increased prices are widespread and sustained, the general price level could increase, which by definition, signals inflation. In addition to reducing the value of fixed-income securities, inflation impedes the pace of consumer spending because workers have to earn more (that is, by working longer) just to afford the same amount of goods and services they used to get at lower prices.

The price index is thus a useful indicator of the potential for inflation, in both the manufacturing sector and the broader economy. According to a recent Report on Business, a price index above 47.1 for a sustained period of time is generally consistent with an increase in the BLS's index of manufacturing prices, which is one of the measures of price inflation on the wholesale level.

As with all sections of the ISM's Report on Business, the anecdotal commentary and remarks following each subindex contribute greatly to this report's value. Because of the detail and insight that the monthly report provides, basic materials and commodities analysts—for example, those covering metals, chemicals, cement, lumber, and paper and packaging—scurry each month to get their hands on a copy.

Investors can benefit by comments such as those in the November 2006 report, which stated that the eight industries paying higher prices for that month were printing and related support activities; food, beverage, and tobacco products; machinery; transportation equipment; computer and electronic products; furniture and related products; miscellaneous manufacturing; and nonmetallic mineral products.

If investors know which industries are paying higher prices during slower economic periods, they can tell that activity in those respective industries may be beginning to turn around. One of the most common characteristics of slower economic times is the inability—and undesirability—of businesses to raise prices. Because slower economic times mean income growth is sluggish and job creation scant, businesses rarely get away with raising prices during such periods. (The only time a company can raise prices during gloomy economic conditions is if that company is selling a necessity, like health or medical care.) So when prices are rising, it's generally a signal of better times to come.

A high correlation also exists between the ISM's price index and the spot price of West Texas intermediate crude oil. Again, this isn't surprising, because manufacturers employ a great deal of oil in the production process. Smelters, kilns, compressors, furnaces, and machinery at countless plants and factories use some form of crude oil or one of its derivatives. So when the price of crude oil rises, so too does the cost of manufacturers' inputs. These increases are usually reflected in the ISM's price index because it is a measure of prices that manufacturers pay. Again, the concern among policy makers is that if input prices are rising, there is an increased likelihood that those prices will be transferred to the final product, which would mean a higher cost to the end user, the consumer.

ISM Supplier Deliveries Index

The ISM's price index isn't the only inflation barometer in the ISM's monthly Report on Business. The ISM's supplier deliveries index, also referred to as the vendor supplier index, provides clues to the future direction of prices.

The supplier deliveries index, which is compiled from the responses to the question regarding delivery performance, is a measure of how long it takes suppliers to deliver parts and materials that are integral to the production process. When the index exceeds 50, it means that delivery has slowed, indicating that greater demand is making it more difficult for suppliers (vendors) to get crucial materials to manufacturers. Sub-50 postings, conversely, indicate faster deliveries.

Lengthened delivery times often result from labor disputes that lead to strikes or lockouts. Such disputes occur more frequently among companies involved in the manufacturing process—particularly those employing machinists, rail workers, dockworkers, and truckers—than in the services sector. An increase in the delivery time for supplies (inputs in the production process) could result in bottlenecks that can, if sustained, in turn result in higher prices because of the inability to fabricate and deliver necessary inputs.

This process is consistent with the basic laws of supply and demand. Impeded deliveries, for whatever reason, limit the amount of production that can be performed and consequently reduce the availability of final goods produced. This, by definition, is a decline in supply. When the supply of a good declines, its price rises. The longer the labor dispute, the longer the delivery time and the greater the potential for inflation. Moreover, any time supplier backlogs develop, the manufacturer incurs greater costs as well as the increased potential for lost business, which may exacerbate the inflationary environment.

Economists look at the ISM supplier deliveries index alongside the *Journal of Commerce*'s industrial materials price index, which

Figure 5.5   ISM's Supplier Deliveries Index Versus Intermediate PPI

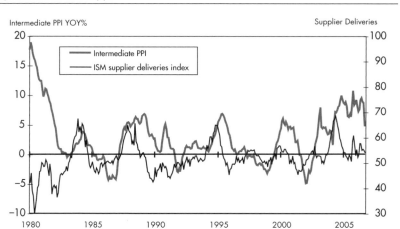

Sources: Institute for Supply Management; U.S. Department of Labor, Bureau of Labor Statistics

is calculated on a daily basis by the Economic Cycle Research Institute and represents eighteen industrial commodity materials, including nickel, cotton, polyester, burlap, copper, red oak, plywood, tallow, steel, crude oil, benzene, and ethylene. When these industrial commodity prices rise, it is often a sign that conditions are improving. Unfortunately this index is not readily available to most traders—particularly those without a Bloomberg terminal. As a proxy we use the intermediate producer price index, which is presented in **FIGURE 5.5**. As the chart illustrates, higher postings in the supplier deliveries index are soon accompanied by increases in the prices of producer prices at the intermediate stage of production. Conversely, precipitous declines and sub-50 postings in the index result in lower industrial price levels.

ISM NONMANUFACTURING INDEXES

Because manufacturing currently accounts for only 20 percent or so of total economic output, not surprisingly, economists have wanted a measure similar to the purchasing managers' index that would address the condition of the businesses constituting the other 80 percent of the economy. In response, the ISM created the Non-Manufacturing Report on Business in July 1997. The nonmanufacturing survey is similar to the manufacturing survey and like its older sibling, possesses some degree of predictive power. It is based on data from responses to questions asked of more than 375 purchasing and supply managers in approximately 62 industries, including entertainment, utilities, hotels, real estate, retail, insurance, finance and banking, accounting, communications, mining, agriculture, engineering, educational services, construction, and health services—in other words, just about anything that doesn't fall under the heading of manufacturing. Because a considerable number of service businesses are represented in this survey, the business press often refers to the nonmanufacturing survey as the ISM services report.

Among the indexes represented in the Non-Manufacturing Report on Business are the following:

- total business activity
- new orders
- backlog of orders
- new export orders
- imports
- prices
- employment
- supplier deliveries
- inventory sentiment
- inventory change
- customers' inventories

Like the ISM manufacturing report's purchasing managers' index, the nonmanufacturing report has a headline index called total business activity. This index is frequently referred to as the nonmanufacturing, or services, purchasing managers' index. Unlike the manufacturing report's purchasing managers' index, however, the nonmanufacturing total business activity index is not a composite index or a weighted average of subindexes.

Because the nonmanufacturing report is, relatively speaking, in its infancy, the monthly report—usually released two business days after the manufacturing report, or the third business day of the month—

Figure 5.6   ISM's Non-Manufacturing PMI and Consumption Spending on Services

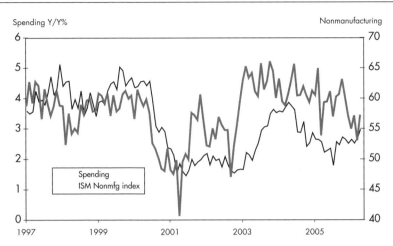

Sources: Institute for Supply Management; U.S. Department of Labor, Bureau of Labor Statistics

doesn't possess the same ability to move the financial markets as its older, more esteemed manufacturing counterpart. Its predictive nature isn't exactly known, considering that the number of economic downturns since its initiation in 1997 has been rather limited.

FIGURE 5.6 shows how closely the ISM's nonmanufacturing purchasing managers' index tracks the Commerce Department's twelve-month rate of consumption of services in the economy. This relationship is to be expected because services dominate the nonmanufacturing sectors surveyed. Economists have found that an index reading of 50 equates to a growth rate of about 3.5 percent (year-over-year) in the consumption of services.

The indexes in the nonmanufacturing survey clearly possess a high degree of correlation with a considerable portion of U.S. economic activity. There's no doubt that the ISM's nonmanufacturing survey will eventually become a top-tier economic indicator, especially because the United States has steadily evolved from a smokestack industrialized economy to a more services-dominated one. But before than can occur, a longer history, as well as a weighted composite index similar to the Manufacturing ISM Report on Business purchasing managers' index, will be needed.

How to Use What You See

The stock market tends to react in sync with movements in the purchasing managers' index and production index. This is understandable because manufacturing activity, despite its reduced role, has proved to be a good representation of total economic conditions. When businesses foresee stronger consumer demand—as evidenced through declining inventories and acceleration in consumer spending—they pick up the pace of production. So, upticks in the purchasing managers' index or the production index and postings higher than 50 usually portend better things for equity issues, because greater demand usually results in higher sales and subsequently, profitability.

Normally, the fixed-income market would react adversely to large increases in the purchasing managers' index. In other words, higher postings, above 50, would be regarded as inflationary, thereby eroding the value of fixed-income securities, sending prices of bonds lower (and yields higher). Bear in mind that the ISM Report on Business also contains the price index, which also captures the attention of bond traders. The higher the value of the price index, the greater the inflation fear and the greater the sell-off in bonds. So, to better understand the fixed-income market reactions, Wall Streeters usually look squarely to the price index and the direction of any movement within as the ultimate inflation barometer of this report.

Tricks from the Trenches

When economists get their hands on a proven set of economic indicators like those contained in the ISM Report on Business, they tend to get creative and conjure up their own indicators, usually derivations of the more successful components in the series. One of the more popular tricks performed by Wall Streeters is to take the difference between the ISM's new orders index and the inventories index. The resulting statistic, depicted in **FIGURE 5.7**, has exhibited a relatively strong correlation with the year-over-year percentage change in real GDP.

Figure 5.7   ISM'S "New Orders Minus Inventories" Index Versus Real GDP

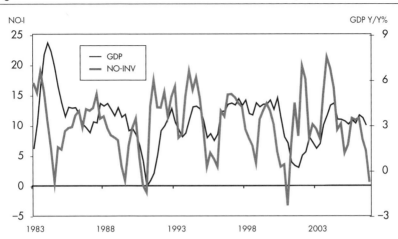

Sources: Institute for Supply Management; U.S. Department of Commerce, Bureau of Economic Analysis

Because gross domestic product is reported on a quarterly basis and is prone to rather lengthy delays, some economists find this "new orders minus inventories" index a timely (available monthly as opposed to quarterly) and accurate depiction of the economic growth rate.

Like the many diffusion indexes examined in this chapter, the "new orders minus inventories" index doesn't project a specific magnitude for real economic growth, or GDP, but it is quite telling about the likelihood of economic contraction or expansion. During some phases of the business cycle when the identification of recession isn't exactly clear, this trick becomes another helpful indicator on the state of economic affairs.

Economists look out for low or negative readings in the "new orders minus inventories" index. Anytime there is no difference between the inventories and new orders indexes, that is, when the "new orders minus inventories" index is zero, the economic growth rate tends to contract. Historically, negative readings have been associated with economic recessions. Readings in the "new orders minus inventories" index of 10 or higher historically have equated to real economic growth rates in excess of 3.5 percent—a rate generally considered to be strong.

Are these levels gospel? Absolutely not. This is nothing more than a crude model and should be used only as a guide to projecting economic activity on a monthly basis (because GDP is not read-ily available). However, as this indicator has, on occasion, possessed something of a leading quality, some economists look for trends in the index to forecast GDP growth.

Another crude model applied by economists looks at the differ-ence between the ISM's new orders index and the price index. The resultant measure has displayed a relationship with the year-over-year percentage change in the total return of the Standard & Poor's 500 index. The possible economic explanation behind this associa-tion may be that the price index is in effect a proxy for costs, and new orders for revenues. The difference between these two mea-sures would be profits. In this case, profits are reflected in the year-over-year total return of the S&P 500. As suggested in **FIGURE 5.8**, there is indeed a close association between these indicators.

Problems with this little-known indicator include the fact that input prices as measured by the ISM price index are not a highly accurate proxy for costs. A number of costs manufacturers incur are not captured by the price index, the largest being labor, for example. Furthermore, new orders are hardly the best representation of rev-enues. Orders aren't always filled, many are delayed, and ultimately different volumes may be shipped. Still, the so-called new orders minus price index provides a "quick and dirty" model for predicting the total return of the S&P 500. A simple regression analysis reveals that the total return on the S&P 500 (on a year-over-year basis) will be positive as long as the difference between the ISM's new orders index and the price index is greater than –20.

Bear in mind that this index doesn't always pan out as the greatest forecasting model of stock market levels. Despite the aftermath of the burst stock market bubble in early 2000, the "new orders minus price" index began to register some hefty readings in early 2001, suggesting the total return of the S&P 500 would be strong. Clearly this was a false signal, as stocks continued their descent well into 2003. Nev-ertheless, as Figure 5.8 suggests, for a simple back-of-the-envelope forecast, the tool isn't too bad a predictor of stock market returns.

Regional economists and all those who are looking for a more detailed, targeted representation of manufacturing conditions are

Figure 5.8   ISM's "New Orders Minus Price" Index Versus S&P 500 Growth Rate

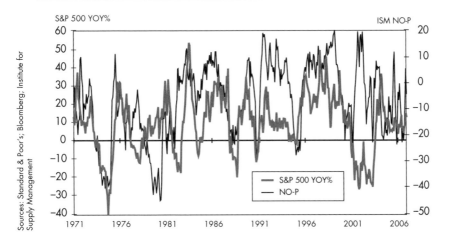

encouraged to visit the ISM's website and view the various regional business survey reports. These surveys are conducted by the many local purchasing management associations, and should not be confused with the national survey that has been examined in this chapter. Some of the more popular regional reports observed by Wall Street include the Arizona, Austin, Buffalo, Chicago, Cleveland, Dallas, Denver, Georgia, Houston, New York, Northwest Ohio, Pittsburgh, and Western Washington reports.

These reports have helped many Wall Street economic departments create a mock beige book. The real beige book, so called by the Street because of the color of its cover, is one of the three books that the Federal Reserve creates and uses during its eight-times-a-year monetary-policy deliberations. It is the only information at those meetings released to the public; this generally occurs two weeks prior to the Federal Open Market Committee meeting.

Formally known as the *Summary of Commentary on Current Economic Conditions by Federal Reserve District*, the beige book contains anecdotal commentary that has been accumulated by each of the twelve Federal Reserve districts. The regional ISM surveys frequently provide information to those summaries and generally offer excellent insight into the manufacturing and economic climate in each region.

Manufacturers' Shipments, Inventories, and Orders   6

T HE MANUFACTURERS' SHIPMENTS, Inventories, and Orders
(M3) survey is one of the most respected economic indicators
on Wall Street. Published monthly by the U.S. Department of
Commerce's Census Bureau, the report measures current activity and future commitments in the U.S. manufacturing sector.
Using data supplied by some forty-seven hundred reporting units
of businesses in eighty-nine industry categories, it provides statistics on the value of factories' shipments, new orders, unfilled
orders, and inventories. The survey is closely followed by economists, members of the business community, and various government organizations, including the Bureau of Economic Analysis
(BEA), which employs the survey's figures in preparing its gross
domestic product (GDP) report, particularly the investment and
inventory sections.

The M3 survey is published in two parts. The advance report
on durable goods is released about four weeks after the reference
month, on about the eighteenth business day of the month (the date
varies somewhat to avoid overlapping with other economic releases).
The revised and more comprehensive Manufacturers' Shipments,
Inventories, and Orders appears about a week later, providing greater
detail about production, by industry group, as well as including for
the first time information about nondurable, in addition to durable,
goods. In both the advance and the later report, it is the orders component that garners the most attention from market participants.

Manufacturing orders constitute a leading economic indicator,
because they reflect decisions about optimal inventory levels given

the demand businesses anticipate based on their economic forecasts. In this regard, new orders for durable goods have proved to be particularly accurate predictors, because demand for such products is especially dependent on economic health.

Manufacturing is an important sector of the U.S. economy, accounting for roughly 20 percent of GDP and about the same percentage of overall employment. But the significance of the demand and pace of production figures for trading-floor economists and traders is even greater than those percentages imply. Trends in production are usually experienced as well by the services sectors associated with shipments of manufactured goods and can be quite accurate in marking turning points in the overall economy. For that reason, the Conference Board's index of leading indicators includes components of the M3 survey: manufacturer's new orders for non-defense capital goods and manufacturers' new orders for consumer goods and materials.

The M3 survey can be found on the Department of Commerce's Economic and Statistics Administration website, www.economicindicators.gov, together with the historical series for all its components. Larger increases—of the magnitude of 1 percent or more—in the monthly percentage change of new orders for durable or factory-produced goods are usually interpreted as positive for equity markets and somewhat undesirable for fixed-income security holders. Businesses order goods only if they expect demand to increase. Conversely, declines in new orders are perceived as indicating slower times to come, and generally cause the stock market to decline and bond prices to rally. Investors must keep in mind that both reports are extremely volatile and hard to predict, so the markets may not always place the utmost emphasis on the month-to-month postings.

EVOLUTION OF AN INDICATOR

The M3 survey grew out of the Department of Commerce's Current Industrial Report (CIR) program, in place since 1904. In 1939, the Commerce Department's Office of Business Economics, working through the CIR program, established the first monthly Industry Survey. The forerunner of the M3 survey, it contained broad-based measures of inventory changes and information about the ratio of new and unfilled orders to current sales. In following years, various changes were made in how the data were calculated and presented, as well as in which industry groups were represented and their composition. Revisions instituted from 1947 to 1963, for example, included adding seasonally adjusted dollar estimates of the data to better reveal nonseasonal features, distinguishing durable from nondurable and household from business-related goods, and breaking down market categories into final products and materials. Seasonal effects include a decline in motor vehicle production during summer months as factories retool for the new model year, and the increase in the production of heating oil during September ahead of the winter special season.

In 1997, as part of a broader revision involving many Commerce Department economic reports, the Census Bureau responded to the development of new products and industries by switching the M3 series of data to the more current and generally accepted North American Industry Classification System (NAICS) from the outdated Standard Industrial Classification (SIC) system. These systems are simply uniform systems of classification. By adopting the NAICS, manufacturing, trade, and inventory data can be compared throughout all of North America, rather than just the United States. Use of the NAICS resulted in a number of regroupings. For example, some activities that were not previously classified as manufacturing under the SIC system—such as bottling spring water, retail baking, and software reproduction—are now formally counted under the new NAICS. During this benchmark reclassification, data were revised only back to February 1992, when the U.S. economy was in the process of emerging from the 1990–1991 recession. Because the NAICS data are available only from that date and previous data are classified by different SIC industries, historical analysis is limited.

DIGGING FOR THE DATA

The Census Bureau obtains its data on domestic manufacturing through surveys of manufacturing companies with annual shipments totaling $500 million or more. Participation is voluntary, and responses may be submitted over the Internet, by telephone, or by fax. Relevant data received by the eighteenth day of the month following the month covered by the survey are included in the advance report on durable goods. Additional data, collected through the thirtieth of the month, are consolidated with the previously reported data and included in the more complete Manufacturers' Shipments, Inventories, and Orders.

The reports contain both seasonally adjusted and nonadjusted figures for the record month and for the previous three months, together with percentage changes from month to month. All the values are nominal, given in constant-dollar terms.

The Census Bureau presents the collected data both by industry category, such as industrial machinery and computers, and by topical series. Topical series aggregate industries into broad market groupings, such as home goods and apparel, and into special series, such as nondefense capital goods and defense capital goods. For example, the nondefense capital goods series includes small arms; farm machinery and construction equipment; turbines, generators, pumps, and compressors; oil- and gas-field machinery; computer storage devices; office and institutional furniture; and medical equipment and supplies. Wall Street industry analysts monitor the topical series carefully. Aerospace and defense analysts, for instance, watch defense capital goods closely, whereas hardware and peripheral equipment analysts scrutinize the information technology series.

DURABLE GOODS REPORT

Durable goods are goods expected to last three years or more. They include lumber and wood products; furniture and fixtures; stone, clay, and glass products; and industrial machinery and equipment. These products tend to be quite pricey and are not usually purchased on a regular basis. As a result, data connected to their manufacture fluctuate significantly from month to month and are difficult to predict. This is particularly true with regard to defense-related goods, such as ships and aircraft, whose valuation is exceptionally complex.

The advance report on durable goods contains four categories of data: shipments, new orders, unfilled orders, and inventories. The table in **FIGURE 6.1**, from the October 2006 report, illustrates how the seasonally adjusted data (and the monthly percentage changes) for shipments and new orders of durable goods in different sectors are reported. Another table in the report (not shown) presents the same breakdown for unfilled orders and total inventories.

Shipments comprise products actually sold by establishments. The dollar figures reported are the net sales values of domestically manufactured goods shipped to distributors during the record month. (For larger goods with lengthy fabrication schedules, such as aircraft and tanks, the reported figures are estimates of the value of work performed during the survey period.)

Some of the larger categories of shipments include capital goods (products, such as machinery, that are used to make other products), representing 35 percent of the total; transportation products, representing 26 percent; and machinery, 13 percent. (The percentages don't add up to 100 percent because the categories overlap, that is, both nondefense capital goods and machinery include textile and paper industry machinery.)

New orders are product orders received during the record month, including both those to be filled during the month and those for goods to be delivered sometime in the future. Because these figures indicate businesses' intentions with regard to purchases, they are the most forward looking in the release. **Unfilled orders** are orders that haven't yet been shipped or reported as sold. They are a measure of order backlog.

Businesses understandably want to keep information regarding the level of new orders close to their vests. Because some survey participants (in this voluntary survey) are reluctant to provide this information, the Census Bureau is forced to estimate the level of new orders.

Figure 6.1 Manufacturers' Shipments and New Orders for Durable Goods ($ in millions)

Item	Seasonally Adjusted					
	Monthly			Percentage Change		
	Oct 2006	Sep 2006 (r)	Aug 2006	Sep– Oct	Aug– Sep (r)	Jul– Aug
DURABLE GOODS						
Total:						
Shipments......................	$209,941	$208,769	$214,555	0.6	–2.7	2.1
New orders	209,974	229,021	210,645	–8.3	8.7	0.0
Excluding transportation:						
Shipments......................	155,211	154,375	157,774	0.5	–2.2	0.8
New orders	150,229	152,752	151,951	–1.7	0.5	–1.3
Excluding defense:						
Shipments......................	200,037	199,366	204,689	0.3	–2.6	1.9
New orders	200,338	214,073	199,373	–6.4	7.4	–0.4
Manufacturing with unfilled orders:						
Shipments......................	146,370	147,698	150,590	–0.9	–1.9	2.1
New orders	154,112	173,843	153,476	–11.3	13.3	–0.8
Primary metals:						
Shipments......................	19,045	19,297	19,958	–1.3	–3.3	0.0
New orders	19,115	18,908	19,503	1.1	–3.1	–2.7
Fabricated metal products:						
Shipments......................	24,661	24,610	25,037	0.2	–1.7	1.3
New orders	24,425	25,044	25,595	–2.5	–2.2	2.7
Machinery:						
Shipments......................	28,343	27,817	28,169	1.9	–1.2	1.7
New orders	30,018	29,602	28,608	1.4	3.5	–1.0
Computers and electronic products:						
Shipments......................	34,858	34,466	35,745	1.1	–3.6	1.0
New orders	27,575	30,722	30,040	–10.2	2.3	–2.1
Computers and related products:						
Shipments......................	4,715	6,276	6,710	–24.9	–6.5	–3.2
New orders	4,766	6,410	6,354	–25.6	0.9	–10.1
Communications equipment:						
Shipments......................	5,944	5,974	5,910	–0.5	1.1	10.5
New orders	5,526	6,652	6,700	–16.9	–0.7	12.2
Communications equipment:						
Shipments......................	5,944	5,974	5,910	–0.5	1.1	10.5
New orders	5,526	6,652	6,700	–16.9	–0.7	12.2
Semiconductors:						
Shipments......................	7,709	5,893	6,796	30.8	–13.3	–1.1
New orders	(NA)	(NA)	(NA)	(NA)	(NA)	(NA)

Figure 6.1 (continued)

| Item | Seasonally Adjusted | | | | | |
| | Monthly | | | Percentage Change | | |
	Oct 2006	Sep 2006 (r)	Aug 2006	Sep– Oct	Aug– Sep (r)	Jul– Aug
Electrical equipment, appliances, and components:						
Shipments......................	10,249	10,023	10,367	2.3	–3.3	0.8
New orders	10,838	10,316	9,859	5.1	4.6	–8.9
Transportation equipment:						
Shipments......................	54,730	54,394	56,781	0.6	–4.2	5.6
New orders	59,745	76,269	58,694	–21.7	29.9	3.6
Motor vehicles and parts:						
Shipments......................	37,203	36,585	39,436	1.7	–7.2	5.1
New orders	37,434	36,932	39,301	1.4	–6.0	3.7
Nondefense aircraft and parts:						
Shipments......................	8,199	8,863	8,158	–7.5	8.6	9.2
New orders	13,207	23,802	7,981	–44.5	198.2	–19.2
Defense aircraft and parts:						
Shipments......................	3,717	3,427	3,614	8.5	–5.2	6.4
New orders	3,546	2,976	3,301	19.2	–9.8	8.2
All other durable goods:						
Shipments......................	38,055	38,162	38,498	–0.3	–0.9	0.2
New orders	38,258	38,160	38,346	0.3	–0.5	–0.5
Capital goods:						
Shipments......................	74,575	75,773	76,398	–1.6	–0.8	2.4
New orders	80,978	100,237	79,237	–19.2	26.5	–0.8
Nondefense capital goods:						
Shipments......................	66,371	67,940	68,173	–2.3	–0.3	2.0
New orders	73,165	86,733	69,569	–15.6	24.7	–2.0
Excluding aircraft:						
Shipments..................	61,010	61,928	62,940	–1.5	–1.6	1.3
New orders	63,289	66,662	64,617	–5.1	3.2	1.1
Defense capital goods:						
Shipments......................	8,204	7,833	8,225	4.7	–4.8	5.9
New orders	7,813	13,504	9,668	–42.1	39.7	9.1

NA   Not Available   (r) Revised

Source: U.S. Department of Commerce, Bureau of the Census

New orders numbers are derived by adding together the dollar values of shipments and of unfilled orders from the current month and subtracting the value of unfilled orders from the previous month (which can't be "new"). (For nondurable goods, new orders and shipments are generally the same. Because many of these products are perishable, they are usually shipped, and in many cases, consumed, as soon as they are ordered.)

The monthly inventory postings in the M3 survey indicate the dollar value of goods stockpiled at factories and in sales branches, regardless of the stage of fabrication. These manufacturing inventories account for about 40 percent of total U.S. inventories. (The total business inventory position is discussed in detail in Chapter 7.)

FACTORY ORDERS REPORT

The more comprehensive factory orders report contains revisions to the advance report on durable goods, as well as the first presentation of nondurable goods data and greater detail on all of these data by stage of fabrication.

What's a **nondurable good**? An old economist friend once gave the following nontechnical definition: if you leave it outdoors in the elements and after three years it disappears, it's a good bet that it was a nondurable good. Included in this category are food and beverages, tobacco products, textiles, apparel, paper and allied products, chemicals and allied products, and petroleum and coal products.

Nondurables don't enjoy the headline status of their cousins, durables. Durable goods such as turbines, engines, household appliances, and machinery are sexier and easier to visualize as factory-produced goods than are nondurables such as pesticides, tobacco, and paints. That doesn't mean nondurables aren't an integral part of the economy, however. Nondurable goods account for just a little less than half of total manufacturing industry shipments. In October 2006, for example, nondurables made up 46 percent of total shipments, compared with 54 percent for durables.

In addition to industry category and topical series, the factory orders report also groups data by stage of fabrication: materials and supplies, work in process, or finished goods. Most economists like to look at work in progress, because it includes material already in the pipeline. About three-quarters of the products at this stage of fabrication are durable goods. The fabrication of short-lived non-durables tends to be similarly short; these goods are heavily represented in the finished goods numbers.

WHAT DOES IT ALL MEAN?

The M3 survey is a gold mine of economic information for investors, traders, analysts, and economists. The durable new orders data represent a particularly rich lode because of the insight they provide into a large component of personal consumption and capital expenditures.

DURABLE GOODS REPORT

The equity market reacts positively to increases in new orders for durables, because such increases indicate new demand and an optimistic economic outlook. Conversely, a slowdown or decline in new orders implies a softer economic climate and less likelihood of a pickup in corporate profitability, which generally hurts the value of stocks. In the land of fixed income, the situation is reversed: strong monthly postings fuel worries about inflation, which erodes the value of coupon payments and sends interest rates higher, both of which depress bond prices and push yields up. The bond market welcomes weaker data because they are generally associated with a benign inflationary environment.

Interpretation of these data is complicated, however, by their extreme volatility. Postings in the durable goods and factory orders reports whipsaw from month to month. This is illustrated by the chart in **FIGURE 6.2**, which shows the monthly changes in new orders for durable goods. Virtually all the new orders data, whether for fabricated metals, communications equipment, or machinery, exhibit this type of irregular behavior, which inhibits accurate trend spotting.

To correct for this instability, economists adopt two approaches.

Figure 6.2 Month-to-Month Percentage Change in New Orders for Durable Goods

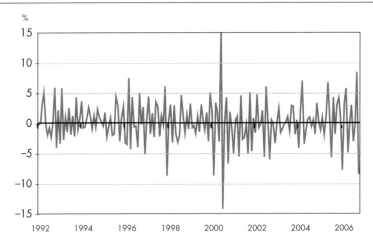

Source: U.S. Department of Commerce, Bureau of the Census

One is to look at the data without the most volatile components: the defense and transportation sectors. Demand for goods such as ships, military armored vehicles, and guided missiles is highly unpredictable and unstable, especially on a monthly basis; an unforeseen order for twenty-five commercial airplanes can really blow an economic forecast. The other approach is to apply some smoothing techniques, such as moving averages, to the data. To compute a moving average, you start by averaging the data over a certain period—for a three-month moving average, for example, you would add together the figures (new orders, say) from three monthly reports and divide by three. To make this average move, you recalculate it each month, dropping the oldest data point and adding the newest one. Another smoothing technique is to look at year-to-year (rather than month-to-month) changes.

The chart in **FIGURE 6.3** illustrates the smoothing effects of two approaches: eliminating the volatile transportation sector and taking the longer year-over-year view. Although the data still reveal plenty of volatility, the sharp swings are minimized.

The chart illustrates another point: the importance of using additional sources of information, such as business reports in newspapers and on television, in interpreting the data. In Figure 6.3, the line graphing new orders bottoms out in October, one

Figure 6.3   New Orders for Durable Goods

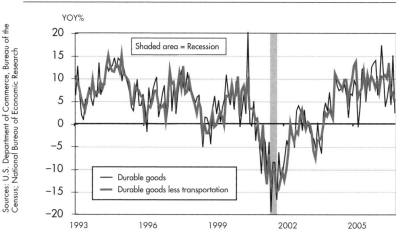

Sources: U.S. Department of Commerce, Bureau of the Census; National Bureau of Economic Research

of the final months of the 2001 recession, and heads higher during the year's final quarter. Anyone following the economic news would know that this recovery was prompted by the zero percent financing that automakers introduced for several makes and models in October 2001. This move sparked the highest automotive demand, production, and sales in history: in October alone, some 21.1 million cars and lightweight trucks were sold. In the period of sluggish economic growth that followed the 2001 recession, big-name retailers such as Home Depot and Sears also offered zero percent financing for up to eighteen months on large durable goods such as washing machines, refrigerators, carpeting, and lawn mowers. These actions served not only to spur activity in the sectors directly involved but also to boost aggregate demand in 2001 and so help keep the recession mild and short-lived. Economists and analysts who took the extra step of investigating the automakers' and retailers' business decisions were able to forecast economic activity more accurately and perhaps avoid being overoptimistic about any continuing impetus from the auto sector, since its strength was somewhat artificial, built on unsustainable zero percent financing and discounts that in effect cannibalized its future sales.

Of the categories represented in the durable goods report, the primary metals sector—which includes iron, steel, aluminum, and copper production—is among those most closely watched by economists. Although shipments of these products represent a relatively small slice of the total for durable goods (about 9 percent in October 2006, as shown in Figure 6.1), the materials are vital ingredients in the manufacturing process. Consequently, increases in new orders for primary metals generally hint at greater future manufacturing activity.

Most of the other categories in the durable goods report involve manufacturing. The goods produced by these sectors are generally expensive, and buyers of them (whether individuals or companies) usually need to finance their purchases. New orders for and shipments of these products are thus very sensitive to interest rates. High rates mean lower numbers. Lower rates, in contrast, boost the new orders figures by making it easier for consumers to buy furniture, appliances, automobiles, and personal computers and for businesses to buy machinery, power transmission generators, and capital equipment. When the Federal Reserve reduces its target overnight borrowing rate, it is attempting to stimulate these sectors.

FACTORY ORDERS REPORT

By the time the report on factory orders comes out, the markets have had time to absorb and react to the critical data in the durable goods report released a week earlier. The more detailed information on inventories and unfilled orders contained in the later report doesn't exactly light a fire under traders. Therefore the markets don't move much when it is released. The report contains several components, however, that provide important measures of current and future demand and so bear careful monitoring.

Unfilled orders are a reasonably accurate gauge of the strength of demand for the particular industry, and so of the strength of the underlying economy. Economists view a rising backlog as a sign of accelerating demand and economic strength, and a declining backlog as an indication of a weakening economy. The story behind this relationship is somewhat complicated. When the economy is expanding rapidly, businesses tend to be optimistic about the future and place large numbers of new orders for goods. They want products on their shelves and in their showrooms when consumers come calling. The manufacturers of these goods attempt to fill as many of the orders as possible but often can't do so expeditiously with their existing staff levels. Most employers put off hiring new workers until they see demand increasing. Companies adopt this "just-in-time" approach to hiring because of the expenses related to employment and employees—perhaps their greatest business costs. Manufacturing is largely unionized, and specialized craftsmen with finely honed skills are often needed to fill skyrocketing new orders. Manufacturers must consult union officials, adopting specific pay rates and work schedules. They are often forced to hire a minimum number of workers. If the economy turns south, triggering widespread order cancellations, the companies are saddled with newly hired workers standing around idled machinery. Only when the union-negotiated contracts expire are they free to eliminate staff. No wonder they're reluctant to add employees until demand makes it necessary. But the process of advertising for, interviewing, hiring, and training new workers is lengthy. In the meantime, backlogs of unfilled orders thus pile up.

How to Use What You See

The basic trading strategy related to the M3 survey data involves identifying potential turning points in demand for U.S. manufactured goods and related products. Obviously, the greater the volume of shipments, the greater the strength of current demand. For future demand, the reasoning is similar: the higher the number of new orders for goods, the greater the probability of strong activity down the road; the lower the number, the bleaker the outlook. Particularly potent in predicting the future are manufacturers' new orders for consumer goods and materials, and for nondefense capital goods. These components have proved so accurate that the Conference Board includes them in its index of leading economic indicators. Remember, however, that in applying this approach, it is best to look at year-over-year

Figure 6.4 Shipments of Nondefense Capital Goods Excluding Aircraft Versus Software and Equipment Investment

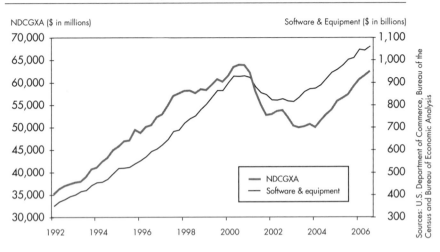

percentage changes as opposed to the monthly figures, which, as noted above, are too volatile to allow accurate trend spotting.

TRICKS FROM THE TRENCHES

This chapter's trick is to watch the value of nondefense capital goods spending excluding aircraft (NDCGXA). The BEA uses the reports' figures for shipments of NDCGXA in determining the equipment and software investment component of the GDP report. As **FIGURE 6.4** shows, the volume of NDCGXA shipments shows a high correlation with the level of software and equipment spending.

Because of this relationship, shipments of nondefense capital goods excluding aircraft can serve as a proxy for the level of total non-residential business investment in the GDP report, also referred to as capital goods investment. This is very useful; because investment in capital drives economic activity, economists want to spot trends in this component as early as possible. But capital-investment figures are available only on a quarterly basis, in the GDP report, and three months is a very long time to wait. NDCGXA shipments are among

Figure 6.5   New Orders for Nondefense Capital Goods Excluding Aircraft
Versus Capital Spending

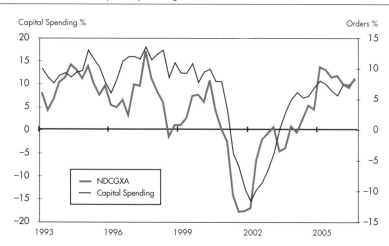

Sources: U.S. Department of Commerce, Bureau of the
Census and Bureau of Economic Analysis

the few monthly surrogates for this important indicator—and the only one that is given in dollar-denominated values, rather than as a representative index, like the industrial production or the Institute for Supply Management's new orders diffusion indexes.

As mentioned above, shipments data paint a picture of current demand; for future trends you have to look at new orders. New orders for nondefense capital goods excluding aircraft are particularly significant. Only when businesses are confident about the economic outlook and future demand will they make costly investments in new machinery and innovative processes. As **FIGURE 6.5** illustrates, NDCGXA new orders anticipate this investment by about three to six months. On a macroeconomic level, prior to the commencement of the recession in April 2001, for instance, new orders began a sharp decline in July 2000, replicated by capital spending during the fourth quarter of 2000.

So watch for trends in the NDCGXA data. These reveal corporate perceptions of the near-term economic outlook and so can help you to predict manufacturing activity and overall economic growth.

Manufacturing and Trade Inventories and Sales 7

TALK ABOUT THE REDHEADED STEPCHILD of economic indicators! Few investors, either professional or lay, pay much attention to inventories. Even popular economics texts largely ignore them. Not so corporate managers and economists. Both these groups are well aware of the importance of inventory levels—and of the dangers of miscalculating them.

Business inventories are "waiting room" goods—products that have been manufactured, processed, or mined but have not yet been sold to a final user. As such, they are very important in the calculation of gross domestic product (GDP) (see Chapter 1). GDP is the total amount of final goods and services produced in an economy in a given period. That includes goods that haven't found a final purchaser—in other words, inventories. Accordingly, the Bureau of Economic Analysis incorporates inventories in the aggregate expenditure formula—$C + I + G + (X - M)$—used to calculate GDP. The I in the formula stands for gross private domestic investment, which includes businesses' spending on inventories. That's one reason economists keep close track of this factor. Miscalculating the value of inventories can throw off an estimate of economic growth by up to 2 percentage points—a mistake that can ruin a Wall Street economist's career.

But inventories' role in the GDP calculation is not the sole reason economists and managements monitor them carefully. Failure to balance inventories against demand can, and has, hurt businesses and destabilized the economy. Companies that overstock their shelves in anticipation of orders that ultimately fail to materialize find themselves in a hole, forced to cut production and lay off workers. Some prominent economists have even implied that the crash of 1929 was provoked, at least in part, by the misalignment of inventory positions. Businesses whose inventories are too lean, on the other hand, miss potential profit during a boom. To avoid such opportunity loss, companies with low stocks may pick up the pace of new orders, spurring manufacture and boosting the economy. Because of their relation to production activity, inventory levels are also of interest to traders. Falling levels, with their promise of increased production and thus higher earnings, can boost equity prices. Fixed-income prices, meanwhile, may decline because of fear of heightened inflation that often accompanies an accelerating economy. On the other hand, rising inventories, implying slowing production, depresses stocks and buoys bonds.

Several economic reports address the inventory position of U.S. companies, but the most comprehensive is the monthly Manufacturing and Trade Inventories and Sales (MTIS) report. The MTIS report, also referred to on the Street as the total business inventories report, contains the most recent available inventory data for the manufacturing, wholesale, and retail sectors. It is assembled by the U.S. Department of Commerce's Census Bureau and released at 8:30 a.m. (ET), about six weeks after the reference month. The report for October 2006, for example, was distributed on December 13. Both the current report and historical data are available on the Commerce Department's website, www.economicindicators.gov.

Despite the importance of inventories to GDP and business management, the monthly MTIS report is generally ignored by the investment community and the business media. One reason is that all the sales statistics it contains and two-thirds of the inventory data—those for manufacturing and wholesalers—have already been reported elsewhere. The only new information is on retail inventories, and all the figures are a month and a half old.

Another reason for the MTIS report's lukewarm reception is the difficulty of making the historical comparisons necessary for extensive analyses. The numbers presented are only for the record month and the preceding one. Moreover, because all the data were converted to the North American Industry Classification System (NAICS) in 2001, the statistical history goes back only to 1992.

These drawbacks notwithstanding, the MTIS report is definitely worth a careful read. Beyond presenting the first monthly numbers for retail inventories, it contains the very useful inventories-to-sales ratios. And its breakdown and presentation of the data make it relatively easy to trace trends and evaluate the significance of movements.

EVOLUTION OF AN INDICATOR

The MTIS survey was originally implemented, and the results published and analyzed, by the Department of Commerce's Bureau of Economic Analysis. The Census Bureau took on those duties in March 1979, with the release of the January inventory and sales data of that year. In 1997 the Census Bureau, responding to the scores of new products and industries that needed to be cataloged, decided to convert to the NAICS from the outdated Standard Industrial Classification (SIC) system. It wasn't until 2001, however, that the data contained in the MTIS report was converted to NAICS. This necessitated some adjustment of data reported under the old system, so that historical comparisons could be made. But the adjustment has been completed back to only 1992.

DIGGING FOR THE DATA

The MTIS report compiles sales data previously reported in the Census Bureau's Advance Monthly Sales for Retail and Food Services report (see Chapter 10) together with inventory and sales information from its Monthly Wholesale Trade Survey and its Manufacturers' Shipments, Inventories, and Orders (M3) survey (see Chapter 6). The only new information, as noted earlier, is on retail inventories, which is obtained from retail firms regarding the value of their end-of-month inventories.

The report organizes the data into three tables. Table 1 contains sales and inventory numbers and inventories-to-sales ratios

Figure 7.1 Estimated Monthly Sales and Inventories for Manufacturers, Retailers, and Merchant Wholesalers

| | Sales ($ in millions) | | |
	Oct. 2006 (p)	Sept. 2006 (r)	Oct. 2005 (s)
Adjusted			
Total business	$1,046,286	$1,047,878	$1,009,800
Manufacturers	389,854	389,406	385,959
Retailers	328,648	329,040	314,307
Merchant Wholesalers	327,784	329,432	309,534

(p) preliminary, (r) revised, (s) adjusted data revised for concurrent seasonal adjustment

for business as a whole as well as for the three primary subgroups: manufacturers, retailers, and merchant wholesalers. The numbers are given, in both seasonally adjusted and nonadjusted form, for the reference month and the month preceding, as well as for the same month a year earlier. **FIGURE 7.1** shows part of Table 1 from the October 2006 report, released in December. In this table, manufacturing accounts for 37 percent of total inventories, retailers for about 31 percent, and merchant wholesalers about 31 percent. These percentages tend to remain relatively stable, although they can be expected to change somewhat as the composition of the American economy evolves.

Table 2 from the report shows the month-over-month and year-over-year percentage changes in sales and inventories (both seasonally adjusted and nonadjusted) for the reference month and the month-over-month changes for the month preceding. Table 3 presents the detail for the retail sector, breaking down the inventory and sales numbers, percentage changes, and ratios by retail business: motor vehicle and parts dealers; furniture, home furnishings, electronics, and appliance stores; building materials, garden equipment, and supplies stores; food and beverage stores; general merchandise stores; and within the last category, department stores excluding leased stores. It also gives two totals: for the retail sector as a whole and for the sector excluding motor vehicles and parts dealers.

Figure 7.1   Estimated Monthly Sales and Inventories for Manufacturers, Retailers, and Merchant Wholesalers (cont'd.)

	Inventories ($ in millions)			Inventories/Sales Ratio		
	Oct. 2006 (p)	Sept. 2006 (r)	Oct. 2005 (s)	Oct. 2006 (p)	Sept. 2006 (r)	Oct. 2005 (s)
Adjusted						
Total business	$1,365,943	$1,361,086	$1,272,910	1.31	1.3	1.26
Manufacturers	481,078	479,304	449,332	1.23	1.23	1.16
Retailers	491,941	491,908	466,604	1.5	1.49	1.48
Merchant Wholesalers	392,924	389,874	356,974	1.2	1.18	1.15

(p) preliminary, (r) revised, (s) adjusted data revised for concurrent seasonal adjustment
Source: U.S. Department of Commerce, Bureau of the Census

WHAT DOES IT ALL MEAN?

What do the levels of inventories tell economists? The simple answer is, plenty. Low inventory positions may signal an impending acceleration in production and manufacturing activity. Conversely, very high inventories may portend a recession and widespread layoffs. Wall Street equity analysts likewise can learn much from inventories. By monitoring the levels in the industries they cover, they can identify developing imbalances and potential troubles that other indicators may not reveal.

Inventories are informative because they are central to the production process, which in turn is key to the health of individual businesses, sectors, and the broader economy. As an illustration, consider the recent history of the telecommunications industry.

During the dot-com heyday of the late 1990s and early 2000s, companies desperate to keep up with the twenty-first-century Zeitgeist were continually upgrading their Internet infrastructures with the newest telecommunications technologies. Communications and fiber-optic equipment went from blueprint to development and production on what seemed a monthly basis, and businesses and consumers eagerly bought the new products. Competing telecommunications equipment makers, greedy for market share, dropped prices. They also boosted production, both to make up for their shrinking margins and to keep ahead of soaring demand. Then the bubble burst. Everyone had upgraded as far as they needed or could afford to, and the telecommunications manufacturers were left with massive inventories. The only way to deplete these was by selling stock at deep discounts. The resulting downward price spiral squeezed profits. Companies canceled orders for goods they couldn't sell, leading to pullbacks in production and the layoff of thousands of idled workers. Stock prices collapsed, credit deteriorated, companies declared bankruptcy—and the economy fell into recession.

An interested observer could have identified the potential formulation of a bubble in the telecommunications equipment industry by merely observing this sharp increase in inventories. The graph in **FIGURE 7.2** shows that inventories in the nondefense communications industry increased steadily but evenly during the boom time of the mid-1990s, as manufacturers managed to keep just ahead of heavy demand. Around the turn of the century, though, inventories suddenly shot up, reflecting the steep reduction in consumer purchases. The following period of recession was marked by companies slowly clearing their shelves.

Not all accumulation or depletion of inventories is economically significant; some degree of growth or shrinkage is part of the normal course of business. The significance of a change in inventory level depends in part on its cause—whether it was planned or unplanned. The smart economist determines this by talking with cor-

Figure 7.2   Inventories of Nondefense Communication Equipment Manufacturers

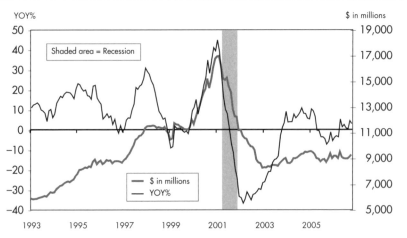

Sources: U.S. Department of Commerce, Bureau of the Census; National Bureau of Economic Research

porate officers in the industry experiencing the growth or depletion of inventories.

INVENTORIES AND THE BUSINESS CYCLE

Inventories are obviously closely tied to economic activity. But are they a lagging, coincident, or leading indicator? The answer is, it depends on how you look at them. The *level* of inventory investment is generally considered a lagging indicator. This is because businesses have traditionally been slow to recognize that demand is drying up and their stock getting dangerously high, and thus don't start to draw down inventory until an economic slowdown is already under way. Once they begin, however, the decline in inventory investment from business cycle peak to trough can be staggering, sometimes actually exceeding that in aggregate demand. At the other end of the cycle, businesses have generally delayed increasing production and restocking their shelves until they're certain a recovery is under way.

Much of this lagging association can be identified in **FIGURE 7.3**, which depicts the month-over-month *change* in manufacturing and trade inventories.

Figure 7.3 Month-to-Month Dollar Change in Inventories

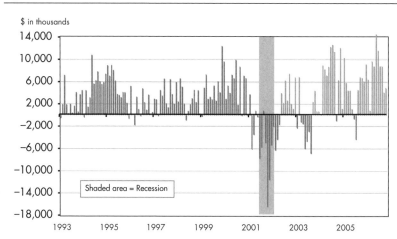

Sources: U.S. Department of Commerce, Bureau of the Census; National Bureau of Economic Research

Changes in inventory levels lead the business cycle insofar as they reflect business expectations. If managements anticipate solid economic growth down the road, they beef up their stocks. Alternatively, if they foresee lackluster demand, they permit current sales to draw down their existing inventories. The object is to maximize inventory levels with respect to anticipated demand. Achieving this goal has become easier in recent years with the advent of technologies such as electronic scanners and supply-chain and related inventory-management systems. These innovations have improved businesses' ability to monitor merchandise levels, so that they don't overorder or understock, and have given businesses greater control over inventory movements. The result has been a gentler business cycle with recessions that are both shorter and milder.

The rate of change in total business inventories is a useful tool in predicting business cycle turning points. But it can be calibrated to an even finer instrument by looking at the numbers for individual industries, some of which have much more relevance than others to economic activity. Inventory levels of nondurable goods such as food, for instance, don't offer much insight into the general economic situation. The demand for these goods is fairly stable, whether recession is imminent or not, and because the products are, by definition, perishable, they never sit long on the shelf. Much more revealing are the inventory levels of more cyclical sectors such as nondefense capital goods, automobiles, and consumer durable goods.

INVENTORIES-TO-SALES RATIOS

Among the most useful numbers in the MTIS report are the inventories-to-sales ratios. They indicate how many months it will take, at the current sales pace, until inventories are entirely liquidated—that is, until nothing is left to be sold. An inventories-to-sales ratio of 1.40, for example, means that at the current sales rate, businesses have 1.40 months of inventories left on their shelves. From 1992 through 2002, the average ratio of total business inventory to sales was 1.45.

Because different types of goods have varied shelf lives, produc-

Figure 7.4   Inventory-to-Sales Ratios: Retail, Wholesale, Manufacturing

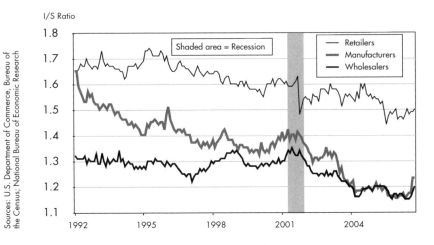

Sources: U.S. Department of Commerce, Bureau of the Census; National Bureau of Economic Research

tion schedules, and sales rates, the inventories-to-sales ratios for different industries normally move within separate ranges. This is clearly illustrated in **FIGURE 7.4**, which graphs the ratios for the manufacturing, retail, and wholesale sectors. The chart shows that from 1992 through 2003, retailers had the highest ratios of the three groups, followed by manufacturers and then wholesale merchants. Security analysts who are aware of the range for their area of specialization can check the MTIS report to see where the current ratio fits within it.

HOW TO USE WHAT YOU SEE

Because the data in the MTIS are dated, it is more productive to look at long-term trends in the inventory numbers than to try to analyze those contained in individual reports. Many Wall Street economists maintain running databases of inventories, sales, and the inventories-to-sales ratios from the reports, updating the numbers with each release. This practice can be a bit tedious, but it is well worth the undertaking.

The economics departments at most Wall Street research institutions provide monthly chartbooks to their security analysts.

These chartbooks catalog data in the Manufacturing and Trade Inventories and Sales report so that potential production changes can be identified. A sustained, abnormal run-up in monthly automobile inventory levels, for instance, could mean a manufacturing slowdown in the industry down the road, together with slashed prices or staff reductions. An analyst or economist noticing such a trend might talk with automotive industry insiders to confirm or refute the apparent production overhangs and identify their causes. It's always useful to have a Rolodex of insiders' numbers.

TRICKS FROM THE TRENCHES

The trick for this chapter involves a different way of looking at data that are there in the MTIS report for anyone to see: the inventories-to-sales ratios. As was noted, these have long been considered good indicators of future economic activity. In the period before the conversion to NAICS, an inventories-to-sales ratio between 1.55 and 1.60 was taken to mean that recession was imminent. That indication no longer seems to be the case. As was also noted, innovations such as just-in-time inventory and supply-chain management systems have given businesses a better grasp of appropriate inventory levels and better control over the production-shipment-inventory process. As a result, no specific inventories-to-sales number can be an accurate recession signal.

Instead, economists look for pronounced movements in the ratio that are sustained over several months, such as the rapid run-up from 1.38 in March 2000 to 1.46 in April 2001. When the inventories-to-sales ratio rises over time, it means that sales are not strong enough to reduce inventories or that goods are being accumulated at too fast a pace. The bottom line is that sales are slower than companies had anticipated. This is a bad sign for the economy. As **FIGURE 7.5** shows, a recession soon followed the 2000–2001 buildup. Conversely, when the ratio of inventories to sales falls over several months, it means that sales are growing faster than inventories and that manufacturers may soon have to boost production. This, of course, is good for overall economic activity.

Figure 7.5   Total Business Inventory-to-Sales Ratio

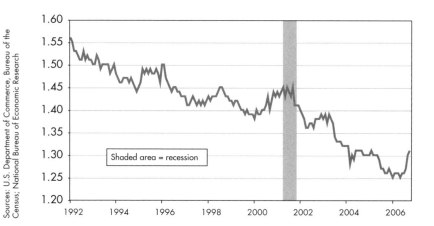

Sources: U.S. Department of Commerce, Bureau of the
Census; National Bureau of Economic Research

New Residential Construction 8

I F YOU LEARN ONE LESSON from this book, let it be this: never underestimate the economic importance of housing. The realization of the American Dream of home ownership is one of the primary drivers of the economy. Housing activity affects the investment (I) component of the aggregate expenditure formula for calculating gross domestic product (GDP) (see Chapter 1): $C + I + G + (X - M)$. The construction of new privately owned residential structures, particularly single-family homes, is very informative about consumer sentiment and the health of the economy. After all, a purchase of this magnitude requires the utmost confidence in one's personal financial situation, including employment security and earnings prospects. It also implies favorable conditions in the broader economy. Beyond personal income, the primary influences on housing activity are the level of interest rates and demographics. When these factors are aligned correctly, a buoyant housing market can boost total economic activity; when they're not, a slumping market can drag the overall economy into deep recession.

How can new housing construction, which accounts directly for only 5 percent of GDP, influence the economy so profoundly? Because of the multiplier effect of related spending and other indirect contributions. Once a home is bought, it must be furnished and decorated. All of this activity means new jobs for construction workers, retail salespeople, and manufacturers; increased tax revenues for local and state municipalities; and greater spending on goods such as carpeting, furniture, and appliances. Of course, these jobs and revenues fail to materialize if unfavorable conditions, such as rising interest rates, stifle demand for new homes.

Several important housing indicators exist, including the Census Bureau's new home sales and the National Association of Realtors' existing home sales. The most influential, however, are housing starts and building permits. These statistics are contained in the New Residential Construction report, which is released jointly by the Census Bureau and the U.S. Department of Housing and Urban Development, at 8:30 a.m. (ET) on approximately the fifteenth day of the month following the reference month. The release, as well as detail on the different stages of the construction process and a description of the methodology used, is available on the Census Bureau's website, www.census.gov/newresconst. The data contained in the New Residential Construction report, informally called "housing starts" by market participants, are among the most respected economic indicators on Wall Street and should be included in any serious model of U.S. economic activity.

EVOLUTION OF AN INDICATOR

Information regarding the origins of the New Residential Construction report is limited. Truth be told, there is little meaningful history to speak of. The Census Bureau assumed the responsibilities of the collection of housing starts data back in 1959. Previously, the duties of aggregating, calculating, and distributing the starts and permits data belonged to the Department of Labor's Bureau of Labor Statistics (BLS). The data that the BLS had gathered dated back to 1889.

The report has remained basically the same, in form and methodology, since 1959. A few minor changes have occurred along the way, such as the inclusion of farm housing and the exclusion of public housing. Some definitions have also been modified. In the wake of Hurricane Andrew in 1992, for instance, the meaning of "housing starts" was expanded to include rebuilding on existing foundations. In the 1990s, a correction was made so that starts without legal permits would be included, resulting in a break in the series. This break has had little consequence on the continuity of the series. In 1968, the bureau began reporting detailed housing characteristics, such as completions. For the most part, however, any and all of these changes have had a negligible effect on the monthly reports.

DIGGING FOR THE DATA

The New Residential Construction report contains data on privately owned residential structures, both single family and multifamily. Each unit in the multifamily structures is counted separately; a building with ten apartments, for example, is counted as ten units. Excluded are public housing, and hotels, motels, group residential structures such as college dormitories and nursing homes, and mobile homes.

The release consists of a summary of the month's figures followed by five tables. Each table corresponds to five stages in the residential construction process. The first contains data on the number of new privately owned housing units for which applications for building permits, required for construction in most U.S. regions, have been filed. The figures are compiled from responses to mail surveys sent to building-permit officials in 8,500 permit-issuing localities, out of a universe of some 19,000 permit-issuing localities.

The Census Bureau derives a sample of 900 permit-issuing places in the Survey of Construction (SOC), which is the source for the housing units authorized but not started, housing starts, housing units under construction, and housing completions (Tables 2 through 5) data. This sample is chosen with respect to the labor force, race and ethnic origin, population change, and family and housing characteristics in the respective permit-issuing localities. Census Bureau field representatives canvass these 900 localities, as well as the less than 3 percent of areas that don't require permits, and estimate the characteristics of the several stages of construction (that is, was the unit started, completed, and so forth).

The second table contains data for units whose construction has been authorized but not yet begun. The Census Bureau produced this table because the majority of new construction typically begins during the month of permit issuance, and is included in Table 1 (which contains data for units authorized).

The third table presents the number of housing starts—that is, the number of units for which excavation of the footings or foundation has begun. This is the headliner of the New Residential Construction report. By this stage, money has generally been exchanged, implying that owners are committed to the construction project. The fourth table includes units "under construction"—that is, where work has begun but not yet been completed. These data closely parallel the changes in residential construction figures contained in the Commerce Department's Value of Construction Put in Place report, referred to on the Street as construction spending. The fifth table analyzes completions.

By breaking down the numbers according to stages in the construction process, the tables allow economists, investors, and other market participants to pinpoint where the strengths and weaknesses lie. For example, should permits, starts, and construction all pick up but completions remain flat, home builders may be running up against troubling economic conditions such as an increase in the unemployment rate that could hinder would-be home buyers from purchasing new homes. Also, a rising-interest-rate environment could create difficulties for those buyers attempting to obtain financing at reasonable terms.

The tables present twelve months of data—preliminary figures for the record month, revisions for the two previous months, and final figures going back a year—in both seasonally adjusted annualized form and as unadjusted monthly numbers. They also include the unadjusted annual numbers for the previous two years and the year-to-date totals for the current year and the year before, as well as the adjusted annualized percentage changes between the record month and the previous month and between the record month and the same month a year earlier.

The numbers of units at each stage of construction are given for the entire United States as well as for four regions: the Northeast, the Midwest, the South, and the West. The figures for the entire country are broken down by size of structure, into single-family dwellings, residences with two to four units, and those with five or more units.

WHAT DOES IT ALL MEAN?

Residential housing investment has a ripple effect on the overall economy that is far greater than its direct contribution to GDP. This is because of the amount of labor and the number and volume of products involved in constructing and furnishing a home. Just consider the following list, from the National Association of Home Builders (NAHB), of resources used in an average 2,000-square-foot single-family home:

- 13,127 board feet of framing lumber
- 6,212 square feet of sheathing
- 13.97 tons of concrete
- 2,325 square feet of exterior siding material
- 3,100 square feet of roofing material
- 3,061 square feet of insulation
- 6,144 square feet of interior wall material
- 120 linear feet of ducting
- 15 windows
- 13 kitchen cabinets, 2 other cabinets
- 1 kitchen sink
- 12 interior doors
- 7 closet doors
- 2 exterior doors
- 1 patio door
- 2 garage doors
- 1 fireplace
- 3 toilets, 2 bathtubs, 1 shower stall
- 3 bathroom sinks
- 2,085 square feet of flooring material, such as carpeting, resilient sheet, resilient tile, ceramic tile, or wood plank
- 1 range, 1 refrigerator, 1 dishwasher, 1 garbage disposal, 1 range hood
- 1 washer, 1 dryer

Of course, those timbers have to be joined, the concrete poured, the sheathing, siding, roofing, wall material, and insulation applied, and the windows, doors, appliances, and other amenities installed. The NAHB has concluded that building 1,000 single-family homes generates 2,448 full-time jobs, $79.4 million in wages, and $42.5 million in government revenues.

Even after houses are built and furnished, they can continue to stimulate economic activity—and not just through remodeling and other forms of upgrading. People's homes are often their largest assets, and thus their largest potential sources of capital. When mortgage rates fall, home owners refinance at the lower rates, either reducing their monthly payments or increasing the amount of their loans, or some combination of the two.

Research has shown that most of the savings realized are poured back into the home. It should thus come as no surprise that do-it-yourself home centers such as the Home Depot Inc. and Lowe's Companies Inc. performed so well during the mortgage-refinancing boom of the late 1990s and early 2000s. Furthermore, because consumer spending is a large component of GDP, the entire economy benefits from this activity. In fact, many economists credit the mildness of the recent recession to the surge in mortgage refinancings driven by the low interest rates during the period.

INFLUENCES ON RESIDENTIAL CONSTRUCTION

Clearly, housing investment has a profound effect on the economy. The reverse is also true: residential construction is one of the most economically sensitive and cyclical sectors. Two important influences on housing are interest rates and demographics.

Because their homes are the most expensive purchases that most people make, borrowing is almost a certainty—unless, of course, they're big lottery winners. It's not surprising, therefore, that housing starts are correlated with the level of interest rates: the lower the 30-year fixed mortgage rate, the rate at which most wannabe home owners borrow, the less onerous the loan and the higher the number of housing starts. **FIGURE 8.1** shows the relationship between

Figure 8.1 Privately Owned Single-Unit Housing Starts and
the 30-Year Fixed Mortgage Rate

Sources: Federal Home Loan Mortgage Corporation;
U.S. Department of Commerce, Bureau of the Census

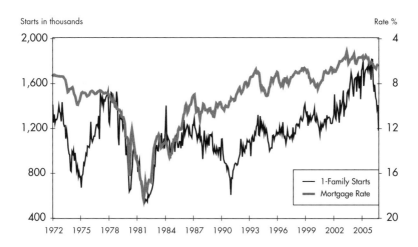

mortgage rates and housing starts (an inverse one—note the inverted right-hand scale). A general rule of thumb is that as long as income and employment are both growing steadily and home prices remain reasonable, mortgage rates of 7.25 percent or lower will boost housing activity.

Because it indirectly influences the 30-year rate, the Federal Reserve Board has the power to boost or dampen housing activity. When economic growth threatens to spark high inflation, the Fed may attempt to slow things down by raising its overnight borrowing rate (see Chapter 1). This increase usually travels along the maturity spectrum, eventually resulting in higher mortgage rates. The consequent reduction in house building and sales, combined with retrenchments in other capital spending caused by the Fed's tightening, slows economic growth. If the Fed is overzealous and raises interest rates too high, a recession can set in. On the other hand, when the economy is sluggish, the Fed often acts to stimulate it by lowering its target overnight rate, which bolsters demand for, and construction of, new homes.

Also important in determining housing activity are the size and composition of the population. Obviously, the more people there are of home-buying age, the greater the potential activity. Economists have found that the number of people between thirty and fifty-nine years of age has the strongest correlation with the number of new and existing home sales, as well as with the pace of single-family residential construction. Remember, it generally takes a while after graduation for an individual to accumulate enough money for a down payment on a home. Furthermore, earnings for individuals in their twenties generally don't amount to much.

People between the ages of twenty and twenty-five and those age sixty and above are more closely linked to multiple-unit construction, because recent graduates and the elderly tend to reside in multifamily structures, such as apartment buildings. The first of the 77 million or so baby boomers—Americans born between 1946 and 1964—reached the average home-purchasing age, thirty-two, in 1978. This demographic shift not only boosted the housing market over the past quarter century but also played an integral role in greater economic activity in general.

Immigration increases the population and thus the demand for housing. The Federal National Mortgage Association (FNMA) has found that newcomers to the United States typically realize the American Dream about ten to fifteen years after arriving. Given the incredible improvement in immigrant incomes and the interest-rate environment over the last twenty years, recent immigrants might become first-time home owners a bit quicker than that. Already, the tsunami of immigration in the late 1900s and early 2000s has buoyed new construction activity, with some home builders crediting the housing boom of late as being related more to improvements in immigrant welfare than to near-record-low interest rates.

Because of their sensitivity to interest rates, demographics, and other factors, such as taxes and weather, monthly housing data are very volatile. To discern trends more easily, economists smooth out this volatility by looking at new construction activity on a quarterly or a trending three-month basis.

Figure 8.2   Regional Composition of New Residential Construction,
November 2006

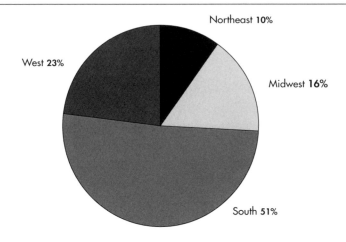

Northeast 10%

West 23%

Midwest 16%

South 51%

Source: U.S. Department of Commerce,
Bureau of the Census

REGIONAL DIFFERENCES

Many of the factors that can affect construction activity vary considerably from region to region across the United States. Midwestern agricultural communities, for instance, will typically suffer disturbances in employment and income growth at different times and under different economic conditions from those in areas with more manufacturing industries, such as the Rust Belt, and the West Coast with its concentration of technology companies. Weather conditions also vary regionally, with hurricanes in the Southeast, cold winters in the Northeast and Midwest, and flooding and drought in the South and Southwest. Furthermore, although monetary policy, which determines interest rates, is national, other policy matters, such as tax incentives, differ from state to state. Not surprisingly, then, there is a great disparity between the housing statistics for the different regions represented in the New Residential Construction report.

As shown in **FIGURE 8.2**, during November 2006 the Northeast accounted for less than 10 percent of the total of new private housing starts. The Midwest, West, and South, meanwhile, contributed approximately 16, 23, and 51 percent, respectively. This composition has remained fairly constant throughout the 1990s and the early 2000s.

HOUSING AND THE BUSINESS CYCLE

The preceding sections described the close two-way relationship between housing and the economy. But what does housing activity—and more precisely, the statistics contained in the new construction report—tell us about different stages and turning points in the business cycle?

Housing's relationship to the business cycle may best be described as "first in, first out" (FIFO): housing is one of the first industries to head south before a downturn and among the first to pull out of recession. In other words, it is something of a leading indicator. Not all the stages of construction, however, have the same predictive power; nor do they receive the same attention.

The number of permit applications is the most forward looking of all the statistics in this report. It is so forward looking, in fact, that the Conference Board includes it in the index of leading economic indicators (see Chapter 2). Although permit applications don't always result in starts, economists assume that contractors won't go through the trouble, time, and expense of applying for a permit unless they are very serious about building a home. Because this statistic is a gauge of future demand for construction and housing, equity analysts covering home builders and real estate investment trusts (REITs) should keep an eye on it.

Economists have found that privately owned housing units authorized by building permits generally precede housing starts by about one month, and sales by about three. The number of permit applications peaks as much as twelve months before the onset of a recession and bottoms out, for the most part, almost simultaneously with the overall economy.

The number of units authorized for construction, representing a later stage in the process, is slightly more accurate than the number of applications as a measure of future building activity. Economists have found that this indicator leads housing starts by about two months. Units under construction depict the current state of construction activity, construction industry employment, and the demand for building materials.

Housing completions can point to problems brewing in the economy. A significant gap in the number of units under construction and the number completed may be due to inclement weather—hurricanes in the South and blizzards in the Northeast and West frequently cause lengthy delays in the building process. But a lag in completions can also mean that a large number of builders or buyers cannot afford to finish their projects. That in turn may signal financial weakness in the overall economy.

SINGLE-FAMILY HOUSING STARTS

Although the statistics for the other stages of construction are informative, the headliner of the New Residential Construction report is the number of housing starts—more specifically, those relating to single-unit structures. Wall Street focuses on single-family residences rather than multiunit homes because the figures for the latter are more volatile. Multiunit structures typically include apartments, condominiums, and townhouses. As noted earlier, each apartment in one of these buildings is counted as a separate unit. So when construction of a five-hundred-apartment building is started or canceled, five hundred units at a time are added to or eliminated from the monthly tally. This can cause extreme month-to-month swings.

Multiunit housing is also more sensitive to tax policy. The U.S. government, for instance, provides incentives for building in underdeveloped neighborhoods; these incentives usually involve multi- rather than single-unit structures. Because such incentives change with the political landscape, they can add to the volatility of the multiunit numbers. Finally, the pace of multiunit construction may be partly a function of the growth rate of single-family housing. In the late 1990s and early 2000s, for instance, many apartment dwellers left their apartments to buy single-family

Figure 8.3 Total and Single-Unit Housing Starts

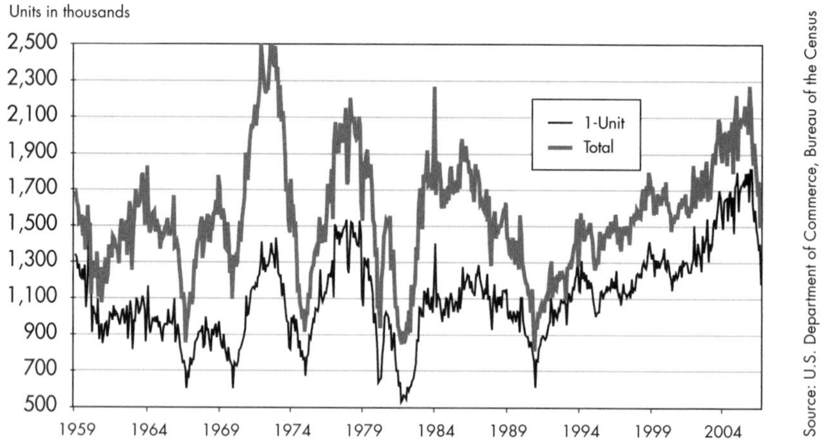

Source: U.S. Department of Commerce, Bureau of the Census

homes, which had become much more affordable. This boosted single-unit numbers and depressed multiunit figures.

Single-family starts, as illustrated in **FIGURE 8.3**, typically account for close to 80 percent of all new private housing starts. This statistic may be the ultimate gauge of consumer confidence; and because consumer activity accounts for upward of 70 percent of total U.S. economic output, single-family starts deserve the attention they get.

Why is the level of single-family housing starts such an excellent barometer of the health of the consumer sector? Simply put, when people are concerned about their economic situation, they may still spend on other products, but they won't even consider buying homes. This is another reason the housing market is such an excellent indicator of business cycle activity.

Before the 2001 recession, housing starts were the most reliable and accurate measure of U.S. economic health. Every post–World War II economic recession was accompanied by a precipitous decline in housing starts and housing activity in general, which triggered similar reductions in consumer expenditures for related goods and in the employment of workers in associated industries.

The 2001 recession broke this pattern. Housing starts remained strong during the downturn because historically low inflation kept mortgage rates low. Multidecade lows in the unemployment rate and soaring personal incomes from the torrid pace of payroll growth during the 1990s helped fuel future (that is, recession-period) home and related purchases. The same factors—plus the mortgage refinancing mentioned earlier—kept consumer spending in positive territory. In fact, the worst showing for expenditures, occurring during the second quarter of 2001, was a 1.4 percent increase. Not coincidentally, a great deal of this spending was on home-related goods, along with renovations, additions, and other home improvements. All this kept the 2001 recession very mild.

Another reason that home purchases and related spending remained strong during the recession and through 2002 was the dismal performance of the stock market. Recognizing that they could do little or nothing to improve their portfolios' value, people worked to increase the value of their greatest assets, their homes. It is important to remember that at this time, home owners (67 percent of U.S. households) outnumbered shareholders (50 percent) in the United States. Home ownership is defined by the Census Bureau as the proportion of the number of households that are owners to the total number of households. After the September 11, 2001, attacks, moreover, Americans became nesters, vacationing within a hundred miles of their homes and eliminating unnecessary business travel. They also started buying second homes as getaways from primary residences in, or near, big cities. Many of the purchasers were baby boomers looking toward retirement, whose second homes could become their primary postretirement residences.

How to Use What You See

As always, one of the goals for market pros is to get a jump on the market-moving statistics in the report. In the case of the New Residential Construction report, one strategy would be to gather anecdotal evidence from the home builders themselves. Many of the nation's largest builders—including KB Home, M.D.C. Holdings Inc., Pulte Homes Inc., Toll Brothers Inc., Lennar Corp., the Ryland Group Inc., Hovnanian Enterprises

Inc., Engle Homes, LP, and Beazer Homes USA Inc.—talk about the issues they are facing in their quarterly statements or in frequent presentations, which are available on their websites. In addition, the NAHB provides excellent statistical measures of the housing market, remodeling trends, and housing affordability. The Mortgage Bankers Association (MBA) has created a few of the Street's most respected economic indicators on mortgage applications for purchases and refinancings. It's also a good idea to keep an eye on the loan and default data on the Federal Reserve's website, which can provide early signals of troubles in the industry. Reluctance by loan officers to extend housing credit may signal that banks are having problems collecting on extended loans. Specifically, interested readers should watch the household detail in the Federal Reserve's Senior Loan Officer Opinion Survey on Bank Lending Practices. It is available on their website, www.federalreserve.gov.

TRICKS FROM THE TRENCHES

Economists have found that the difference between the number of privately owned housing units authorized by building permits and the number of privately owned housing starts yields a crude gauge of housing activity that is more informative than the number of starts by itself. Permits here can be seen as a proxy for housing demand and starts as a proxy for housing supply. The resulting "spread" is most useful as an indicator of boom conditions in the housing sector.

A negative spread, with permits lagging behind starts, is characteristic of a normal or even moderately expansionary housing market. As **FIGURE 8.4** shows, such a spread existed from 1992 to 1997. During this six-year period, new housing starts averaged about 1.4 million units (annualized), a reasonably strong pace by historical standards.

Positive spreads, when permits exceed starts, existed from 1998 to early 2006. Economists interpreted these as signals of a boom in future housing activity. When housing demand exceeds supply by a

Figure 8.4 Difference Between Housing Permits and Starts

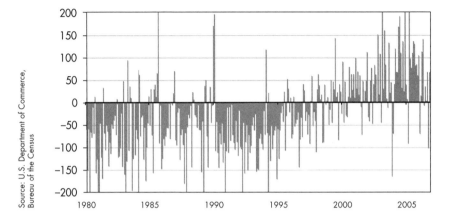

Source: U.S. Department of Commerce, Bureau of the Census

significant amount, prices generally rise. From 1995 to 2006, median new home prices surged 110 percent. A boom generally occurs when all economic cylinders are firing, inflation and interest rates are low, and incomes and employment are on the rise.

Conference Board Consumer Confidence and University of Michigan Consumer Sentiment Indexes

9

"**M**OST, PROBABLY, OF OUR DECISIONS to do something positive, the full consequences of which will be drawn out over many days to come, can only be taken as a result of animal spirits—of a spontaneous urge to action rather than inaction, and not as the outcome of a weighted average of quantitative benefits multiplied by quantitative probabilities." These words—by pioneering economic theorist John Maynard Keynes in his 1936 opus, *The General Theory of Employment, Interest, and Money*—may be the first written recognition of the importance of consumer sentiment in economics. The need to quantify these "animal spirits" is the motivating force behind the consumer confidence measures of today.

When it comes to the economy, consumers are king, accounting for roughly two-thirds of gross domestic product through their spending on items from abacuses to Zip disks. It is always good to know how the king is feeling. When people feel confident about their financial situation and future, they are usually reacting to some positive economic fundamental, such as solid employment growth or rising personal incomes. It is not surprising, then, that measures of consumer attitude have produced an impressive record of predicting economic turning points.

Many surveys of consumer confidence and sentiment exist. Some research institutions and investment firms have even created their own, to get the data into their systems and transformed into forecasts and strategies as quickly as possible. Although differing in specifics, the various surveys share one crucial characteristic: they ask everyday people from different walks of life simple questions that probe their feelings about the current and future state of the economy, inflation, and their plans for vehicle and home purchases. The survey participants may not know the difference between recession and depression, but their answers provide insights into the likelihood of these situations occurring.

Of all the surveys and measures, the best known and most respected are the Conference Board's consumer confidence index and the University of Michigan's index of consumer sentiment. (The weekly ABC News/*Money* magazine consumer comfort index is another outstanding measure with exceptional links to consumer retail sales activity, but it is less popular than the other two, possibly because its weekly schedule makes it extremely volatile and therefore less of a market mover.)

The Conference Board's confidence index is generally released on the last Tuesday of each month and made available to the investing public (in a limited version) on the Conference Board's website, www.conference-board.org. A more detailed version, as well as its history, is available by subscription directly from the Conference Board.

The University of Michigan usually issues its consumer sentiment index on the second to last Friday of each month, followed by the revised *final* estimate two weeks later. This survey is available by subscription only. A historical series of the consumer sentiment index and the inflation expectation index is available at the Federal Reserve Bank of St. Louis website at http://research.stlouisfed.org/fred2/. The results that come across the newswires or are posted at the more popular business news websites are sufficient for most readers' purposes.

Every Wall Street economics department that is serious about forecasting growth subscribes to these surveys. They are also frequently cited by Federal Reserve and White House officials and are the objects of countless studies by government agencies seeking to determine if economic policies are working as intended. After the Federal Reserve lowers the overnight interest rate, for instance, it will want to know if this move has encouraged consumers to buy interest rate–sensitive goods, such as houses and automobiles. The answer could well determine whether the Fed will lower rates further.

The markets generally react most sharply to the confidence measures when the business cycle is close to a turning point. The indexes won't indicate how much the economy may grow or contract. But when the indexes decline sharply, you can bet on tough economic sledding ahead. Conversely, when the indexes spike upward, you can look forward to more prosperous times.

EVOLUTION OF AN INDICATOR

George Katona, a Hungarian-born psychologist and economist with the Survey Research Center of the University of Michigan, started asking questions about consumer intentions in the 1940s. The university began conducting its survey in 1946, using many of the same questions that it does today. The survey, originally an annual event, switched to a quarterly schedule in 1960 and then a monthly schedule in 1978.

Throughout the 1940s and 1950s, Katona and University of Michigan economics professor Eva Mueller were virtually alone in the field, together producing a weighty corpus of studies of consumer attitudes, incomes, and spending habits. The Conference Board started conducting bimonthly surveys of consumer attitudes only in 1967. It too converted to a monthly schedule ten years later, in June 1977.

DIGGING FOR THE DATA

Although both the Conference Board's and the University of Michigan's indexes measure consumer confidence and expectations, the underlying surveys pose different questions and poll sample groups of different size and breadth. For its indexes, the University of Michigan's Survey Research Center polls five hundred households in the lower forty-eight states by telephone, asking participants about their personal finances, general business conditions, and planned purchases. The entire survey consists of more than two dozen core questions, which serve as the basis for several indexes. The index of consumer sentiment (ICS) is created from the responses to five of the questions, those asking respondents (1) if they're better or worse off financially than a year ago; (2) whether the year to come will be better or worse for them financially; (3) how businesses will fare in the next twelve months; (4) whether the country during the next five years or so will experience good times or widespread unemployment and depression; and (5) whether it is a good or bad time to buy major household items. Responses are classified as positive, neutral, or negative. Two subindexes are formed from different subsets of the five responses: the index of current economic conditions (ICC), from replies to questions 1 and 5, and the index of consumer expectations (ICE), from questions 2, 3, and 4.

These three indexes are all constructed using diffusion methodology: the positive responses are added together and the result divided by the sum of positive and negative responses, to yield a relative value. The index values are calculated relative to a base month of January 1966, whose value is set at 100.

The survey on which the Conference Board bases its indexes is conducted by Greenwich, Connecticut–based NFO Research Inc. NFO polls a panel of about five thousand households on their assessment of current economic conditions, their expectations for the future, and their plans for major purchases in the next six months. Like the University of Michigan's Survey Research Center, the Conference Board constructs three diffusion indexes from the responses to five of these questions. These five ask respondents (1) how they rate general business conditions in their area; (2) what conditions they foresee in six months; (3) how they would characterize current job availability in their area; (4) how they think availability will compare in six months; and (5) how they think their family income in six months will compare with their current income. The consumer confidence index is constructed from the responses to all five questions; the present situation index from answers to questions 1 and 3; and the expectations index from questions 2, 4, and 5. All three indexes are calculated relative to the base year 1985, whose value is set at 100. Unlike the Survey Research Center, the Conference Board adjusts the survey statistics for seasonal variations.

The Conference Board receives preliminary results eighteen to twenty-one days into the record month, so the indexes reflect the conditions of the month's first three weeks. Any late surveys are retained and used in the revision contained in the next month's release. The index numbers in the monthly report are kept secret until the official release. The only exceptions are for the Conference Board officials charged with writing the accompanying commentary, the Federal Reserve, and the Council of Economic Advisors (CEA). The Fed and the CEA receive the report after 4:00 p.m. (ET) the day before the official release. The Conference Board also releases, separately, consumer confidence data for nine geographical regions.

WHAT DOES IT ALL MEAN?

The differences in the methodologies used by University of Michigan's Survey Research Center and the Conference Board are small but still important enough to produce indexes with somewhat divergent characteristics and strengths. On the one hand, many economists feel that the larger pool sampled in the NFO survey makes the Conference Board's indexes more significant statistically. They also believe that eliciting expectations for the next six months, as the NFO survey does, is more realistic than the University of Michigan's practice of asking for a five-year perspective. On the other hand, the longer history and the twice-monthly reporting of the sentiment indexes make the University of Michigan's report one of Wall Street's favorites. Serious investors would be best served by subscribing to both surveys.

That said, the similarities between the two sets of indexes are in many ways more important than their differences. The most obvious similarity is that they all move closely with the business cycle.

FIGURE 9.1 shows the University of Michigan's index of consumer sentiment charted against the Conference Board's coincident in-

Figure 9.1 The University of Michigan's Consumer Sentiment Index and the Conference Board's Coincident Index

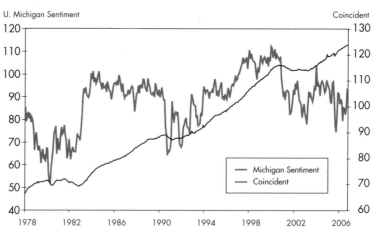

dicators index. As explained in Chapter 2, the coincident index reflects the current condition of the economy; it rises during periods of expanding economic activity and declines during recessions or periods of retarded growth. Note that current economic activity, as measured by the coincident index, flatlines or declines each time the University of Michigan's index of consumer sentiment falls below 80. When the index is below that level for a sustained period, the economy is extremely sluggish. Such was the case from late 1978 through early 1983. During that stretch, the economy was mired in recession, plagued by some of the poorest economic fundamentals in history: inflation topped 14 percent, unemployment broke 10 percent, and both the prime rate and the federal funds rate exceeded 20 percent. No wonder consumer confidence tumbled. Consecutive index readings above 90, conversely, coincide with periods of relative prosperity, marked by a rising trend in the coincident index.

The picture is similar for the Conference Board's consumer confidence index. Lynn Franco, the director of the Conference Board's Consumer Research Center, says that a reading of 100 or above indicates the economy is expanding. During the 120 months from April 1991 through March 2001, which marked the longest eco-

Figure 9.2 The Conference Board's Consumer Confidence Index and Recessions

Sources: The Conference Board; National Bureau of Economic Research; Bloomberg

nomic expansion in U.S. history, the confidence index stood above 100 for 69 months and above 90 for 81 months. At the onset of a recession, in contrast, the index usually dips below 80. This is illustrated in **FIGURE 9.2**, which shows the confidence index overlaid by highlighted bars representing recessions, as identified by the National Bureau of Economic Research (NBER), the official arbiter of U.S. business cycles. Note that during the 1981–1982 recession, the index was below 80 for fifteen of the sixteen months, and during the 1990–1991 recession for five of the eight months.

Figures 9.1 and 9.2 also illustrate one drawback of the two indexes as economic indicators: because of their strong links to consumer activity, they may fail to identify turning points that are not consumer driven. Figure 9.1, for example, shows that the University of Michigan's consumer sentiment index badly lagged the 1991 economic recovery, remaining in the 60s and 70s even as the economy was steadily improving. This "hangover" reflects the fact that the job market remained stagnant for more than two years after the official end of the recession in March 1991. Labor conditions have a profound effect on consumer attitudes.

The Conference Board's confidence index has also missed the mark from time to time, as evidenced by its behavior during the 2001 recession, represented in Figure 9.2. During the entire seven months from April 2001 to November 2001 that the economy was in recession, the index never fell below 80. In fact, its lowest reading during the recession was 84.9, recorded in November 2001. This reflects the fact that unlike other post–World War II downturns, the recession of 2001 was the result of a precipitous decline in business investment rather than a retrenchment in consumer spending. In fact, spending was buoyed by low (4.6 percent) unemployment, mild (2.5 percent) inflation, and similarly low interest rates.

Another potential source of misleading sentiment readings is the lag that occurs between conducting the surveys and releasing the indexes. The Conference Board indexes reflect the conditions during the first three weeks of the month. Any earth-shattering news occurring after the twenty-first of the month will not be reflected in the confidence level recorded in the release. A dramatic example of this was the stock market crash of 1987. Black Monday, when the Dow Jones Industrial Average tumbled a record 508 points, was October 19. Many responses to the NFO survey were elicited before this date. As a result, the confidence index fell a mere 0.6 points in October, to 115.1 from 115.7 in September. By November, everyone was aware of the crash, and the index declined nearly fifteen points, to 100.8. Of course, 100 is still far from 80, the usual recession level. The confidence index was thus one of the few indicators that accurately predicted economic prosperity after the stock market crash.

THE EXPECTATION INDEXES

Although the overall confidence and sentiment indexes possess moderate predictive power, as illustrated in the preceding example, they are more likely to move in synchrony with the business cycle. The true powerhouses of predictability are the two expectations indexes constructed by the Conference Board and the University of Michigan. In fact, the University of Michigan's index of consumer expectations is included in the Conference Board's leading economic indicators index. The University of Michigan's consumer sentiment index predates the Conference

Board's measure and was used in the leading index prior to the Conference Board's formal acceptance of the calculation, publication, and caretaking responsibilities of the Business Cycle Indicators report in 1996.

Before a recession, the two expectations indexes typically experience considerable declines for about five to six months. There is no specific reading or percentage drop associated with either index that signals a definitive downturn. However, large declines in either index generally alert analysts to a probable economic downturn. For example, prior to the commencement of the August 1990 recession, the Conference Board's expectations index tumbled from a reading of 100.3 in May to 74.2 in August. The index continued to decline into the 50s throughout the remainder of the year. Declines in the Conference Board's expectations index of this magnitude have historically preceded downturns in the economy by an average of about three months, and declines in the University of Michigan's index have preceded downturns by two months. The longest lead for both indexes was six months, before the beginning of the downturn in April 2001.

The indexes are most accurate in predicting recessions when their movements over an entire year are considered. The expectations indexes tumbled an average of 24 percent and 18 percent, respectively, over the twelve months leading up to the 1980, 1990, and 2001 recessions. Interestingly, the headline confidence and sentiment indexes are also strongly predictive when looked at in this way. In the twelve months before those same recessions, the Conference Board's consumer confidence index declined 20.9 percent on average and the University of Michigan's consumer sentiment index 14.4 percent.

The expectations indexes tend to possess less predictive powers when it comes to recoveries. For example, when the 1990–1991 recession ended in March 1991, the Conference Board's expectations index bottomed in January 1991 with a reading of 55.3, and followed with gains in February to 63.3 and a tremendous surge in March to 100.7. Similarly, the index bottomed in October 2001 with a reading of 70.7, a month before the "official" end of the recession in November, when the expectations index had a reading of 92.4. The expectations indexes clearly identify recoveries, but with little lead time.

CONFIDENCE AND DURABLES SPENDING

People generally buy big-ticket durable goods, such as stoves, refrigerators, and autos, on credit, which means committing to principal and interest payments over a long period of time. In making such purchases, therefore, consumers need to take stock of their financial future. That entails considering their employment status, potential income growth—even the state of the economy. These are the very considerations covered in the forward-looking questions of the Conference Board and University of Michigan surveys. It's hardly surprising, then, that the two expectations measures possess a strong relationship to durable goods purchases, as illustrated in **FIGURE 9.3**.

Recognizing this relationship, the big automakers, producers of some of the priciest durable goods, keep a watchful eye on the consumer indexes. Ford Motor Company's sales-analysis manager underlined the importance attributed to these numbers by the in-

Figure 9.3 The Conference Board's Expectations Index Versus Consumer Spending: Durable Goods

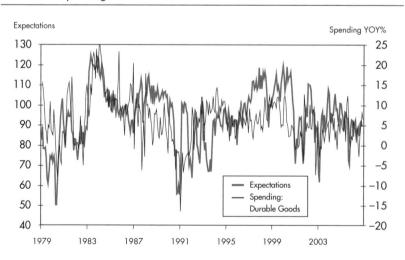

Figure 9.4   The University of Michigan's Consumer Sentiment Index and the Federal Reserve's Industrial Production of Autos Index

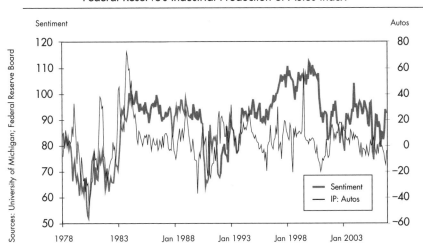

dustry when he told the *Wall Street Journal* in January 2001 that the drop in the University of Michigan's sentiment index to 93.6 in that month's report from 98.4 the previous month had "played an important role" in the company's decision to cut back on North American production.

The automakers' close reading of the indexes is reflected in **FIGURE 9.4**, which shows that for much of the 1980s and especially in the 1990s, automobile production paralleled the sentiment index. This relationship broke down a bit in the early 2000s because of the zero percent financing deals that automakers offered in the fall of 2001. Consumers simply could not ignore such incredible deals. Still, this relationship has been steady over time, and all analysts are encouraged to keep this index in their toolkits.

HOW TO USE WHAT YOU SEE

Any indicator becomes a more useful tool when you understand the factors that affect it. Such knowledge can aid in both interpreting and anticipating the indicator's readings. Measures of consumer attitude, however, differ from other indicators because the former deal not with something tangible—such as the number of computers produced, the level of aircraft orders, or the value of construction put in place—but with psychology. Using consumer sentiment measures effectively thus requires knowing how consumers' emotions are brought into play and whether these emotions are sufficiently strong to change spending habits and thus have an impact on the general economy.

EMPLOYMENT AND SENTIMENT

In the United States, employment status has deep psychological resonance. You are what you do. When people meet at a cocktail party or at a bar, their first question after exchanging names is usually, "Where do you work?" Not having a proper response can be upsetting.

People who are uncertain about their job security or hear of relatives or neighbors being laid off become pessimistic, the depth of pessimism depending on the breadth of job losses and the length of unemployment. During a recession, jobless claims and widespread layoff announcements usually garner headlines, producing anxiety even among those that still have jobs. All this is reflected in the consumer confidence and sentiment indexes. As **FIGURE 9.5** illustrates, confidence falls steeply when nonfarm payroll growth slows, and plummets when that measure moves into negative territory. Watching the employment numbers can thus help you anticipate the next month's sentiment numbers or just as important, interpret current readings. As the confidence index's behavior during the 1991 recovery illustrates, high unemployment can keep confidence low even when other fundamentals are picking up.

NONECONOMIC INFLUENCES ON SENTIMENT

Consumers react to many things besides employment and perceptions of general economic health. War, peace, and politics can all shake or bolster consumer confidence. The emotional ride is particularly turbulent today because of the tremendous growth

Figure 9.5 The Conference Board's Consumer Confidence Index and Nonfarm Payroll Growth

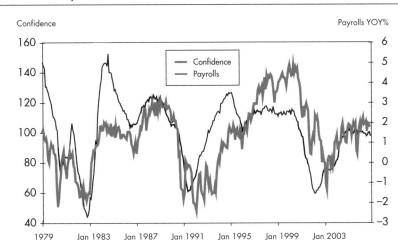

Sources: The Conference Board; U.S. Department of Labor, Bureau of Labor Statistics; Bloomberg

in news outlets on the Internet and cable, and the almost instantaneous dissemination of information over these channels. The result is often a false economic signal. Economists, analysts, and traders must learn to differentiate between news that will stimulate or stop spending and information that consumers will simply find uplifting or irritating.

Consider the 1990s. The flood of investment advice, technical and fundamental information, and live securities prices flowing through financial websites and news channels fed stock market fever in the general populace. Not surprisingly, consumer attitudes closely paralleled monthly changes in stock prices. Consumers frequently confuse stock market activity with economic activity, and differentiating between the two can be difficult for those analysts interpreting the confidence measures. Rather than look at the mounting excesses in the underlying economy and the irrational stock market valuations, consumers clung to the false sense of enthusiasm generated by business journalists that were attempting to scoop one another with respect to new investment trends. It was this subsequent rising stock market wealth that was reflected in the rising confidence measures of the 1990s, not the heavily burdened economic foundations.

News, of course, affects confidence in both directions. Just as the dot-com news festival propelled sentiment to some of the highest levels ever recorded, so too did reports of President Bill Clinton's possible impeachment, the "hanging chad" presidential election of 2000, and the anthrax terrorist scares of 2001 drive the confidence numbers down into the cellar.

When President Clinton was threatened with impeachment in December 1998, Americans were gravely concerned about the leadership of the nation, its direction, and the possible consequences this action would have on their personal situations. The same holds true for the 2000 presidential election, when Al Gore won the popular vote and George W. Bush the electoral vote. There were suspicions of widespread scandal in Florida's ballot counting and doubts about the legitimacy of the electoral process. Both events affected consumer sentiment negatively, but because neither really had anything to do with the economy, economic activity was generally unaffected.

Impeachment and election uncertainty are mild disturbances compared with war and terrorism. These can have devastating effects on consumer confidence. The Iraqi invasion of Kuwait in August 1990, which sparked the Gulf War in January 1991, sent fears of casualties throughout U.S. households. The Oklahoma City bombing in 1995, with its unexpected threat of domestic terrorism, similarly shocked the country. These episodes rattled confidence but didn't constrain spending.

Even more psychologically crushing were the attacks of September 11, 2001. Americans feared for their safety, their finances, and their jobs. The U.S. financial markets and banking system were closed for the greater part of a week, prompting fears about their soundness. In the face of all this, consumer confidence slumped to a six-year low. The drop was interpreted as a recession signal, especially given the economic context, with the nation's airports, borders, ports, and terminals shut down; domestic and international commerce brought to a screeching halt; and workers idled in hundreds of industries. Miraculously, however, recession was actually a month away from ending, not beginning.

The moral is that not every crisis of confidence presages an economic downturn, nor every swell of optimism an economic expansion. This is not a problem for the indexes. Rather it is a challenge to the interpreter, who must learn to distinguish between changes in confidence that affect consumer spending and those that leave it untouched.

TRICKS FROM THE TRENCHES

One way economists use the sets of consumer sentiment indexes to predict economic peaks and troughs is to chart the spread, or difference, between the Conference Board's expectations and present situation indexes. The reasoning behind this strategy is simple: if the expectations index is less than the present situation index, generating a negative spread, the implication is that people are happier with where they are now than with where they see themselves in the near future. That attitude is bound to constrain spending and so dampen economic growth. Conversely, a positive spread implies a belief that greater prosperity lies just around the corner, a good sign for spending and the economy. The wider the spread in either direction, the drearier or dreamier future conditions are expected to be relative to the present.

As **FIGURE 9.6** shows, the expectations–present situation spread generally bottoms out just before a recession begins and peaks just after it ends. In February 2001, the spread widened considerably, putting it into record negative territory. Apparently consumers were spot-on with their concerns, because a recession began two months later and lingered eight months, to November 2001. Consumers retrenched as their incomes dwindled and stock markets fizzled. In response, the Bush administration instituted immediate tax relief in the form of individual tax rebates ($300 per worker, up to $600 per working family) and longer-term relief through reductions in the marginal tax rate.

Also in many economists' bag of tricks is another index based on the same survey as the University of Michigan's sentiment index and

Figure 9.6 The Conference Board's Expectations–Current Situation Spread and Recessions

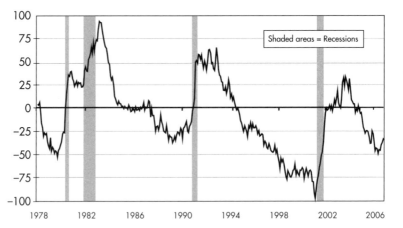

Sources: The Conference Board; National Bureau of Economic Research

its associated subindexes but constructed from a different subset of responses. The price expectations index is based on two questions asking respondents whether they believe prices will rise, fall, or remain stable in the next twelve months and by what percentage they expect them to change. The end product, as **FIGURE 9.7** demonstrates, is a highly accurate predictor of near-term inflation. Because inflation influences both consumer spending and the fixed-income market, this is a very useful and highly respected indicator.

Throughout the twenty-five years covered by the graph, growth in the price expectations index was almost identical to growth in the consumer price index, a proxy for inflation. Only in 1979–1981 and 1990–1991 did the actual inflation rate differ significantly from consumers' expectations. During both periods, the U.S. economy was mired in recession. In the first, inflation unexpectedly topped 10 percent. At the time, no economist on Wall Street foresaw price growth of that magnitude, so consumers' predictive failure shouldn't be surprising.

Figure 9.7 Change in the University of Michigan's Price Expectations Index and the Consumer Price Index

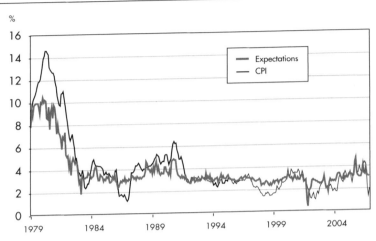

Sources: University of Michigan; U.S. Department of Labor, Bureau of Labor Statistics; Bloomberg

Advance Monthly Sales for Retail and Food Services *10*

T HE CENSUS BUREAU of the U.S. Department of Commerce releases the Advance Monthly Sales for Retail and Food Services report, known on Wall Street simply as the retail sales report, about two weeks after the end of the record month, at 8:30 a.m. (ET). The report, which presents preliminary estimates of the nominal (non-inflation-adjusted) dollar value of sales for the retail sector, as well as the month-to-month change in that value, is available on the Census Bureau's website, www.census .gov/retail. These releases are avidly followed by economists and analysts and have been known to generate serious jolts to the financial markets.

The reason for the intense interest in the retail sales report is that retail spending provides a great deal of insight into personal consumption expenditures—the largest contributor to gross domestic product (GDP)—both in the aggregate and with respect to several industries and sectors. These data, moreover, are available up to two weeks before the Bureau of Economic Analysis releases its monthly Personal Income and Outlays report, the source for the consumption-expenditure statistics incorporated into the GDP report (see Chapter 11). The retail sales report, despite covering a narrower range of data than the Personal Income and Outlays report, is therefore a timely index of current and future economic health.

Not surprisingly, the report has a significant effect on the financial markets. Stocks react favorably when it shows an increase in total retail sales, which generally equates to greater corporate profitability. Higher sales numbers may also, however, imply higher prices. Because inflation erodes the value of fixed-income coupon and principal payments, a strong report depresses bond prices and boosts bond yields, which move inversely to price. Sluggish retail sales activity, on the other hand, portends weak profit performance and few inflationary pressures. In this situation, stocks slump, bonds rise, and yields fall.

If the total retail sales numbers are significant for the markets as a whole, the figures for various components of the report can move related sectors or even individual stocks. Noteworthy increases in retail sales at electronics and appliances stores, for example, may lift the shares of Best Buy Co. Inc. and Circuit City Stores Inc., whereas lower postings at clothing and accessory stores may hurt AnnTaylor Stores Corporation and the Talbots Inc.

EVOLUTION OF AN INDICATOR

The Census Bureau began collecting data on retail sales in the early 1950s. The first Monthly Retail Trade Survey, published in March 1952, contained estimates of sales at retail stores beginning with January 1951.

In mid-1997, the Census Bureau significantly modified its collection procedures. Hoping to reduce the magnitude of revisions necessary between preliminary and final statistics, the bureau redefined the sample used in its surveys based on the results of the 1992 Census of Retail Sales and instituted a system of polling all the thirteen thousand companies included each month. Previously, only the largest companies were surveyed monthly, with smaller companies divided into three rotating panels, each of which was polled once every three months. In mid-2001, the Census Bureau instituted another major change, converting the data for this report, as it had for other of its economic reports and surveys, from the old Standard Industrial Classification (SIC) system to the North American Industry Classification System (NAICS). The goal was to facilitate comparisons of retail numbers for the whole continent. Because of the size of the task, however, data were converted to the new system only back to 1992, thus reducing the scope of possible historical comparisons and analyses.

DIGGING FOR THE DATA

The Census Bureau compiles the Advance Monthly Sales for Retail and Food Services report from responses to a survey it mails out to approximately five thousand companies about five working days before the end of the reporting month. These five thousand companies are a subsample of the thirteen thousand or so companies polled for the later Monthly Retail Trade Survey. The principal business of all the survey participants is selling goods that are intended for personal or household consumption.

Replies, which are weighted and benchmarked to give an accurate representation of the more than 3 million retail and food services companies in the United States, indicate what these establishments earned during the record month from merchandise sales and for providing services that, as the Census Bureau puts it, are "incidental to the sale of the merchandise." In other words, repairs offered at auto retailers are included, but life insurance and taxi rides are not. In this respect, the retail sales figures paint a less complete picture of consumer spending than the Personal Income and Outlays report, which does incorporate service expenditures.

Included in the retail sales receipts are excise taxes—such as those levied on alcohol, tobacco, and gasoline—that are paid by manufacturers or wholesalers, passed along to retailers, and bundled into the price of goods. Excluded are sales taxes paid by customers.

The bureau aggregates the survey data into total sales figures for the month. It also breaks down some of the numbers by type of business, using the NAICS categories and subcategories. This report is similar, but not identical, to the table shown in **FIGURE 10.1**, and by two subgroupings: total sales excluding motor vehicles and parts, and general merchandise, apparel, furniture, and other (GAFO).

All the figures provided are both unadjusted and adjusted for seasonal, holiday, and trading-day variations. The report consists of a short summary of the survey findings followed by several charts and tables. These present retail sales, adjusted and unadjusted, both in nominal dollars and as percentage changes from the previous month and the previous year. In addition to total sales, figures for all the cat-

Figure 10.1   Major Categories of Retail and Food Services Companies, with
Percentage Each Contributes to Total Sales

Major Category Percentages of Total Retail and Food Services Sales*		
Total retail and food services sales (unadjusted)		
Motor vehicle and parts dealers		20.08%
Automobile and other motor vehicle dealers	*18.28*	
New car dealers	*16.56*	
Auto parts, accessories, and tire stores	*1.80*	
Furniture and home furnishings		2.79
Furniture stores	*1.43*	
Home furnishing stores	*1.36*	
Electronics and appliance stores		2.24
Appliance, TV, and camera	*1.83*	
Computer and software stores	*0.41*	
Building material and garden equipment and supplies		8.43
Building material and supplies dealers	*7.54*	
Food and beverage stores		12.65
Grocery stores	*11.22*	
Beer, wine, and liquor stores	*0.88*	
Health and personal care stores		5.30
Pharmacies and drug stores	*4.51*	
Gasoline stations		9.38
Clothing and clothing accessory stores		4.92
Men's clothing stores	*0.25*	
Women's clothing stores	*0.90*	
Family clothing stores	*2.01*	
Shoe stores	*0.59*	
Sporting goods, hobby, book and music stores		1.77
General merchandise stores		12.57
Department stores (excluding leased departments)	*4.69*	
Department stores (including leased departments)	*4.80*	
Other general merchandise stores	*7.88*	
Warehouse clubs and superstores	*6.92*	
All other general merchandise stores	*0.96*	
Miscellaneous store retailers		2.83
Nonstore retailers		6.77
Electronic shopping and mail-order houses	*4.47*	
Food services and drinking places		10.25
Percentage of Total Retail and Food Services Sales		**100.00%**

* Percentages as of December 2006
Source: U.S. Department of Commerce, Bureau of the Census

egories, subcategories, and subgroupings are given—advance figures for the record month, preliminary figures for the previous month, and final figures for the month before that. The report also contains revised year-earlier numbers for the record and previous months.

In its breakdown of sales numbers according to NAICS business classification, the retail sales report differs from the Personal Income and Outlays report, which categorizes spending activity not by where it occurred but for what it was used—whether a service, or a durable or nondurable good. To illustrate, the purchase of a refrigerator from Best Buy would be included in durable goods spending in the income and spending report but recorded as a sale at an electronics and appliance store in the retail sales report.

Organizing the retail data according to the NAICS simplifies the survey process for the respondents. A reporting company simply records its total sales for the period and sends the form back; there is no need to break receipts down by type of merchandise or service involved. Unfortunately, the easiest collection method doesn't necessarily produce the most informative data. Consider that refrigerator purchase again. It happened to be made at an electronics and appliance store. But a consumer could just as well buy a refrigerator at a furniture store, a building material and supplies center, a warehouse club, a department store, or an Internet retailer or mail-order house. Because the report organizes sales data by point of purchase, it reveals nothing about the level of refrigerator sales each month.

That said, analyzing sales numbers by business classification can be very informative for retail equity analysts. Economists, moreover, can glean important insights into consumer attitudes by looking at the numbers for the retail subgroupings. In the immediate aftermath of the 2001 recession, for instance, consumer confidence indexes slipped, suggesting economic frailty. At the same time, however, sales at food services and drinking places remained strong. Seeing this, savvy economists concluded that confidence was not really that low: if consumers are truly upset about the economic future and their personal financial situations, they don't head out to restaurants and bars.

SURGING SUBCATEGORIES: SUPERSTORES AND E-COMMERCE

In just a few years, new business models can significantly alter the retail landscape. Two such models are represented in a couple of retail subclassifications: warehouse clubs and superstores, and electronic shopping and mail-order houses.

In the past decade, discount wholesalers have had a profound impact on the economy as a whole, and on retail prices in particular. The percentage that warehouse clubs and superstores contribute to total retail sales excluding motor vehicles and parts nearly tripled from 2.5 percent in 1992 to 7.5 percent in 2006. This is testament to the growing popularity of stores such as Costco, BJ's Warehouse, and Sam's Club.

According to Leonard Nakamura, a research adviser at the Federal Reserve Bank of Philadelphia, conventional supermarkets accounted for 73 percent of supermarket sales in 1980. By 1994, this share had tumbled to a mere 28 percent. Dominance was lost to superstores (stores with in-store butchers, bakeries, pharmacies, and so forth) and warehouses (large discount supermarkets).

The Internet and Web shopping sites have also upended traditional business models, with significant effects on both the retail sector and on the broad economy. Census Bureau statistics show that e-commerce made up about 5 percent of total retail sales in 2006. This may seem a small contribution, but it is still significant and it is growing.

According to the Census Bureau, the number of American households with access to the Internet has soared in recent years—from 26 percent of all households in 1998 to 42 percent (approximately 44 million households) in August 2000. There's no doubt that these numbers have climbed considerably in the years between 2000 and 2007, when this book was written, given the increased affordability of personal computers. Many schools and libraries provide free access. With a few keystrokes on their computers, consumers are now able to locate hard-to-find merchandise, search thousands of stores, and compare prices, any time of day and any day of the week. All retailers want to make their merchandise known to as many potential buyers as possible, and e-commerce allows them to do just that: they can post their entire universe of products on their websites, together with the latest prices and availability, inform consumers of sales and new arrivals, and maintain up-to-the second inventory levels, all at an incredibly low cost. The result: a several-fold increase in profitability.

Because of the growing importance of this sales channel, the Census Bureau in 1999 began issuing the Quarterly Retail E-Commerce Sales report. This enumerates all sales of goods and services that are negotiated over an online system (whether they're paid for online or through traditional channels). The methodology for the Retail E-Commerce Sales report is basically the same as that used for the monthly retail sales report, except that only electronically sold merchandise is counted. As you can see in **FIGURE 10.2**, the total estimated value of quarterly e-commerce retail sales has rocketed from approximately $4.6 billion in the last quarter of 1999 to about $27.5 billion in the third quarter of 2006.

E-commerce has transformed retailers' way of doing business. It has also had beneficial effects on inflation. Using the Internet, consumers can search for the least expensive set of tires, shortwave radio, or hockey stick in a matter of minutes. Companies from Bangkok

Figure 10.2 Retail E-Commerce Sales

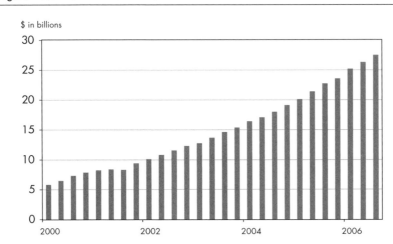

Source: U.S. Department of Commerce, Bureau of the Census

to Boston have been compelled to either reduce prices or risk losing business. This has undoubtedly played a vital role in suppressing price increases during the later half of the 1990s and the early 2000s.

WHAT DOES IT ALL MEAN?

The sales figures for individual business classifications are a rich lode of information for those conducting retail equity analysis. Economists mine the whole report for precious insights. The Street, however, focuses on two numbers: the monthly percentage changes in total retail and food service sales and the change in total sales excluding motor vehicles and parts.

TOTAL RETAIL AND FOOD SERVICE SALES, NOMINAL AND REAL FIGURES

As noted earlier, the advance retail sales total creates a stir in the markets because of the insight it provides into consumer spending, one of the major forces driving the U.S. economy. Traders focus on the month-to-month percentage change in the total, and in the total "ex-auto" retail sales, rather than the monthly change in the dollar amount. The primary reason is that a $10 million monthly increase in 1993 isn't the same as a $10 million increase in 2003. Analysis of monthly percentage changes eliminates this distortion. For the determination of longer trends, and a further refinement of month-to-month swings, analysts look at the year-over-year percentage change.

The picture it paints of general economic activity is a bit distorted, however. Beyond the fact that retail sales don't include expenditures on certain services, they are also given in nominal terms. Because the numbers are unadjusted for inflation, it is impossible to determine if growth is the result of larger sales volumes or of price hikes. For this reason, some economists adjust the retail sales data for inflation by subtracting the year-over-year percentage change in the consumer price index (see Chapter 12). As shown by **FIGURE 10.3**, the real growth rate in retail sales is generally lower than the nomi-

Figure 10.3 Growth in Real and Nominal Retail Sales

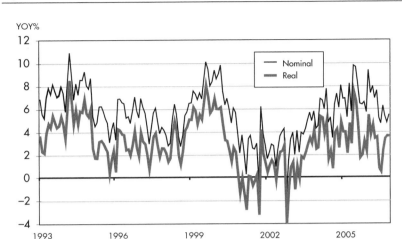

Sources: U.S. Department of Commerce, Bureau of the Census; Federal Reserve Bank of St. Louis

nal one, even dropping into negative territory during the economically difficult early 2000s.

The consumer price index has a significant flaw as an inflation deflator for retail sales—namely, it includes expenditures for services such as health care, education, transportation, and housing (the largest component of the CPI), all of which are largely absent from the retail sales data. Still, CPI-adjusted sales figures produce economically sensible estimates of real growth.

TOTAL SALES EXCLUDING MOTOR VEHICLES AND PARTS

Motor vehicle and parts dealers are responsible for a very large portion of retail sales, ranging from 20 to 27 percent since 1992. The advance retail sales total is thus heavily influenced by the numbers generated at auto shops. Because motor vehicle sales, like those of all expensive goods, can vary considerably from month to month, the total retail numbers including these sales are also highly volatile. This extreme volatility makes it difficult to discern long-term trends in the retail numbers. Accordingly, economists often focus on total sales excluding motor vehicles. As **FIGURE 10.4** illustrates, the total "ex-autos" year-over-year growth trend is relatively smooth,

Figure 10.4 Growth in Total Retail Sales and in Total Sales Excluding Autos

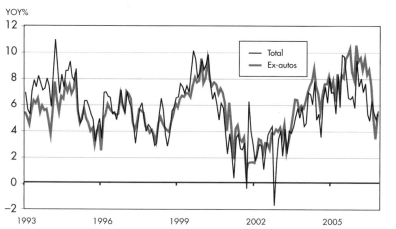

eliminating, for instance, the extreme spikes and dips manifested by the total sales numbers in late 2001 and late 2002.

GENERAL MERCHANDISE, APPAREL, FURNITURE, AND OTHER

The motor vehicle business is not the only one represented in the retail sales figures that is subject to wide price swings. Similar volatility afflicts building materials dealers, health and personal care stores, food and beverage purveyors, and gasoline stations, whose dollar sales figures rise and fall with the highly mutable markets for lumber, pharmaceuticals, food, and petroleum. As an example, consider petroleum. Should the government decide to raise the gasoline tax or require additives in the summer months to reduce pollution, the dollar value of service station sales will rise. The cause of the increase is higher prices, not greater demand, but this would be hard to price out from the numbers. Because the components of the consumer price index and its associated weights differ greatly from those of the retail sales report, "deflating" the retail sales report with the CPI is not a perfect process. The same issue arises with sales of building materials and health and personal care products. In addition, as with auto sales, the volatility of these components is transferred to the sales total, making trends hard to read.

Figure 10.5 Growth in GAFO, Total, and Ex-Auto Sales

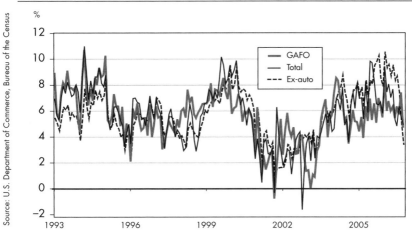

Source: U.S. Department of Commerce, Bureau of the Census

The solution: general merchandise, apparel, furniture, and other. This subgroup excludes the volatile sectors just discussed, in addition to motor vehicle sales. Also omitted are food services and drinking establishments, because they are considered for this purpose services rather than goods. Sales growth in the GAFO businesses—which include furniture and home furnishings stores; electronics and appliances shops; clothing and clothing accessories purveyors; sporting goods, hobby, book, and music stores; general merchandise stores; and office supplies, stationery, and gift stores— is considered the "core" retail growth rate, similar to the core inflation rate (see Chapter 12). As shown by **FIGURE 10.5**, the trend line of year-over-year growth in GAFO sales is noticeably smoother than the jittery movements in the total retail and food service sales and the retail sales excluding motor vehicles and parts.

HOW TO USE WHAT YOU SEE

As with the indicators discussed in other chapters, analysts and traders strive to get an early lock on the retail sales numbers. Forecasting these figures is difficult, largely because of a paucity of information. Several sources do exist, however, that may give insight into what the report will show and definitely help in interpreting the figures when they do appear.

To gain a more accurate perspective on industry-specific activity and trends, economists and retail equity analysts often supplement the data in the monthly retail sales report with anecdotal evidence. As baseball legend Yogi Berra once said, "You can see a lot just by observing." Many analysts and traders head out to malls and shopping centers every Saturday and Sunday during the crucial Christmas holiday season to get an idea of how strong, or weak, the pace of spending is. Some count cars or empty parking spaces. That's obviously a very crude measure, however. People frequent malls for reasons other than shopping—teenagers go to hang out, for instance, and elderly "mall walkers" go to get some exercise protected from extreme heat or cold. Many shoppers, moreover, take mass transportation rather than private cars. Even if the car count reflected the real number of shoppers, moreover, it wouldn't indicate which types of stores were being patronized. Short of actually consulting with store managers and asking what's selling and what's not, the most effective method of estimating mall sales is to count the number of bags that consumers are carrying, noting the store logos on them. People don't generally carry unnecessary baggage, so the presence of a bag implies that a purchase has been made.

Analysts and economists also consult chain store announcements, looking for advance insights into consumer activity. Early each month—often as early as two weeks before the retail sales report—and in some cases every week, retail chain stores report on their sales activity. In addition to indications of individual retailers' strengths or weaknesses, perspectives on total economic activity can be gleaned from the comments of giant retailers such as Wal-Mart. Because of their growing popularity, wholesale discounters also provide important indexes of retail activity. Finally, retail trade groups such as the National Retail Federation and the International Council of Shopping Centers issue informative reports on seasonal spending patterns and trends, most of which are available on their websites.

In interpreting these data, traders and other analysts should take climate into account. Hazardous storms close stores, disrupt transportation routes, and reduce hours worked. All of this means lost retail business, offset somewhat by increased sales of shovels, generators, snowblowers, and related merchandise. That said, the role of nature has been reduced by the advent of the Internet, which enables consumers who can't get to the store to pursue their shopping online.

SAME-STORE SALES

Early each month, usually during the first week, the nation's largest retailers announce their same-store sales, or "comps," for the preceding month. These announcements can be useful in forecasting what trends the advance retail sales report will reveal for major business categories. For instance, it's a fair bet that the building materials and suppliers group will post activity in the advance report similar to that announced earlier by the Home Depot Inc. and the Lowe's Companies Inc.—not necessarily the same magnitude but the same direction. In like manner, announcements made by companies such as AnnTaylor Stores Corporation, the Sports Authority Inc., and CVS Caremark Corporation provide clues to the retail sales numbers for the clothing, sporting goods, and health and personal care categories, respectively.

Same-store sales figures do have some drawbacks as predictive tools. For one thing, they don't include sales by stores that have been open less than a year. This is an important omission. New outlets are carefully sited and heavily promoted by the parent companies and consequently often show the strongest sales activity. Second, only year-over-year growth is reported, so the figures provide little insight into the monthly activity reflected in the retail sales report. To interpret same-store sales, moreover, you must know what retail conditions prevailed in the comparison, or base, month. For instance, if sales were at all-time highs in December 2006, lower numbers in December 2007 wouldn't necessarily mean that activity was sluggish in that month, just slower than the record pace of a year earlier.

SEASONALITY

It should come as no surprise that many retail sectors cycle with the season, which is accounted for in the seasonally adjusted data. Apparel and accessories sales, for instance, usually surge in August and September, when young kids are heading back to school and older students off to college. College freshmen, in particular, need to stock up on new clothes, personal computers, and other electronic must-haves. Similarly, February shows strong candy, cards, flowers, and restaurant sales. The reason, of course, is Valentine's Day. In fact, a very large portion of retail activity is holiday related. A good or bad holiday season can make or break the entire year for a retail sector. No wonder economists and retail analysts keep an eye on where in the calendar movable fetes like Thanksgiving and Easter are scheduled to occur.

Timing is important. Easter, for instance, may fall either in March or in April, boosting retail sales that month, particularly at apparel stores. This can make for misleading comparisons. Say Easter occurs in March one year and in April the next. By comparison with year-earlier numbers, the sales for March in the second year will appear weak, whereas those in April will seem strong.

The timing of Thanksgiving is also important, because the following Friday is the unofficial start of the Christmas shopping season. Because Thanksgiving always falls on the fourth Thursday of November, this season ranges between twenty-six and thirty-two days. The assumption is that the longer the stretch, the stronger the holiday sales numbers will be. Of course, most people must buy a particular number of presents, whether they have twenty-seven or thirty shopping days in which to do so. But the longer time span (together with expanded holiday hours) does mean more spending on everyday items, such as gasoline, groceries, and bar and restaurant visits.

TRICKS FROM THE TRENCHES

Holiday sales are good gauges of economic health and consumer well-being. If the numbers are robust, people are probably feeling secure both financially and in their jobs. A pullback, on the other hand, may reflect consumers' fears about finances and the labor market. The sales numbers for Thanksgiving, Easter, and even Halloween and Valentine's Day are all significant in this regard. But not surprisingly, the real make-or-break shopping season is Christmas.

Because of the importance of Christmas sales, economists, analysts, and traders have developed different ways of estimating these numbers from the monthly retail sales reports. Some extrapolate holiday sales from the total for November and December. Others use the total excluding motor vehicles and parts—a reasonable approach, because few autos appear under the Christmas tree (at least outside Mercedes Benz commercials). Still others look only at the December figures, reasoning that in many years November contains only a few real holiday shopping days and that most Americans every year wait until the last moment to buy their presents. The two most popular proxies for holiday sales, however, seem to be the combined November and December totals excluding autos and food services, and the two months' combined GAFO sales.

Which is the better proxy? It depends on your definition of "holiday sales." If you believe that spending at motor vehicles and parts shops is not holiday related but that sales of gasoline, food and beverages, health and personal care items, and building materials and garden equipment are, the first approach is for you. If you think only purchases of general merchandise qualify, the GAFO method is more realistic.

Most economists favor the GAFO proxy. After all, how many holiday wish lists include oak paneling, carpeting, or prescription drugs? On the other hand, the hot housing and refinancing markets of the late 1990s and early 2000s did create a ravenous demand for home-improvement equipment, tools, and do-it-yourself merchandise, and many of these items may have been Christmas gifts. All the parties given in November and December undoubtedly beef up food and beverage store sales as well as restaurant and bar sales. Finally, if not for stores like Walgreens, CVS, Rite Aid, the Body Shop, and Sephora, where would people get their perfume and cosmetics stocking stuffers?

Figure 10.6 Holiday Retail Sales Using GAFO Approach
(November and December)

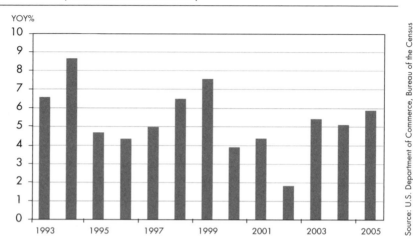

Whatever method they choose, economists estimate holiday sales because of the relationship they bear to the broader economy. This relationship is illustrated in **FIGURE 10.6**, which charts the year-over-year growth in holiday sales, estimated using the GAFO approach. Note that sales increased steadily in the last half of the 1990s. In this period, GDP was growing strongly and the stock market surging. Sales then fell off sharply in the early 2000s, at a time when consumers were struggling with recession and a jobless recovery.

Personal Income and Outlays 11

THE MONTHLY PERSONAL INCOME and Outlays report, produced by the Bureau of Economic Analysis (BEA), contains incredible detail on income-related measures, as well as spending data for virtually every imaginable good and service. Commonly referred to on Wall Street as "income and spending," the report consists largely of income statistics, but the underlying detail on spending may just be the most comprehensive of all economics statistics.

What more could an economist—and those who trade on economic news—ask for in an economic indicator than timely detail on what consumers earn and what they spend their earnings on? And all on a monthly basis: the Personal Income and Outlays report is released about four weeks after the record month, on the first business day following the release of the gross domestic product (GDP) data, at 8:30 a.m. (ET). It's available on the BEA's website (www.bea.gov) within minutes after the formal release, and is extremely helpful in the analysis of macroeconomic and microeconomic trends.

Because spending and income data are coincident indicators, they don't rank high as market movers. Unexpected postings, however, have occasionally given the financial markets a considerable jolt.

The BEA uses the spending data in the report in compiling the consumption expenditures portion of the GDP report. Consumer expenditures, as noted in Chapter 1, account for about 70 percent of all economic activity in the United States. Strong spending is a sign of an expansionary climate; slower spending signals softer economic conditions. The income data, meanwhile, provide insight into future spending and thus future economic activity.

Although economists generally draw the inference that rising incomes eventually result in greater spending, quantifying this relationship is less clear-cut. Conceptually, the income-spending relationship is somewhat leading, yet graphically that relationship is more of a coincident association. Strong income growth usually means an expanding economy, whereas declining income may signal weaker times ahead. Disposable income (what's left of wages and salaries after taxes and certain other payments) is particularly important in identifying the likelihood of greater spending. Rising income from transfer payments, such as unemployment insurance, can signal an economy that is spinning its wheels. (The report also contains personal savings data, derived by subtracting expenditures from income, but this is generally less revealing than the other information.)

The market reaction to the monthly percentage change in the income and spending figures is generally subdued, unless of course the figures deviate greatly from the Street's expectations. Stronger-than-expected increases in income or spending are a sign of a strengthening economy, which would bode well for the general economic climate, corporate profitability, and subsequently the valuation of stock prices. Weaker spending and incomes generally result in softer stock prices. The bond market usually reacts unfavorably to strong postings in income and consumption, and favorably to sluggish income and spending growth. Considerably strong releases spark unease in the stock and bond markets because of the fear of a possible tightening of monetary policy by the Federal Reserve Board.

EVOLUTION OF AN INDICATOR

Because the GDP report draws on data in the monthly Personal Income and Outlays report, you might expect the two to have similar origins. Well, they do. The income and spending report, however, goes a little further back in time, to the 1920s. In 1921 Wesley Clair Mitchell, together with his staff at the National Bureau of Economic Research (NBER), which he helped found and for which he served as its first director of research, published *Income in the United States: Its Amount and Distribution 1909–1919.*

This two-volume work set out a framework for measuring national income and quantitatively describing its composition, industrial sources, and distribution. The data used in the report were collected from sources as obscure as American Telephone & Telegraph town rent surveys and the Department of Agriculture's annual crop estimates. It was an impressive achievement, especially because the NBER received its charter only in 1920. The calculations, however, were relatively crude, and the reports available only on an annual basis. It was up to Simon Kuznets, a student of Mitchell's, to bring the project to maturity. In the 1930s, Kuznets, as described in Chapter 1, created the national income and product accounts, from which comes the GDP report, for the Department of Commerce. The department published the first national income statistics in 1934.

It wasn't until the comprehensive revision of 1958 that quarterly estimates began to appear and both income and outlays data were formally presented. Over the next four decades, there were several revisions, modifications, and definitional improvements that served to make the Personal Income and Outlays report a first-class gauge of household activity.

DIGGING FOR THE DATA

Like the GDP report, the monthly Personal Income and Outlays report contains data from both the income and the production sides of the economy. Every month, these data are analyzed and displayed in typically about eleven tables, one of which (from the November 2006 report) partially appears in **FIGURE 11.1**. The tables show personal income and its disposition—that is, how it is distributed among tax and nontax payments, personal outlays, and personal savings—in terms of both dollar amounts and percentage changes from previous months, quarters, and years. Expenditures and disposable income are expressed in current (nominal) and chained (real) dollars. (See Chapter 1 for a discussion of *chained*, *nominal*, and *real* values.)

Figure 11.1 Personal Income and Its Disposition (Months)
($ in billions; months seasonally adjusted at annual rates)

	September 2006 revised	October 2006 revised	November 2006 revised
Personal income	$11,021.7	$11,057.4	$11,091.2
Compensation of employees, received	7,557.7	7,593.7	7,620.5
Wage and salary disbursements	6,087.6	6,116.7	6,137.8
Private industries	5,061.1	5,087.7	5,105.9
Goods-producing industries	1,184.9	1,190.5	1,191.8
Manufacturing	736.5	739.8	739.5
Services-producing industries	3,876.2	3,897.2	3,914.2
Trade, transportation, and utilities	1,006.3	1,009.4	1,011.9
Other services-producing industries	2,870.0	2,887.8	2,902.2
Government	1,026.5	1,029.0	1,031.9
Supplements to wages and salaries	1,470.1	1,477.1	1,482.7
Employer contributions for employee pension and insurance funds	1,004.5	1,009.5	1,013.8
Employer contributions for government social insurance	465.6	467.5	468.9
Proprietors' income with inventory valuation and capital consumption adjustments	1,017.4	1,023.2	1,024.3
Farm	26.4	29.2	30.1
Nonfarm	991.0	994.0	994.3
Rental income of persons with capital consumption adjustment	83.4	79.5	77.3
Personal income receipts on assets	1,690.6	1,701.3	1,712.2
Personal interest income	1,035.9	1,039.7	1,043.4
Personal dividend income	654.6	661.6	668.8
Personal current transfer receipts	1,625.5	1,617.6	1,617.5
Government social benefits to persons	1,589.8	1,581.7	1,581.4
Old-age, survivors, disability, and health insurance benefits	939.7	937.2	937.1

Figure 11.1 (continued)

	September 2006 revised	October 2006 revised	November 2006 revised
Government unemployment insurance benefits	27.3	27.0	27.3
Other	622.8	617.6	617.0
Other current transfer receipts, from business (net)	35.7	35.9	36.1
Less: Contributions for government social insurance	952.9	957.9	960.6
Less: Personal current taxes	1,370.1	1,384.5	1,391.4
Equals: Disposable personal income	9,651.6	9,672.8	9,699.8
Less: Personal outlays	9,718.1	9,744.3	9,794.8
Personal consumption expenditures	9,348.5	9,374.7	9,425.2
Durable goods	1,072.3	1,079.1	1,091.8
Nondurable goods	2,726.2	2,711.0	2,729.2
Services	5,550.0	5,584.6	5,604.2
Personal interest payments	241.2	240.7	240.1
Personal current transfer payments	128.3	128.9	129.5
To government	79.5	80.1	80.6
To the rest of the world (net)	48.8	48.8	48.8
Equals: Personal saving	–$66.5	–$71.4	–$95.0
Personal saving as a percentage of disposable personal income	–0.7%	–0.7%	–1.0%
Addenda:			
Disposable personal income:			
Total, billions of chained (2000) dollars	$8,386.2	$8,422.7	$8,445.4
Per capita:			
Current dollars	32,175	32,218	32,280
Chained (2000) dollars	27,957	28,054	28,106
Population (midperiod, thousands)	299,972	300,233	300,485

Source: U.S. Department of Commerce, Bureau of Economic Analysis

PERSONAL INCOME

The BEA calculates **personal income** by adding together income from seven major sources and then subtracting personal contributions for unemployment, disability, hospital, and old-age survivors' insurance. The largest income source is wages and salaries, which accounts for about 55 percent of the total. The BEA obtains data for this category from Internal Revenue Service (IRS) reports. Transfer receipts—government disbursements such as Social Security payments, veterans' benefits, and food stamps—usually constitute about 15 percent of total income. The Social Security Administration and the Bureau of Labor Statistics supply the data for this category. The remaining 30 percent or so of total monthly income comes from personal interest and dividend income, which contributes 15 percent; proprietors' income, 9 percent; other labor income (such as group health insurance and pension and profit-sharing), 0.3 percent; and rental income, 1 percent. (The actual percentages vary somewhat from month to month but remain relatively close to the levels indicated here.)

By subtracting contributions for government social insurance and personal current taxes, as well as payments such as donations, fees, and fines from personal income, you arrive at **disposable personal income**. This figure is generally regarded as more useful than (unadjusted) personal income, because it represents the money that households have available to spend or to save.

PERSONAL CONSUMPTION EXPENDITURES

The BEA defines personal consumption expenditures as the goods and services individuals buy, the operating expenses of not-for-profit institutions serving individuals, and the value of food, fuel, clothing, rentals, and financial services that individuals receive in kind. The primary source for these data is the Census Bureau's monthly retail sales report.

The largest portion of consumer expenditures, accounting for 55 percent of the total, is for services. The U.S. economy is service dominated. Approximately 80 percent of all workers in the United States are employed in a service profession. U.S. consumers spend incredible amounts on insurance, repair, transportation, investment advice, and medical care. Legal services are involved in virtually every aspect of American life, from buying a home to getting a divorce to writing a will. Entrepreneurial endeavors, such as setting up a small business or writing a book, require accounting and legal advice. Other service expenditures include school tuition and spending on hotel and motel accommodations, sporting and theater events, and telephone and cable television services.

The next-largest category, representing 30 percent of total expenditures, is spending on nondurable goods. Nondurable goods are products with relatively short life spans. They are divided into four major groups: food; clothing and shoes; gasoline, fuel oil, and other energy goods; and the catchall "other," which encompasses products such as perfumes, cleaning preparations, film, and greeting cards. Durable goods, which account for the remaining 15 percent of expenditures, are those intended to last a minimum of three years. (Most do, and if they don't, they contribute to spending on repair services.) Durables include automobiles, refrigerators, washing machines, televisions, furniture, and other big-ticket items, such as jewelry, sporting equipment, and guns. Because durables are expensive and (because of their "durability") are purchased infrequently, spending on these items as a percentage of total expenditures can vary considerably from month to month.

Personal outlays is one of the subcategories of the personal income report. To compute personal outlays, the BEA adds net transfers to the rest of the world and personal interest expense to personal consumption expenditures. **Net transfers** include payments sent abroad by U.S. residents, such as remittances from foreign workers to their home countries. **Interest expense** comprises what consumers pay on credit cards and on auto and personal loans (but not mortgage interest, because housing is regarded as an investment).

PERSONAL SAVINGS

The BEA includes **personal savings** and the personal savings rate in Table 1 of the income and spending report. Personal savings is defined as the difference between consumers' disposable incomes—the money they have available to spend—and what they actually spend, their personal outlays. This figure expressed as a percentage of disposable income is the **personal savings rate**. The November 2006 computation of the personal savings rate, for example, was:

Disposable personal income		$9,699.8 billion
less personal outlays	−	$9,794.8 billion
equals personal savings	=	−$ 95.0 billion
expressed as % of disposable personal income		
−$95.0 ÷ $9,699.8 × 100		
equals personal savings rate		approximately −0.9%

This figure suggests that consumers have a negative savings rate. That is, they spend more than they earn. How does this happen? The answer can easily be found by looking at the Federal Reserve's reports on consumer credit. Consumers have many channels through which they can borrow.

WHAT DOES IT ALL MEAN?

The two top attention-getters from the income and spending report are the monthly percentage changes in nominal personal income and nominal personal consumption expenditures. These month-to-month changes receive the most attention of any number in the report from the financial markets. Because the dollar values of these two series are so large—in the trillions—they tend not to fluctuate too greatly from month to month. In other words, the month-to-month changes tend to be of the magnitude of 0.1–0.3 percent. Monthly announcements of 0.2 percent changes in personal income or consumption can, as a result, be a bit of a wet firecracker. The real story is in the detail, however, specifically that underlying the income and consumption numbers. By analyzing those details and the relationships between the personal income and expenditure figures, economists and investors are able to identify possible turning points and developing trends in the economy.

PERSONAL INCOME

The financial media tend to pay less attention to income than to expense data. You are more likely to hear a business journalist comment on the monthly increase in services spending, for example, than on an unexpected gain in dividend income. The reason for this lack of interest is most likely due to the indirect effect of income on the economy. Income doesn't always have to be spent—it may be saved. Conversely, the spending data are quite telling about what consumers are actually doing with their income. Another reason for the preference of expenditures data over income data is that stock market traders can directly determine what consumers are spending on. The income data don't provide market traders with such detailed information. That doesn't mean personal income data are less meaningful, however. On the contrary, they provide important insights into the financial health of consumers, a group that, as we have seen, has tremendous impact on all sectors of the economy.

Because some level of income is necessary for all economic activity, trends in income growth should theoretically permit inferences about future spending patterns. Unfortunately, theory doesn't always mesh with reality. As the chart in **FIGURE 11.2** illustrates, personal income tends to move in sync with, rather than lead, expenditures.

One reason for this synchronicity is that wages and salaries tend to get spent rather quickly. Some people live paycheck to paycheck, spending their earnings immediately and saving smaller and smaller amounts. In addition, personal income includes not only wages and salaries but also dividend and interest income and transfer payments, such as health insurance and unemployment benefits. These

Figure 11.2   12-Month Changes in Personal Incomes and Consumption
Expenditures

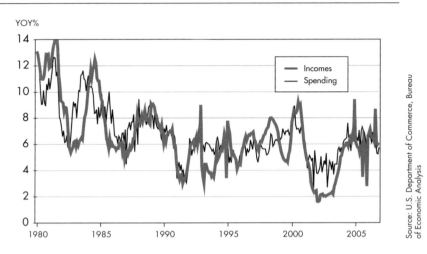

crucial disbursements of unemployment benefits are generally spent
immediately on basic necessities, such as food and rent.

Because these payments are spent on necessities rather than
on durable goods and services, they have relatively little influence
on macroeconomic activity. Economists trying to judge economic
strength therefore focus on wage and salary income.

Still another explanation for the coincidence of income and
spending growth may lie in a source of income that is not included
in the monthly report: consumer credit. Consumer credit is a critical source of income in the United States, capable of altering the
amount of spending in the economy. It's not exactly clear how wide
or narrow the gap between income and spending growth would be
without a formal credit channel. Perhaps income growth would assume a more leading nature because consumers could not make as
many purchases with only wages and salaries. The existence of the
credit transmission mechanism permits greater access to funds, en-
hancing spending without respect to wage and salary growth. No
doubt, consumer credit plays some role in the leading-lagging quality of incomes. Because of this important economic role, economists, retail analysts, and money managers keep a keen eye on the

section of the Federal Reserve's monthly consumer credit release (G.19) that shows the current amount of outstanding consumer credit, including personal, auto, and education loans, as well as the amount of revolving credit on credit cards. The Fed's consumer credit report doesn't contain consumer loans secured by real estate, such as mortgages or home equity lines of credit. All these data and their histories are available on the Federal Reserve's website, www.federalreserve.gov.

Another factor that influences personal income but is not included in the monthly reports is mortgage refinancing. During the late 1990s and into the early 2000s, mortgage rates plunged to their lowest levels in recorded history. Americans refinanced their existing mortgages—some doing so two or three times—to reduce their interest burden. The skyrocketing pace of mortgage refinancings affected economic activity in two respects: first, it freed up income that had previously been earmarked for interest payments; second, several homeowners took advantage of the equity that they had already paid off in their original loans, permitting them to take out even bigger loans—and purchase larger homes—yet make the same monthly payment as the pre-refinancing loan. The savings and capital thus created, which amounted to hundreds of billions of dollars, were not recorded as income. But they did fuel spending. This too has caused some discrepancy between the leading-lagging characteristic of incomes.

Consumer credit and mortgage refinancings can thus increase consumption expenditures. Nevertheless, the amount of income from these two sources—and consequently, the influence they exert on spending—is tiny compared with total personal income as measured in the BEA reports. To predict the economically crucial consumption expenditures figure, it is necessary to understand the factors that influence the level and growth rate of total income—in particular, total disposable income. The most important of these factors are employment, tax structure, and the general economic climate.

As noted earlier, wage and salary disbursements is the largest source of personal income. To earn a salary, one must generally perform some service. (OK, some people manage to receive compensation for doing absolutely nothing, but let's just consider the overwhelming majority

Figure 11.3   Disposable Personal Incomes and Employment

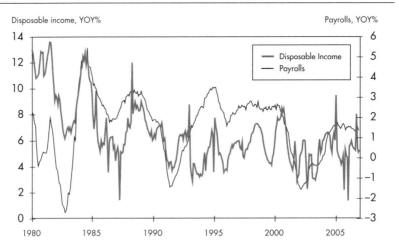

Sources: U.S. Department of Commerce, Bureau of Economic Analysis; U.S. Department of Labor, Bureau of Labor Statistics

of Americans.) So job growth should be an important determinant of income growth. The associated chart in **FIGURE 11.3** highlights some incongruities, which may be credited to a number of factors including changes in tax policy and the comeuppance of nonwage sources of income like stock distributions and stock options.

Growth in payrolls encourages spending not only by increasing disposable income but also by lifting consumers' spirits. Another important influence on consumer expenditures is the level of taxation. When marginal tax rates are low, disposable personal incomes rise. With more of their earned income left over, people have a greater propensity to spend; and because consumer spending accounts for almost 70 percent of all economic activity, and the United States is traditionally a nation of spenders, economic growth will expand.

CONSUMER SPENDING

The connection between consumer expenditures and economic growth has already been well established. But not all spending is equally revealing of economic trends. Spending on nondurable goods such as food and home-heating fuel tends to be fairly constant, remaining positive even in trying economic times. In con-

Figure 11.4   Spending on Consumer Durables and Recessions

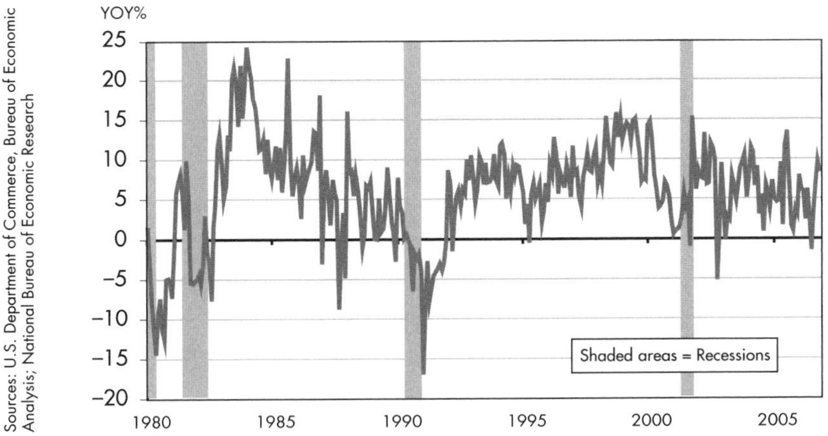

trast, spending on durable goods, which are relatively expensive and long-lived, requires good economic conditions to flourish. In less flush times, consumers aren't going to head out to buy stereos, furniture, or new china. Therefore, of all the subcomponents in the Personal Incomes and Outlays report, durable goods spending might be considered the most effective in calling turning points in the economy.

The chart in **FIGURE 11.4** shows that three of the last four recessions identified by the National Bureau of Economic Research—1981–1982, 1990–1991, and 2001—were accompanied by simultaneous declines in the growth rate in consumer spending on durable goods. The 2001 recession broke this pattern, as automakers and certain other retail giants kept consumers buying their products by offering zero percent financing, hefty discounts, and other incentives. Spending on consumer durables barely fell below zero in 2001.

PERSONAL SAVINGS RATE

Americans spend. The nation as a whole just can't seem to "save for a rainy day," despite the warnings of previous generations. As the chart in **FIGURE 11.5** illustrates, this propensity has worsened in the past five years.

Americans' declining savings rate can be explained in part by demographics. Baby boomers—people born between 1946 and 1964—are the first generation that stands to inherit a significant amount of wealth. The baby boomers' grandparents, born in the late nineteenth century, lost most of their accumulated assets during the Great Depression. Even when the economy picked up, they retained memories of the hardscrabble times and raised their children in households of frugality, saving everything they could. As the Depression survivors began to die off in the mid-1990s, their children, the boomers, inherited the homes, investments, jewelry, cars, autographed baseballs, and other assets they had amassed. This was occurring during some of the best economic conditions in about five decades—rock-bottom unemployment of around 3.9 percent, virtually nonexistent inflation, and a skyrocketing stock market. No wonder the boomers didn't find savings crucial.

Economists generally worry when the personal savings rate slows. This usually signals that consumers are dipping into their savings to make ends meet. Depleted savings are most disturbing during soft economic times, such as those of the early 2000s, when unemployment was on the rise. The hardships posed by the loss of a job—and

Figure 11.5 Personal Savings as a Percentage of Disposable Personal Income

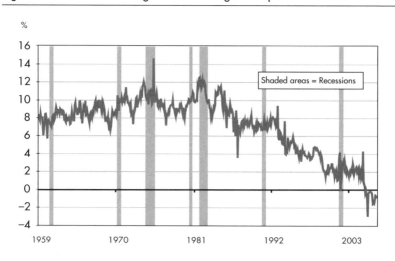

Sources: U.S. Department of Commerce, Bureau of Economic Analysis; National Bureau of Economic Research

of its associated income—are exacerbated when the worker is already overextended. That is why it is important to keep an eye on the pace of consumer credit. If it is rising during a weak economy, a very dangerous situation may be developing, which could result in a double-dip recession as the consumer spending that initially brought the economy out of the recession disappears.

HOW TO USE WHAT YOU SEE

The data in the monthly Personal Income and Outlays reports supply the raw material for the analyses in the quarterly GDP report. To come up with the quarterly figures, the BEA simply averages the monthly numbers recorded for each data category. Because the GDP report isn't published until about a month after the end of the record quarter, economists (as well as some analysts and money managers) keep a running tab of the monthly consumer spending figures to approximate the value of this important contributor to economic activity.

Because personal incomes and expenditures are so critical to the overall pace of economic activity, economists attempt to predict what the report will show before it is released. One way they do this is to go straight to the data sources. The largest source for monthly expenditures information is the Advance Monthly Sales for Retail and Food Services report. Spending on some retail goods, though, is more significant than that on others. Durable goods, as noted above, are more economically sensitive than nondurables. Among durable goods, some are better as predictors of macroeconomic conditions. Wall Streeters, for instance, watch the "RV indicator." Recreational vehicles, or RVs, are usually purchased out of discretionary or unessential income. When expenditures on these vehicles slump, it's a good bet that the economy will soon slow. Conversely, when sales begin to accelerate, the economy is expected to expand.

RVs may still be regarded as luxuries by many Americans. Cars, in general, are not. Every teenager dreams of owning a sports car, and virtually every adult has fond memories of his or her first automobile. (For the record, my first was my grandfather's 1965 forest

Figure 11.6   Spending on Motor Vehicles and Parts as a Percentage of Durable Goods Expenditures

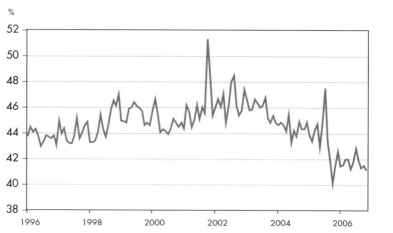

Source: U.S. Department of Commerce, Bureau of Economic Analysis

green Chevy Impala with a 283—the best engine GM ever made.) It's not surprising, then, that purchases of motor vehicles and parts constitute one of the largest components of consumer spending. As the chart in **FIGURE 11.6** shows, motor vehicle spending accounts for a great deal of durable goods spending. In fact, at least since 1997, this component never accounted for anything less than 40 percent of total durable goods spending.

Knowing this, economists like to look at the monthly pace of auto sales. Several indicators of motor vehicle demand exist. The most relevant are contained in the advance retail sales report, because they are measures of spending, and the monthly sales reports of individual car companies (available on their websites). By assessing the pace of automotive sales, investors are able to get a good idea of activity in durable goods as a whole and thus of consumer spending in general and of overall economic conditions.

TRICKS FROM THE TRENCHES

This chapter's tricks involve factors that influence levels of spending and that economists and investors can use to foretell what those levels will be. What determines how much consumers spend? What doesn't? Some people spend because it's Saturday night. Gloomy days often prompt spirit-boosting trips to malls. But rain crimps sales at the beaches and shores, and blizzards keep everyone inside, preventing even determined shoppers from getting to a store and spending. Meanwhile, closed stores prevent hourly workers from earning income. Weather, time of week, time of year, and many other factors affect spending. For economists, however, three influences are predominant: wealth, prices, and employment.

THE WEALTH EFFECT

Many economists identify a **wealth effect**: as individuals' wealth rises, the reasoning goes, so does the level of spending. This seems logical. But how do you measure individuals' wealth? One way is to look at the Federal Reserve's quarterly flow of funds release (available on the Fed's website, www.federalreserve.gov/releases/Z1/), which tracks financial and physical asset flows in the U.S. economy. The Fed's report contains detailed information regarding outstanding levels of household ownership of several types of assets such as U.S. government securities, mutual fund shares, and corporate equities. Unfortunately, these data are provided solely on a quarterly basis and delayed for about three months, rendering them useless for analyzing high frequency, or monthly trends. First-quarter data, for example, are not released until the middle of June—and they undergo wide-ranging revisions.

Given these drawbacks, economists have developed their own more timely way of measuring the consumer confidence implied by the wealth effect. They divide the dollar value of the Wilshire 5000—a stock market index composed of the equities of all the companies headquartered in the United States—as of the end of the quarter by the level of disposable personal income. When the ratio of the Wilshire 5000 to disposal personal income—our proxy for wealth—rises, the stock market wealth is on the rise. This increase makes consumers feel wealthier and so willing to spend more. Through econometric analysis, some economists have determined that for every $1.00 increase in the level of stock market wealth, consumer spending increases by $0.03 to $0.07 per year.

Some economists argue against the wealth effect, pointing out that only about 50 percent of American households have a link (direct or indirect) to the stock market. In other words, our proxy would explain the gain or loss in wealth for only about 50 percent of all households. This might explain the disconnect between the two series prior to 1997 and after 2002 in **FIGURE 11.7**. Because our wealth-effect ratio does parallel trends in the year-over-year growth rate of consumer spending for the better portion of 1997 through 2001, when stock prices skyrocketed and then tumbled, it might be the case that the wealth effect works only during periods of high stock market participation. It seems reasonable, though, that even people who don't invest in equities feed off the positive atmosphere of a rising market and pick up the pace of spending. Newspapers, evening news programs, and radio stations broadcast the daily stock

Figure 11.7 Wealth Ratio Versus Consumer Spending

market gains and the reasons for them—usually upbeat signals about the economy given by the indicators described in this book. Higher stock market valuations result from higher earnings expectations, which in turn imply increased business spending and the increased likelihood of hiring. When job creation increases, consumers are more upbeat, and incomes and spending rise.

PRICES

Another obvious relationship exists between spending and prices. This is summed up in one of the first laws that every economics student learns: the law of demand. In rough terms, this states that the higher the price of a good is, the lower the demand for it will be, and conversely, the lower the price, the greater the demand. Consider gasoline. When the price of a gallon rises to $3.00 or more, consumers demand less of it. Commuters who usually drive to work may carpool or use alternative means of transportation like the bus, train, or ferry. Families might postpone vacation plans until fuel prices recede to more affordable levels. **FIGURE 11.8** illustrates the inverse relationship between price

Figure 11.8   Growth in Real Consumer Spending on Gasoline Versus Growth in Consumer Price of Gasoline

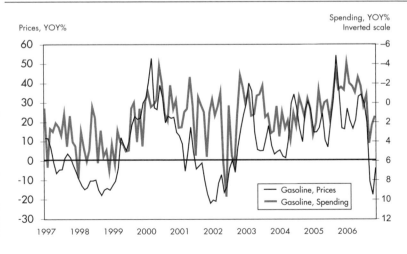

Sources: U.S. Department of Commerce, Bureau of Economic Analysis; U.S. Department of Labor, Bureau of Labor Statistics

and demand (notice the inverted scale). The time span covered includes three periods of high inflation in gasoline prices: 2000, 2003, and 2006. During all three of these episodes, the growth rate of consumer spending on gas declined. Readers can obtain these data—in amazing detail—on the BEA's website, www.bea.gov.

Investors should get into the habit of knowing the underlying price trends for several major spending categories such as healthcare, medicine, apparel, food, housing, tuition, and transportation. Obviously the higher the prices of these goods, in many cases necessities, the less money there will be available for spending on other things. The detail regarding the consumer prices of all these goods and services—and thousands more—are available on the Bureau of Labor Statistics website, www.bls.gov. The price measures will be discussed in Chapter 12.

EMPLOYMENT

Stock market losses and rising prices may dampen consumers' enthusiasm, but they tend to merely slow spending growth rather than stop it altogether. There's one influence that will cause consumers to virtually cease all nonessential spending: the loss of a job.

FIGURE 11.9 illustrates the incredibly tight relationship between the growth rate of nonfarm jobs and the rate of spending. Nothing is as economically depressing as the loss of employment or the fear of losing a job. It isn't just that unemployed people don't have earned income to spend. They may also despair of finding a job anytime in the near future. This is particularly true during weak economic times, when several hundred people might be applying for the same advertised position. When consumer confidence measures tumble before and during recessions, they are capturing this discouragement. The feeling can paralyze spending.

Figure 11.9 shows a bit of disconnect in 2001 to 2002, when payroll growth was contracting, yet spending registered some reasonable solid gains. This is a rarity; the 2001 recession was the first in post–World War II history during which consumer spending did not decline. This anomaly can be credited to the sound implementa-

Figure 11.9 Growth in Real Consumer Spending Versus Payroll Growth

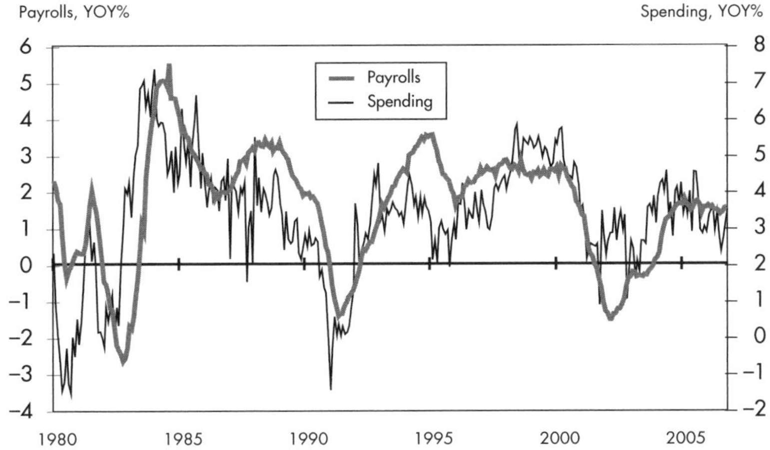

Sources: U.S. Department of Commerce, Bureau of Economic Analysis; U.S. Department of Labor, Bureau of Labor Statistics

tion of fiscal and monetary policy. Expeditious tax cuts by the Bush administration and the preemptive lowering of interest rates by the Fed fueled incomes and kept spending on the rise.

Knowing that the level of employment is critical in the determination of spending, investors should always keep an eye on the pace of job creation. The stronger the rate of growth in employment, the stronger the pace of spending will be. Employment data and its detail can also be found at the Bureau of Labor Statistics website. The employment situation is discussed in detail in Chapter 3.

Consumer and Producer Price Indexes   *12*

A<small>N INCREASE IN THE PRICES</small> of goods and services is called inflation. A certain level of inflation in the economy is normal, even healthy. Accelerating inflation, however, can cause severe problems, sometimes sparking recession. No wonder the financial markets keep a close eye on price measures and their growth rates. For this purpose, many traders and economists, including those at the Federal Reserve Board, favor the implicit price deflators contained in the gross domestic product (GDP) report (see Chapter 1). That report appears only quarterly, however. For more timely—and detailed—inflation indicators, most market participants turn to the reports on the consumer price index (CPI) and the producer price index (PPI).

The Bureau of Labor Statistics (BLS) calculates, maintains, and reports on the consumer price index and the producer price index. (The bureau also produces a third set of indexes in the international import and export price report, but the market doesn't react to these, so they will not be discussed in this book.) The consumer price index and producer price index reports are released around the middle of the month following the record month, the producer price index usually at least one business day before the consumer price index. The releases—which hit the newswires at 8:30 a.m. (ET) and are available on the BLS website, www.bls.gov—often create quite a stir in the financial world, especially the fixed-income market.

The **consumer price index** tracks the change in price, at the consumer level, of a weighted basket of a few hundred goods and services. The composition of this basket reflects households' typical monthly purchases, as revealed in the Consumer Expenditure Survey, which the Census Bureau conducts for the Bureau of Labor Statistics. The weight given each item is determined by its percentage of total household expenditures. The index reading represents how much the basket has increased in value since 1984, the base year. A reading of 130, for instance, indicates that the current average cost of the goods and services is 30 percent greater than it was in 1984.

The consumer price index has two basic versions: the CPI-U, which reflects the buying habits of all urban consumers, and the older CPI-W, which relates only to urban households that include a wage earner or clerical worker. The two versions employ data from the same survey and are constructed using the same methodology. They differ only in the weight given certain basket components. The CPI-W is used by the private sector in price-escalation clauses in contracts and by the government in computing cost-of-living adjustments for Social Security. Wall Street and the media focus on the CPI-U, because it represents roughly 87 percent of the noninstitutionalized population, compared with the CPI-W's mere 32 percent. National and local governments, businesses, and organizations employ the CPI-U in forming and implementing policies. Economists use it to adjust nominal-dollar-based indicators, such as retail sales, for inflation. All of the discussions of the consumer price index in this book refer to the CPI-U.

The **producer price index**, also known as the wholesale price index, tracks changes in the selling prices of some 3,450 items, at various stages of manufacture, that are received by the producers of those items. Price figures are collected monthly and for the most part, are those recorded on the Tuesday of the week containing the thirteenth day of the record month. Components are weighted according to their contribution to GDP. As for the consumer price index, readings represent price changes from the base year 1984.

The producer price index incorporates data about prices before the retail level is determined. It covers items not in the consumer price index, such as raw materials and intermediate goods. Economists looking at the producer price index data can thus see how far in the production process inflation pressures have traveled and how close they are to emerging in the retail or consumer sector. They can also get a feel for whether any rise in business costs is driven by demand or by supply.

Because of these characteristics, and because of its earlier release date, the producer price index is used by some analysts to predict consumer price index readings. This can be misleading, however. The two indexes are very different, both in the way they are constructed and in the items they include. The producer price index, for instance, doesn't contain any information on prices for services, the largest part of the U.S. economy. On the other hand, it does incorporate information about the prices of raw materials, which are extremely sensitive to weather conditions. As a result, monthly readings of the producer price index are extremely volatile and can be quite different from those of the consumer price index, although the two indexes do show a high degree of correlation over the longer term.

EVOLUTION OF AN INDICATOR

The origins of the producer price index and consumer price index, unlike their release dates, are widely separated in time. They were created not only at different times but to serve different purposes, and so each index evolved quite differently.

PRODUCER PRICE INDEX

In the late nineteenth century, the U.S. Senate authorized the Bureau of Labor Statistics to start collecting and reporting wholesale prices, so that the Senate could assess the economic effects of tariff laws. The first wholesale price index (WPI), the index's official name for nearly eight decades, was published in 1902. It was an unweighted index of about 250 commodity prices, covering the period from 1890 through 1901. A weighting scheme was adopted in 1914; it was later refined in 1952 and 1967.

The original purpose of the index was to reveal price activity at the earliest stage of production. It was believed that this was best accomplished by compiling the prices that domestic producers or importers of the goods and commodities received. The original method, unfortunately, involved skewed sampling techniques in which responses from large companies dominated the sample. Over time, this resulted in a misrepresentation of prices. This initial method overemphasized the prices of goods produced by larger firms and underrepresented the prices of goods produced by smaller firms. By the 1940s, moreover, the original weighting scheme was outdated, giving too little importance to certain mining and manufactured products that by then accounted for about half (in dollar value) of all goods used in the production process. These wrinkles were eventually ironed out through the recategorization of data and constant revision to sampling methods and weighing systems.

In 1978, the BLS overhauled the index again, emphasizing the categorization of prices by stage of processing, rather than by commodity or industry, and stressing finished goods over those at other stages. The bureau also changed the name of the index from "wholesale" to "producer" price index.

CONSUMER PRICE INDEX

Compared with the producer price index, the consumer price index is a newcomer. Prices on the consumer level were first collected during World War I, to estimate cost-of-living adjustments to wages. From 1917 through 1919, the BLS collected data from ninety-two industrialized population centers and analyzed spending patterns to create weighted indexes of consumer expenditures.

Profound changes in consumer buying habits, particularly during the Roaring Twenties and the Great Depression in the 1930s, led to a comprehensive overhaul of the weights and composition of the indexes in 1940. World War II–related rationing and shortages necessitated similar revisions. In 1953, the consumer price index underwent its greatest makeover up to that time, including improvements in methodology and collection procedures, as well as new sources of data and a more representative list of items. This process of refinement and restructuring continued through the late 1990s.

In December 1996, a commission created by the Senate Finance Committee to study the consumer price index and its framework released a highly publicized report concluding that the consumer price index, as currently constituted, overstated the true level of inflation by about 1.1 percentage points and suggesting several remedies. The Boskin Report (so-called after the commission chair, Michael Boskin) set the financial world abuzz: because cost-of-living adjustments in employee compensation and pensions are linked to the growth rate of the consumer price index, a reduction in the index's growth rate would lower disbursements to retirees, Social Security recipients, and civil service workers, and so restrict their spending power. Due to the political, economical, and social nature of these findings, there hasn't been any serious adjustment to the consumer price measures.

DIGGING FOR THE DATA

Just as the origins of the two indexes differ, the data sources for the consumer price index and producer price index and the methodologies used in compiling them also differ considerably.

CONSUMER PRICE INDEX DATA SOURCES

The consumer price index represents prices on the retail, or demand, side of the economy. To gather the data used to construct the index, field economists from the BLS visit supermarkets, department stores, gasoline filling stations, hospitals, and other establishments in eighty-seven urban areas all around the nation, recording prices of food, fuel, beverages, apparel, health care, and other goods and services. Additional prices are obtained via mail survey.

The prices gathered are organized into eight expenditure categories: housing, transportation, food and beverages, recreation, medical care, education and communication, apparel, and "other," which includes such items as personal care products and tobacco. The goods and services included in the survey are based on the re-

Figure 12.1   Composition of the CPI-U

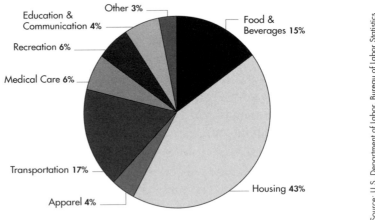

Source: U.S. Department of Labor, Bureau of Labor Statistics

sults of the Consumer Expenditure Survey, as are the weights given to the various categories in computing the index. These weights, which reflect the portion of their incomes that consumers spend on the items in the category, range from 42.4 percent for housing and 17.4 percent for transportation through 6.0 percent for education and communication to 3.5 percent for "other" and 3.8 percent for apparel (see **FIGURE 12.1**).

The index's basket of goods and services does not, of course, capture every individual's or every group's consumption pattern. The elderly, for instance, probably spend more of their monthly allowances on health care, whereas the younger generation spends more on tuition and apparel. The categories and their weights, however, present a fairly accurate picture of Americans' *average* monthly spending habits.

Calculating the average prices for items and categories isn't as simple as it may sound. For goods like toothpaste, alcoholic beverages, tires, or a ticket to a sporting event, the process is straightforward. Services are a different matter. Housing, the largest component of the consumer price index, is particularly complex. The index measures the cost of using services, not of obtaining assets, such as condos or houses. The BLS accordingly recognizes two categories of housing costs: residential rent and owners' equivalent of residential rent. The BLS defines the latter as "the cost of renting housing services equivalent to those services provided by owner-occupied housing." This definition removes the investment component of ownership. Price information for the housing category is obtained through interviews with landlords, tenants, and owner-occupants.

From the monthly pricing data, the BLS calculates values for the headliner all-items index (covering the entire basket) and for various subindexes, including one for each of the eight expenditure categories and several "special" subindexes. Tables throughout the report present values for the various indexes and subindexes, both adjusted and unadjusted for seasonal variations. What draw the most attention are the percentage changes—from month to month, from year to year, and over a three-month period—which represent inflation rates for the relevant periods and categories of items.

The top three special indexes are for energy, food, and all goods and services except food and energy. The last of these, referred to as core CPI, is particularly influential.

Energy and food prices are extremely volatile. Tensions in the Middle East, unusually cold or hot weather, and changes in production schedules, particularly among OPEC countries, are just a few factors that can send oil and gas prices soaring or plummeting. Similarly, food prices can move violently on news of droughts, storms, or late frosts that destroy crops. Removing these components and their erratic movements makes it easier to discern longer-term inflationary trends. The result is termed "core inflation." (Economists at the Federal Reserve Bank of Cleveland have gone one step further in reducing consumer price index "noise," lopping off those components with the biggest gains or declines in a given month; the so-called median index—also referred to as the Cleveland Fed index, the median CPI, or the Cleveland Fed's median CPI—is available on the Cleveland Fed's website, www.clevelandfed.org, and has become a Wall Street favorite.)

PRODUCER PRICE INDEX DATA SOURCES

The producer price index tracks price trends from a seller's, or supply-side, perspective. Every month, the BLS collects prices for about 100,000 goods at various stages of production, from voluntary surveys completed by some 30,000 businesses. Using these prices, the BLS compiles around 8,000 indexes in three major categories: commodity indexes, which organize data according to end use or material composition (farm products, textiles and apparel, transportation equipment, for instance); industry indexes, which are organized according to several different classification systems and whose components are weighted by "net output," or the value of shipments outside the industry (railroads, the U.S. Postal Service, tour operators); and stage-of-processing indexes, which are grouped by the amount of processing of the good and the purchaser's class. The last category is the focus of the producer price index report and the one most often cited in the business press and on trading floors.

The stage-of-processing system classifies items as crude materials for further processing, intermediate components, or finished goods. *Crude materials* are commodities that have not been refined or processed, such as raw cotton, hides and skins, and copper and aluminum base scrap. *Intermediate materials* have undergone some processing but have not completed the fabrication process. Popular goods in this category include industrial textile products, leather, glass containers, and synthetic rubber. *Finished goods* are ready to be sold to the final user (consumers and businesses) without further refinement.

The stage-of-processing category is divided into two major groups, with weights consistent with the contributions to total economic activity in the national income and product accounts: *consumer goods*, which are weighted in line with the composition of personal consumer expenditures (accounting for approximately three-quarters of all finished goods) and are themselves divided into food and nonfood items; and *capital equipment*, a representation of the value of business purchases. (**FIGURE 12.2** shows the finished goods

Figure 12.2   PPI Finished Goods Components•

Crude foods	1.688%
Processed foods	18.583
Finished consumer foods	**20.272**
Nondurable goods less foods	40.114
Durable goods	*14.884*
Nonfoods	**54.998**
Finished consumer goods	**75.270**
Manufacturing industries	6.662
Nonmanufacturing industries	18.068
Capital equipment	**24.730**
FINISHED GOODS	**100.000%**

Source: U.S. Department of Labor, Bureau of Labor Statistics
*All percentages as of November 2006

components and subcomponents.) Finished goods include apparel, roasted coffee, textile machinery, commercial furniture, and railroad equipment. Because these items are the closest to the retail level, the Street focuses on their price indexes. When the media, economists, or analysts refer to producer prices, wholesale prices, or the producer price index, they are referring to the inflation rate or percentage change in the finished goods indexes.

The monthly producer price index news release contains only the key aggregate indexes of about two hundred or so seasonally adjusted and unadjusted indexes. The BLS publishes more than five hundred industry price indexes, eight thousand specific product-line and product-category subindexes, and thirty-two hundred commodity price indexes. The complete series of indexes, as well as their histories, are on the BLS website and in the BLS's monthly PPI Detailed Report, available by subscription.

CALCULATING THE INFLATION RATE

You can use the following formula to determine the rate of inflation between two periods implied by any of the index values in the consumer price index or producer price index reports:

$$R_{Inf} = 100 \times (I_{CP} - I_{PP}) \div I_{PP},$$

where R_{Inf} is the rate of inflation, I_{CP} is the current index value, and I_{PP} is the previous index value.

To illustrate, suppose you wanted to figure out the twelve-month inflation rate for pulp, paper, and allied products as of November 2006. For that month, the unadjusted index for pulp, paper and allied products was 212.3, versus 203.8 in November 2005. Plugging those values into the formula, you get

$$R_{Inf} = 100 \times (212.3 - 203.8) \div 203.8$$
$$= 8.5 \div 203.8$$
$$= 4.17 \text{ percent,}$$

or approximately 4.2 percent inflation, year over year.

WHAT DOES IT ALL MEAN?

The inflation rate can tell us a great deal about economic conditions. When the economy is strengthening, companies experience increased demand for their products and so can charge higher prices for them. As a result, revenues increase, lifting profits and permitting companies to boost capital investment and create new jobs. At the same time, however, the higher prices squeeze consumers, who may have to choose where to allocate limited funds: the more they pay for one good or service, the less they have for others. It's a delicate balance. Too little inflation, and corporate profits tumble, curtailing capital spending and causing unemployment; too much, and consumers can't afford to buy. The results are the same, only the course is different.

That said, the producer price index and the consumer price index aren't generally considered leading indicators. Changes in the general price level aren't as predictive of business cycle turning points as are many of the indicators discussed in previous chapters. They do tell a great deal about the microeconomic conditions of individual commodities or industries, however. Just don't read too much into a single month's activity. Price indexes, even those excluding energy and food, can be affected by any number of influences. Legislation and taxes, for example, can push up prices on items like liquor and tobacco quite dramatically from one month to the next.

PRICE TRENDS

Prices can display three trends: **inflation**, a sustained increase in prices; **disinflation**, a slowing of the rate of increase; and **deflation**, a sustained decrease. **FIGURE 12.3** illustrates all three phenomena. First, inflation. The line graphing year-over-year changes in consumer prices remains above zero for the entire chart. That means the inflation rate was positive for the whole period. In other words, 1970 through 2003 saw rising prices for consumer goods. The increases have not been uniform, however. The price-growth line falls sharply from 1972 to 1974, 1975 to 1977, 1980 to mid-1983, and then again from 1991 to 1992. Those drops indicate slower rates of price growth—that is, disinfla-

Figure 12.3   Consumer and Producer Price Indices

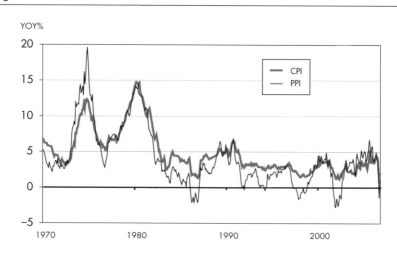

Source: U.S. Department of Labor, Bureau of Labor Statistics

tion—in consumer goods. To see a graphic representation of deflation, you have to turn to the more volatile producer prices (the only serious bout of consumer price deflation that ever occurred in the United States was during the Great Depression). As the PPI-growth graph shows, since 1975 the twelve-month inflation rate in producer prices has fallen into negative—deflationary—territory several times during 1986–1987, 1992, 1994, 1997–1999, 2001–2003, and again in 2006.

Deflation is as damaging to economic health as high inflation. When prices are falling, consumers postpone purchases in anticipation of even lower prices in the future. Without the engine of consumer expenditures (the largest component of GDP), economic growth slows and may even contract if the situation continues. Deflation also hurts corporate profits, causing companies to cut production and reduce staff.

In recent years, economists have fretted about the possibility of deflation in the United States. Growing globalization has sent production facilities to low-wage nations such as China and India, which send incredibly low-priced toys, textiles, computer parts, and foods back to the United States. Prices of nonimported services, such as education, medical care, housing, and electricity, however, have been rising. So, although certain industries have experienced deflation, the economy as a whole has not. In a true deflationary period, all prices decline, at both the consumer and the producer level. The only hint of deflation has been in the producer price index. One reason for this is that no services are included in the producer price index. Moreover, the core rate of producer price growth—which excludes the volatile food and energy components—has fallen into negative territory only once, and that barely. (Core PPI deflation exists only during prolonged periods of manufacturing weakness.)

PRICE INDEXES AND THE MARKETS

To bondholders, inflation is public enemy number one. Bond buyers are actually lending the security's purchase price to the issuer; in return for their loans, they get coupon payments at regular intervals for the life of the bond (unless they sell or it is called). Inflation erodes the purchasing power of future payments. Suppose a 10-year bond pays a 6 percent coupon. If inflation rises to 4.5 percent, the investors' real (inflation-adjusted) rate of return is only 1.5 percent—not very good over a ten-year period. No wonder that, at the slightest whiff of inflation, investors sell their fixed-income securities, sending prices down and yields (which are inversely related to price) up.

Equity investors generally react very little to the inflation reports. Even stockholders, however, can get exercised when the monthly postings differ greatly from expectations or suggest an inflation rate that could impede consumer spending and disrupt economic growth. A series of high inflation numbers—say, three consecutive monthly increases of 0.7 percent in the consumer price index or producer price index—will have both bond and stock investors anticipating a possible tightening by the Federal Reserve.

To cool the economy down and dampen inflationary pressures, the Fed may raise its target for the federal funds rate (the rate banks charge each other for overnight loans used to meet reserve requirements; see Chapter 1). Longer-maturity interest rates usually follow suit. High rates discourage consumers from buying assets, such as houses and motor vehicles, whose purchases are financed with loans. Companies may also put off construction and other projects that would necessitate forays into the debt markets. If rates rise to truly restrictive levels, they may be forced to eliminate workers.

PRICE INDEXES AND THE BUSINESS CYCLE

As with other price measures, the "core" rate of inflation, computed by excluding the volatile food and energy components, is often used for tracing inflation trends. The BLS calculates the core rate for the producer price index: the crude nonfood materials less energy index. The core crude PPI, as it is known, is more obscure than the other core indexes but very useful in tracking the business cycle.

Historically, changes in the prices for raw materials have indicated turning points in the business cycle. Early in a recovery,

Figure 12.4   Core Crude PPI Versus S&P 500 Operating EPS

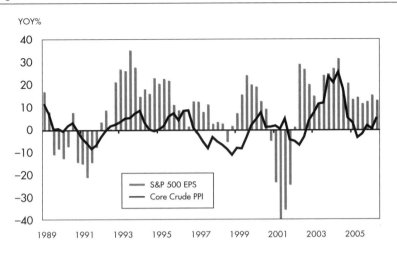

companies prepare for the anticipated pickup in demand for their products by speeding up their own purchases of commodities they need to begin manufacturing. Conversely, at the first sign of a downturn, they protect against slowing demand by reducing their consumption and purchases of crude materials, depressing these items' prices. This relationship is manifested in the correlation, shown in **FIGURE 12.4**, between year-over-year changes in the core crude PPI and the twelve-month growth rate of operating earnings per share for the Standard & Poor's 500 index.

HOW TO USE WHAT YOU SEE

As with other indicators discussed in this book, many of the strategies associated with the inflation reports are aimed at getting a jump on the data in the reports. Economists who want to try to predict the consumer price index and producer price index numbers keep a close eye on material and commodity prices. Increases at that stage can lead to price hikes farther down the production pipeline. This is known as cost-push inflation—an industry experiencing rising costs for materials, capital, labor, or land passes the increase on to another sector of the economy by charging higher prices for its own goods or services. When copper prices rise, for instance, homebuilders and buyers feel the pinch. The Copper Development Association, a trade council, estimates that the average single-family home uses about 439 pounds of the metal, in roofing, flanging, gutters, plumbing, circuitry, wire, fillings, valves, appliances, hardware, and lighting fixtures. Builders pass their increased costs for these items along to buyers. So, when copper prices are on the rise, it's a safe bet that new-housing prices will be rising as well.

The story is similar with natural gas and aluminum. Natural gas not only heats millions of homes in the winter but also is the second-largest resource, behind coal, used in electricity production. One of the most energy-dependent operations is aluminum manufacturing. Higher prices for natural gas can thus push up the price of aluminum. That in turn boosts the prices of goods such as cars, which use aluminum or aluminum derivatives in fenders, motors, axles, bodies, wheels, and other components.

Just about every serious business periodical contains some measure of commodity and raw-materials prices. The *Wall Street Journal*, the *Financial Times, Investor's Business Daily*, the *Economist, Barron's*, and *BusinessWeek* have detailed listings and usually publish graphs of the most pronounced movements in a select group of goods.

One word of caution: it is not enough to discern movements in commodity and raw-materials prices; you must also identify the causes of those movements. Price increases that are due to heightened demand (so-called demand-pull inflation) are more likely to be long term and passed on to end users than those caused by supply-related factors such as strikes, bad weather, factory explosions, and other production disruptions.

TRICKS FROM THE TRENCHES

The price indexes are extremely versatile and are employed in a wide array of circumstances. Economists, for instance, use the core CPI as a deflator—subtracting the year-over-year percentage change in the core CPI from the twelve-month growth rate

Figure 12.5   The Misery Index

Source: U.S. Department of Labor, Bureau of Labor Statistics

in the nominal values of the indicators they track, so that they can discern trends without the distorting effects of inflation. Sometimes analysts tweak, combine, or compare the inflation indexes to produce other findings. The misery index is one product of such tweaking.

Aficionados of soprano recitals are familiar with the aria from Antonio Vivaldi's opera *Griselda*—"Agitata da due venti," or "Battered by Two Winds." Economics has its own battering winds: inflation and unemployment. Acknowledging the buffeting these ill winds can give consumers, businesses, and investors, economists have combined the twelve-month growth rate of consumer price inflation with the Bureau of Labor Statistics' unemployment rate to form the misery index, shown in **FIGURE 12.5.**

When the misery index rises above 13 percent, economic conditions are, well, miserable. During the seven recessions occurring in the forty-plus years covered by the chart, the average index value was 13.25 percent; from mid-1973 through 1984, it was 15.40 percent, with May 1980 recording a dismal 21.9 percent. Expansions, in contrast, are characterized by average misery index values of around 9.7 percent. In recent years, the index has remained mostly in the 7 to 9 percent range.

Yale University economist Ray Fair has shown in several working papers and his book *Predicting Presidential Elections and Other Things* that changes in economic conditions, including inflation and unemployment rates, have an effect on voting outcomes. The high levels of the misery index registered in May 1980, within months of the presidential election, pretty much guaranteed a loss for incumbent President Jimmy Carter. Americans vote with respect to the economy, and economic conditions during this period were the worst in decades.

The Fixed-Income Market *13*

P REVIOUS CHAPTERS HAVE FOCUSED on a particular economic indicator or release. This chapter widens the picture to show
why it is important to become familiar with what's happening in
the fixed-income market and most important, with bond prices
and their respective interest rates. These are major determinants of the pricing and valuation of stocks, the stock market as
a whole, and other investments. Investors often compare returns
on different asset classes and investments (stocks, commodities,
real estate, art, and so forth) to some interest-rate reference like
the yield of the 10-year Treasury note. The level of interest rates
in the fixed-income market also greatly influences household
spending and business decisions to invest, which are the twin
drivers of overall economic activity.

Chapter 2 gave a brief introduction to the yield curve and to
interest-rate spreads, with a discussion of leading economic indicators. The yield curve says a great deal about the perceptions
and expectations that the bond market has about the economy.
Other indicators that investors should be looking at include the
market's expectations for inflation, the pace of the overall economy, and the potential direction of the Federal Reserve Board's
monetary policy.

The U.S. bond market is the Big Daddy of the financial markets. According to the Federal Reserve's flow of funds statement,
at the end of 2006, credit-market debt outstanding totaled $43.5
trillion, easily above the U.S. outstanding corporate equity value
of $19.3 trillion and dwarfing the level of U.S. gross domestic

product, which was hovering around $13.3 trillion. As we shall see, the gargantuan bond market speaks volumes about the economy.

EVOLUTION OF AN INDICATOR

Interest rates have a long and storied history that dates back to the creation of coinage. A thorough examination of the subject can be found in Sidney Homer's *A History of Interest Rates*, a highly recommended read for any student of investment. Homer's book provides detailed insights on credit and interest, including tables of interest rates in Mesopotamia from 3,000 to 400 BC. For our discussion, however, we'll stick to recent twentieth- and twenty-first-century figures.

Economists have come to care about the activity in the bond market first and foremost because of its size—anything as big as the U.S. bond market demands attention. Its behavior reveals a great deal about current and future expectations for the economy, investor sentiment, and the general condition of corporations, municipalities, the U.S. government, and many other entities that issue fixed-income securities.

It is a widely accepted idea that well-diversified investors should have some exposure to fixed-income securities. The recommended percentage differs from portfolio to portfolio, but most professional money managers would agree that bonds are an integral part of investment strategy. This, coupled with the needs of many borrowers to raise capital, explains the enormity of the fixed-income market. With so many transactions taking place between issuers and investors, economists are reasonably assured that the data derived from the fixed-income market is robust, or statistically significant.

Beyond the size of the sample, there is another reason, perhaps even more important, to analyze the bond market for information about future economic conditions. Market-determined data are strong indicators of market expectations about economic fundamentals. We know that the clues contained in the bond market are real because its movements are "backed by money." That is, market participants have actually invested in particular securities on the basis of their expected return on each investment. This type of outlay is predicated on numerous factors, which may include expectations about monetary and fiscal policy, the strength of economic activity, the value of the dollar, the direction of the general price level, and the creditworthiness of those that are borrowing money by issuing bonds.

Market-determined indicators differ from the results of conventional surveys because market participants being polled don't always do as they say. With the purchase or sale of a security, an investor is placing money on the expectation of a particular set of economic conditions, or a series of circumstances. The results of surveys and indicators derived from polls might be very different if they required some sort of payment or wager from the respondents.

In the financial markets, investors make distinct choices, based on a belief, say, that either inflation will be contained and their investments will flourish, or it won't. Moreover, indicators based on investor decisions are useful precisely because investors change their minds, reversing or trading out of their previous positions from one moment to the next. Surveys and polls aren't afforded the luxury of instantaneous revision.

DIGGING FOR THE DATA

Live bond prices and associated interest rates may be obtained during trading hours by subscription to a professional trading system like the Bloomberg Professional service. Delayed quotes may be found on television programs such as those on CNBC and on dozens of financial websites. But if the ultimate use of interest-rate data is economic study and analysis for trading decisions, it is best to have a resource containing a large history of the more relevant series of interest rates. Fortunately, such a resource not only exists but is also free. This veritable gold mine of information is compiled by the Federal Reserve.

The Federal Reserve releases the H.15 Selected Interest Rates report every Monday at 2:30 p.m. (ET). It is generally considered the primary source for interest-rate data and can be found on the Federal Reserve website, at http://www.federalreserve.gov/releases.

Figure 13.1   Federal Reserve H.15 Selected Interest Rates Report

Instruments	2007 Jan 8	2007 Jan 9	2007 Jan 10	2007 Jan 11	2007 Jan 12	Week Ending Jan 12	Week Ending Jan 5	2006 Dec
Federal funds (effective)	5.23	5.25	5.26	5.27	5.22	5.23	5.22	5.24
Commercial Paper								
Nonfinancial								
1-month	5.26	5.26	5.23	5.19	5.24	5.24	5.23	5.23
2-month	n.a.	5.25	n.a.	5.17	n.a.	5.21	5.19	5.20
3-month	n.a.	n.a.	n.a.	5.17	n.a.	5.17	n.a.	5.19
Financial								
1-month	5.25	5.25	5.25	5.25	5.24	5.25	5.25	5.25
2-month	5.24	5.24	5.23	5.25	5.24	5.24	5.24	5.24
3-month	5.23	5.24	5.23	5.24	5.24	5.24	5.23	5.24
CDs (secondary market)								
1-month	5.30	5.29	5.30	5.29	5.29	5.29	5.30	5.31
3-month	5.31	5.31	5.32	5.32	5.32	5.32	5.32	5.32
6-month	5.32	5.32	5.33	5.33	5.34	5.33	5.32	5.31
Eurodollar deposits (London)								
1-month	5.32	5.32	5.32	5.32	5.32	5.32	5.32	5.34
3-month	5.35	5.35	5.35	5.35	5.35	5.35	5.35	5.35
6-month	5.36	5.37	5.37	5.37	5.37	5.37	5.36	5.33
Bank prime loan	8.25	8.25	8.25	8.25	8.25	8.25	8.25	8.25
Discount window primary credit	6.25	6.25	6.25	6.25	6.25	6.25	6.25	6.25
U.S. government securities								
Treasury bills (secondary market)								
4-week	4.75	4.81	4.85	4.89	4.89	4.84	4.71	4.78
3-month	4.95	4.95	4.96	4.98	4.96	4.96	4.92	4.85
6-month	4.93	4.93	4.93	4.95	4.96	4.94	4.90	4.88
Treasury constant maturities								
Nominal								
1-month	4.87	4.90	4.94	4.99	4.98	4.94	4.81	4.87
3-month	5.08	5.08	5.09	5.11	5.09	5.09	5.05	4.97
6-month	5.13	5.13	5.13	5.15	5.15	5.14	5.09	5.07
1-year	5.01	5.02	5.02	5.05	5.06	5.03	4.98	4.94
2-year	4.78	4.79	4.81	4.86	4.88	4.82	4.76	4.67

Included in this report are the daily and weekly averages of interest rates for selected U.S. Treasury and private money market and capital market instruments. **FIGURE 13.1** is the H.15 report released on January 16, 2007.

Figure 13.1   (continued)

Instruments	2007 Jan 8	2007 Jan 9	2007 Jan 10	2007 Jan 11	2007 Jan 12	Week Ending Jan 12	Week Ending Jan 5	2006 Dec
Treasury constant maturities								
Nominal (continued)								
3-year	4.70	4.70	4.72	4.78	4.81	4.74	4.68	4.58
5-year	4.66	4.65	4.68	4.73	4.76	4.70	4.65	4.53
7-year	4.66	4.65	4.68	4.73	4.76	4.70	4.65	4.54
10-year	4.66	4.66	4.69	4.74	4.77	4.70	4.66	4.56
20-year	4.84	4.83	4.87	4.92	4.96	4.88	4.84	4.78
30-year	4.74	4.74	4.77	4.82	4.86	4.79	4.76	4.68
Inflation indexed								
5-year	2.42	2.43	2.46	2.50	2.53	2.47	2.40	2.28
7-year	2.42	2.42	2.46	2.50	2.53	2.47	2.41	2.28
10-year	2.38	2.39	2.42	2.43	2.49	2.42	2.37	2.25
20-year	2.37	2.38	2.41	2.46	2.50	2.42	2.35	2.26
Inflation-indexed long-term average								
	2.34	2.35	2.38	2.43	2.47	2.39	2.32	2.23
Interest rate swaps								
1-year	5.32	5.33	5.34	5.36	5.39	5.35	5.30	5.25
2-year	5.13	5.14	5.18	5.20	5.23	5.17	5.12	5.02
3-year	5.05	5.06	5.10	5.13	5.17	5.10	5.05	4.94
4-year	5.04	5.05	5.08	5.11	5.16	5.09	5.04	4.93
5-year	5.05	5.06	5.09	5.12	5.17	5.10	5.05	4.94
7-year	5.07	5.08	5.12	5.16	5.20	5.13	5.08	4.97
10-year	5.12	5.14	5.17	5.21	5.26	5.18	5.14	5.03
30-year	5.25	5.25	5.30	5.33	5.38	5.30	5.27	5.18
Corporate bonds								
Moody's seasoned								
Aaa	5.29	5.29	5.32	5.37	5.41	5.34	5.31	5.32
Baa	6.25	6.25	6.28	6.33	6.36	6.29	6.27	6.22
State & local bonds				4.21		4.21	4.15	4.11
Conventional mortgages				6.21		6.21	6.18	6.14

n.a. Not available.

Source: Board of Governors of the Federal Reserve

The **federal funds rate** is the rate of interest charged by depository institutions within the Federal Reserve System that lend their surplus reserves to each other overnight. The Federal Open Market Committee sets a desired target, but the market determines the actual level. The weighted average of daily trades is known as the *effective* federal funds rate.

Commercial paper (CP) is broken down in the H.15 report into financial and nonfinancial instruments. CP is simply a bill or note, issued by a corporation, with a maturity of up to 270 days. The average maturity is closer to thirty days.

A **CD**, formally known as a certificate of deposit, is a money market instrument usually issued by a commercial bank that pays a specified fixed rate of interest with a specific maturity. The terms range from thirty days to five years, and the holders are generally restricted from withdrawing funds prior to maturity. The H.15 report includes only maturities of less than one year. Such shorter-term CDs are considered money market instruments and can be traded in a secondary market.

Eurodollar deposits are U.S. dollar-denominated deposits held at banks outside the United States. These deposits, which are not associated with the Federal Reserve, became known on Wall Street as Eurodollars because they were largely held by European banks and financial institutions.

The **bank prime loan rate** is the interest rate charged by the majority of the nation's top domestic commercial banks to their most creditworthy (prime) clients. It is used as a reference when those banks make commercial and consumer loans. Usually loans are made with respect to some "spread" over or under the bank prime rate, that is, prime plus x percent or prime minus x percent.

The **discount window primary credit rate** is set by the Federal Reserve for commercial banks and other depository institutions that borrow at the Federal Reserve's discount window lending facility. This is usually an overnight borrowing rate.

U.S. government securities are fixed-income instruments issued by the U.S. government to raise money. The U.S. Treasury website, http://www.treas.gov, gives an excellent explanation of how the government raises funds and sells securities, as well as of the entire quarterly refunding process.

Inflation-indexed securities are government issues whose principal is tied, or indexed, to the consumer price index (CPI). Inflation erodes the value of the principal of a traditional bond. Inflation-indexed bonds are protected from such erosion.

Interest-rate swaps are agreements between two parties to exchange fixed-rate interest payments against floating-rate payments. The terms and conditions for swaps can vary immensely. The rates provided in the Federal Reserve's H.15 report are for receivers of 3-month Libor (London interbank offered rate).

Corporate bonds, in the report, refer to average yields on Aaa- and Baa-rated bonds as provided by Moody's Investors Service.

State and local bond yields are obtained by the Bond Buyer index and refer to general-obligations bonds, with mixed credit qualities and maturities of twenty years or longer.

Conventional mortgages, which refer to contract interest rates on commitments for fixed-rate first mortgages, as compiled by the Federal Home Loan Mortgage Corporation, are considered the benchmark for mortgage rates.

In addition to this report, the Federal Reserve's website also provides a deep and detailed history of interest rates. Most Wall Street economists get their data from this site or from the site of one of the regional Federal Reserve banks. The most popular and easily accessible sources for downloading data into a spreadsheet is the Federal Reserve Economic Database II (FRED II) maintained by the Federal Reserve Bank of St. Louis at http://research.stlouisfed.org/fredII. Another excellent source of information on the size of and trading in the fixed-income markets is the Securities Industry and Financial Markets Association (SIFMA) and its website, http://www.sifma.org/.

The data listed above, and various combinations of them, have enabled economists to form opinions and make forecasts about the current well-being and future direction of the economy.

WHAT DOES IT ALL MEAN?

Just as there are countless influences on an investment in the stock market, multiple factors determine the price—and subsequently the yield—of a bond. In fact, bond prices and their respective interest rates are a primary factor used in many stock market valuation models. Interest rates are a critical explanatory measure, potentially alerting investors to changes in the economy several months before they actually occur. Because economists are so aware of the economic consequences of rising interest rates, data about them form a kind of dashboard of interest-rate conditions that include the historical trends of interest rates during recessions, changes in the yield curve, spreads between certain fixed-income instruments, and of course the slope of the yield curve.

Businesses tend to issue more bonds when they wish to build new factories and plants or purchase new equipment and machinery. If rates become too high relative to historical norms, then some sectors of the economy may experience difficult times. Demand for goods in the most interest-rate-sensitive sectors—durable goods, automobiles, and housing—may suffer if the price of money (interest rates) is too high. Because high-priced goods are often paid for over a period of time, some amount of financing is necessary—the higher the rate of financing (interest rates), the higher the cost. Conversely, when the economy softens, the Federal Reserve may attempt to facilitate greater spending on these types of goods by lowering interest rates, which attracts new borrowers and spenders.

Figure 13.2 5-Year Treasury Note Yields and Recessions

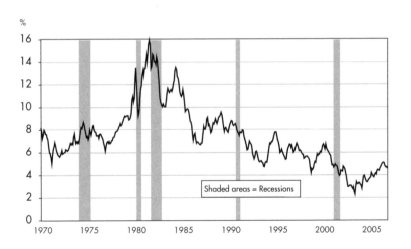

Shaded areas = Recessions

Sources: Federal Reserve Board; National Bureau of Economic Research

The Street commonly refers to a reduction in the Fed's short-term interest rate as an "ease," or an ease in monetary policy.

INFLATION, INTEREST RATES, AND BOND PRICES

Consider **FIGURE 13.2**, which charts both the yield on the 5-year Treasury note and recessions. Notice how interest rates experience some run-up before the economy heads into recession. In each of the last five recessions (1973–1975, 1980, 1981–1982, 1990–1991, and 2001) the yield on the 5-year Treasury note increased by at least 230 basis points. Rising interest rates often take time to affect economic conditions, so these rate increases have operated with long and varying lags. (Notice also that yields have a tendency to issue "false" signs, as they did, for instance, in 1994–1995, when yields ran up over 300 basis points but failed to send the economy into recession.)

Why does this happen? During periods of economic downturns, businesses are less capable of raising prices. So it is widely accepted that a chief characteristic of slower economic periods is lower inflation, or disinflation—meaning an inflation rate that is positive but decreasing. Lower inflation means higher bond prices and lower yields. Because most bonds pay a fixed rate of return, the presence of inflation erodes the value of those future payments. Conversely, when the inflation rate is low, bonds become more attractive and investors bid up the price of those instruments. When the economy starts picking up again, inflation tends to be a dominant concern, as businesses become more confident that rising employment and higher incomes will give consumers sufficient resources to endure an increase in prices.

To thwart rising inflation, the Federal Reserve has typically attempted to cool things down by raising its target overnight borrowing rate, known as the federal funds rate. Investors, knowing that the Fed rarely pushes up its target borrowing rate only once or twice, begin to incorporate into their thinking the expectation of a series of increases, which generally sends longer-term yields upward.

Among other things, the Fed's actions trigger a fear of higher inflation, causing bondholders to sell bonds, which pushes yields higher. The higher levels of interest (the prime rate, mortgage rates, and other loan rates) cause a drop in borrowing activity, and as a result, businesses and households curtail their spending. This reduction in spending will ultimately slow down the economy. During periods of slower economic activity, businesses are less likely to raise prices, so the rate of inflation falls, completing the cycle.

The U.S. Treasury Yield Curve

A yield curve is simply a graphical representation of the yields (effective interest rates) of a particular class of bonds for different maturities. The most common and often-cited yield curve is the U.S. Treasury curve, also referred to as the coupon curve. A representation of this curve, seen in **FIGURE 13.3**, can usually be found in the business sections of newspapers and on business news programs.

A yield curve is said to be upward sloping when yields on shorter-term maturities are lower than those on longer-term issues. The slope of the yield curve changes constantly throughout the trading day, as investor expectations of economic conditions, fundamentals, and policy change. The biggest drivers of price-yield changes have tradition-

Figure 13.3 U.S. Treasury Yield Curve

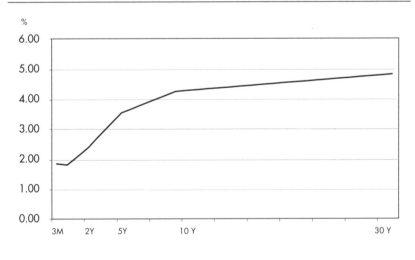

ally been releases of economic data and speeches by Federal Reserve and Treasury Department officials. Because the data or speeches usually reveal something about the future direction of the economy, the market digests that new information and reacts accordingly. On days when little or no economic data are released, the yield curve may not move at all, but that is the exception rather than the rule.

A positive or upward-sloping yield curve is considered "normal" and generally implies solid economic conditions. The reason for this gradual increase in yield as the term of maturity lengthens is the greater risk—and greater expectation of risk—associated with holding a security with a fixed rate of return like a bond for a longer period of time. A lot can happen over the span of ten or thirty years that could alter the value of the security. To compensate for that undetermined risk, bondholders demand higher yields.

Flat yield curves—those with a slope near zero—usually occur when the financial markets are encountering policy shifts. For example, the Federal Reserve may be in the process of, or thinking about, raising or lowering rates at the short end, while longer-dated issues linger at their current levels. This is a difficult time to predict the economy, because the flat curve usually signals a change in the economic landscape.

Inverted, or downward-sloping, yield curves are rare occurrences and typically imply weaker economic conditions, which are also not likely to occur frequently. Here too, the chief culprit behind the change of the slope has historically been the Federal Reserve. An inverted yield curve can develop when market participants expect the Fed to reduce its target overnight borrowing rate in response to slower economic activity. Because the primary reason for a Fed rate cut is to stimulate the economy, investors anticipate that interest rates are going to be lowered (and thus that bond prices will go up), so they begin purchasing bonds, bidding up bond prices and sending yields southward. Longer-dated maturities tend to move more frequently than the Federal Reserve's benchmark rate, which tends to change only during specific meetings. The Federal Reserve's policy-making body—the Federal Open Market Committee (FOMC)—meets eight times a year, about every six or seven weeks. In recent history, the FOMC has rarely altered rates outside these regularly scheduled meetings. As soon as the market believes the economy is moving in a particular direction, it will react accordingly.

Risks and Spreads

There are risks involved in every transaction, financial or otherwise. To estimate the degree of risk, credit-rating agencies like Standard & Poor's and Moody's Investors Service assign values to particular debt issues. These ratings appear for corporations, municipalities, and sovereign governments. The strongest rating is investment grade, and the lowest-quality issues are referred to as high-yield or "junk" bonds, as summarized in **FIGURE 13.4**.

The stronger the financial condition of a company or other borrower, the more secure its ability to repay its creditors and the higher the rating accorded to its bonds. Conversely, the lower the quality of a borrower's ability to repay loans, the lower the rating. It is important to watch the ratings on the lesser-quality issuers because they may be prone to bankruptcy in the event of an economic downturn. Economists try to quantify the level of risk of securities such as corporate bonds by observing the spread over Treasuries.

It's largely assumed that U.S. Treasury securities—those issued and backed by the full faith and credit of the U.S. government—are the safest investment vehicles in the world because the likelihood of default is so remote. An interesting example of the U.S. Treasury market's safe-haven status was seen in the market reaction imme-

Figure 13.4 Bond Ratings

Standard & Poor's	Moody's	Grade
AAA	Aaa	Investment
AA	Aa	Investment
A	A	Investment
BBB	Baa	Investment
BB, B	Ba, B	Junk
CCC, CC, C	Caa, Ca, C	Junk
D	C	Junk

Sources: Standard & Poor's; Moody's Investors Service; Bloomberg

Figure 13.5   Corporate Spreads Over 10-Year Treasury Note Versus S&P

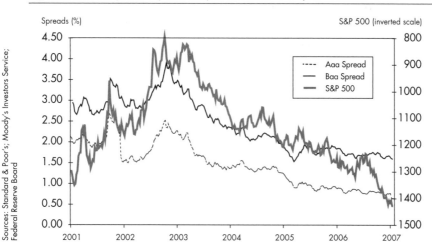

Sources: Standard & Poor's; Moody's Investors Service; Federal Reserve Board

diately following the September 11, 2001, terrorist attacks against the United States. Despite the understandable fears and uncertainty facing the global financial markets, national economies, and individuals around the world, investors flocked to purchase U.S. government bonds. Put another way, what other nation in the world could be attacked and have the entire global investment community scurry to invest in that government's credit? There aren't many countries, besides the United States, that enjoy this status.

FIGURE 13.5 shows the spreads between the average weekly yield on the benchmark 10-year Treasury note and the weekly average yields of the Moody's Aaa- and Baa-rated corporate bonds, as well as value of the Standard & Poor's 500 index (inverted scale).

Spreads of riskier investments such as the bonds of corporations with lower-quality credit (Baa ratings, a notch above junk status) tend to rise sharply prior to, and during, economic recessions. Even the spread of higher-quality (Aaa) issues increases during less promising economic times, although not as much as that of the Baa-rated securities. During periods of strong economic performance, investors have more confidence in the ability of borrowers (issuers) to repay lenders. This sends bond prices up and yields down.

In Figure 13.5, we can also see that the better the underlying economic environment, the lower the yield on corporate bonds. Subsequently, as the spread between corporate issues and the benchmark 10-year Treasury note narrows, economic growth flourishes. On the other hand, when uncertainty about the economy rises, corporate spreads widen. Spreads continue to broaden through recessions or deep economic downturns. Note that the stock market, as measured here by the S&P 500, moves in line with the spreads. Wider spreads are associated with a sinking stock market, whereas narrower spreads correspond with higher stock market prices.

HOW TO USE WHAT YOU SEE

The bond market contains many clues about underlying economic conditions; investors simply have to know where to find them. It also helps to know what is occurring in the economy at the time of the analysis. **FIGURE 13.6** illustrates one of the primary reasons economists look to the fixed-income market for insight into the economy: the close relationship between yields and the overall pace of economic growth. One of the reasons this relationship exists may be the presence of inflation in the nominal growth rate of gross domestic product (GDP). As the economy gathers steam, it tends to generate a whiff of inflation. When investors sense higher

Figure 13.6   Nominal GDP Growth Versus 10-Year Treasury Yield

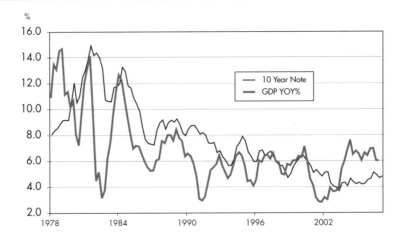

Sources: Federal Reserve Board; U.S. Department of Commerce, Bureau of Economic Analysis

inflation coming, they sell bonds and yields rise. Conversely, weaker economic periods are accompanied by lower inflation, causing investors to buy bonds, which sends yields lower.

This tight correlation held true for most of the period in Figure 13.6. However, in 2002–2003, that relationship broke down, as economic growth accelerated yet the yield on the benchmark 10-year Treasury note continued to trend lower. The best explanation for this divergence was the widespread understanding that the U.S. economy experienced an unprecedented and sustained increase in the level of productivity. Nonfarm business productivity (the level of output per hour worked) held unit labor costs—the largest faced by a company—in check. This kept inflation fears at bay and permitted the economy to expand with little to no inflation pressures.

YIELD CURVES OVER TIME

Some economists swear by the history of the yield curve and its accuracy in predicting turning points in the economy. Others argue that the spread between short- and long-term yields has lost a good deal of its power because there are greater, and many different, factors driving the longer end of the maturity spectrum. To completely remove this instrument from the economist's toolbox however, would be foolish.

A very simple yield curve can be constructed by plotting the yields of any two fixed-income securities of the same asset class with differing maturities. If only two maturities are used, that particular "curve" will simply be a line connecting the two points. Some, like the Conference Board, use the difference between the benchmark 10-year Treasury note and the federal funds rate to determine the slope of the yield curve. Others estimate the slope using the difference between the 10-year Treasury note and the 3-month Treasury bill.

For our analysis of a two-point yield curve, we will use the 3-month–10-year note spread because that is the most common practice on Wall Street. **FIGURE 13.7** depicts the strong predictive power that the yield curve has in estimating economic recessions. In fact, each of the last five recessions has been predicted by an

Figure 13.7   3-Month–10-Year Treasury Note Spread and Recessions

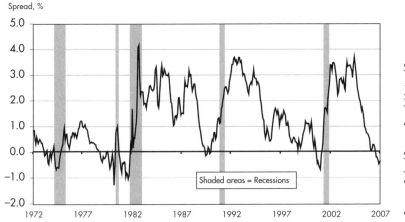

Spread, %

Shaded areas = Recessions

Sources: Federal Reserve Board; National Bureau of Economic Research

inversion (negative slope) of the 3-month–10-year yield curve.

The jury is still out with respect to the inversion that occurred from August 2006 to February 2007. First, that increase in the short end of the curve—which was the primary driver of the inversion—was a result of the Federal Reserve's pushing its overnight rate from an incredibly low 1.0 percent to 5.25 percent, which is not particularly restrictive and more in line with its historical average. Keep in mind that the Fed had dropped its target rate to that low 1.0 percent level—the lowest since the late 1950s—to counter shortages of liquidity resulting from the 9/11 attacks and the 2001 recession.

Second, increased demand for longer-dated Treasury securities, particularly by China, has sent the long end of the curve to historically low levels. In order to peg its currency, the yuan, to the U.S. dollar, the Chinese have had to purchase an inordinate amount of U.S. Treasuries. Also, the trend in bond yields of other countries was set in a downward pattern for several years leading up to 2006. In 2006–2007, global long-term interest rates (in the United Kingdom, France, and Germany) hit a multidecade low. Furthermore, most of the yield-curve inversions have historically been accompanied by slumping equity-market prices. During the 2006–2007 inversion, however, stock prices rallied. In addition, during this period the U.S. economy consistently posted a series of solid 3-plus percent increases in quarterly GDP figures, the unemployment rate was at a cyclical low 4.5 percent, and consumer spending was above 4.0 percent. These are not exactly conditions representative of a downturn or the onslaught of recession. So it may very well be that the inversion of 2006–2007 was a false signal.

Notice that even though the yield curve has flattened several times in the past, most recently in 1995 and 1998, the economy never slumped toward a recession. In fact, both of those most recent flatliners, which show up in Figure 13.7 as low spread values, resulted in heavy economic activity. It takes more than just a flat or an inverted yield curve to indicate that a period of recession is coming. This is why it is important to understand the economic factors that cause the yield curve to behave the way it does.

In mid-2004 the Federal Reserve began hiking its target overnight borrowing rate. Much to the surprise of market participants—as well as the Fed's chairman—longer-term maturities didn't follow suit. In fact, longer-term yields continued to slip, reaching very low levels by historical comparison. This oddity was referred to as "the conundrum." Central bankers, investors, economists, and scholars were left wondering why long-term yields failed to respond to the Federal Reserve's short-term actions. Although the mystery of the conundrum hasn't been solved, many economists have identified high demand by foreign investors for U.S. Treasuries as the primary reason for lower long-term yields. Geopolitical risks were rampant in the early 2000s, and nearly all investors wanted to have some of their assets in the safe haven of the U.S. Treasury market, which contributed to the lower yields. Since the Fed's seventeen 25-basis-point rate hikes commenced when rates were near a historical low of 1.0 percent, the low-interest-rate environment might have had a great deal to do with the irresponsive nature of longer-dated yields. Mild inflation expectations almost certainly played a big role.

In 1996, economists from the Federal Reserve Bank of New York estimated the likelihood of recession, given different values of the yield-curve spread (as measured by the difference in the yields on the 10-year Treasury note and on the 3-month Treasury bill). **FIGURE 13.8** depicts those findings.

Figure 13.8   Estimated Recession Probabilities Using Yield-Curve Spread

Recession Probability (%)	Value of Spread (%)
5	1.21
10	0.76
15	0.46
20	0.22
25	0.02
30	–0.17
40	–0.50
50	–0.82
60	–1.13
70	–1.46
80	–1.85
90	–2.40

Source: Estrella and Mishkin, June 1996

THE TIPS SPREAD

A relatively new favorite indicator from the fixed-income market is known on the Street as the "TIPS spread." In January 1997, the U.S. Treasury Department introduced a new bond called the Treasury inflation-indexed security. Apparently this name was difficult to sell to retail clients, so the terminology was tweaked by salespeople and became the Treasury inflation-protected security, or TIPS. These securities are indexed to the level of inflation, so the investor is *protected* against a rising price environment.

TIPS, like conventional Treasury notes and bonds, are direct obligations backed by the full faith and credit of the U.S. government and are available in several mid- to long-term maturities. The difference is that the par value (principal amount at issuance) is periodically adjusted for changes in the consumer price index for all urban consumers (CPI-U) (see Chapter 12).

Because the primary difference between TIPS and Treasury notes is inflation, or the market's expectation of inflation over the

Figure 13.9   5-Year Treasury–5-Year TIPS Spread

Spread %

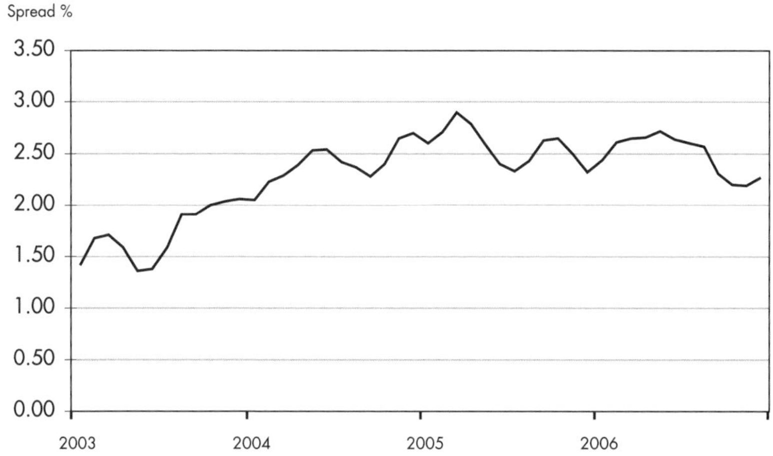

Source: Federal Reserve Bank of St. Louis

remaining time to maturity of the TIPS, economists can in theory measure inflation expectations by subtracting the yield of the TIPS from that of a Treasury security with comparable maturity. This spread makes for a reasonably accurate measure of inflation.

The two most common indicators are constructed using the spread between the 5-year Treasury note and the 5-year TIPS (see **FIGURE 13.9**) and the spread between the 10-year Treasury note and the 10-year TIPS.

From this chart of inflation expectations based on the 5-year Treasury–5-year TIPS spread, the most meaningful inference to be drawn is that since 2003, inflation expectations have not exceeded 3.0 percent. There are several possible explanations for this phenomenon, including rapid gains in productivity, globalization—freer exchange of goods, services, ideas, and money—and technological advances. Some people credit the inflation-fighting resolve of the Federal Reserve in the 1980s through the early 2000s for dampening fears of runaway prices. No matter what the actual reason is, we can say that according to the 5-year-TIPS-spread indicator, the fixed-income market in late 2006 did not see any economically compromising inflation in the near-term future.

Like most indicators, the TIPS spread isn't foolproof. The assumption behind the TIPS spread is that outside of inflation expectations, the yields on the two securities (the conventional Treasury note and the TIPS) should be the same. If there are any influences that disrupt this condition, then bias creeps into the equation, distorting the measure. Many will argue—perhaps successfully—that differences in the liquidity of the two securities (the Treasury note and the TIPS) make an exact comparison impossible. In that view, the TIPS spread wouldn't indicate precise inflation expectations. Nevertheless, it is an important indicator, used in some capacity by virtually all of the economics departments on Wall Street today.

TRICKS FROM THE TRENCHES

Economists have a unique way of identifying market expectations about changes in monetary policy, based on the level of the fed funds futures, which are usually included in some of the more comprehensive business publications. Specifically, this information comes from the table of the fed funds futures contracts. Professional investors can obtain up-to-the-second pricing data on the Bloomberg Professional service.

Fed Funds Futures. A contract on the fed funds future index is an instrument that investors trade in order to hedge or speculate on expected changes in the Federal Reserve's target overnight borrowing rate. The 30-day fed funds future is traded on the Chicago Board of Trade (CBOT) and is based on the expected average effective trading rate for a specific delivery month. Consider the following settlement price table for the 30-day fed funds future in late January 2007.

Contract month	Settle	Implied yield
January	94.75	5.25%
February	94.75	5.25%

The price of the January fed funds futures contract settled, or closed, at 94.75. To better understand this price, one has to subtract it from 100 to get a corresponding yield. Using data from our example, the market's expectations for the fed funds rate during January is 5.25 percent (100 minus 94.75). Similarly, the February contract also settled at an implied yield of 5.25 percent (100 minus 94.75).

What this tells us is that market participants expect the Federal Reserve's target overnight rate to average 5.25 percent during the months of January and February. Since the actual fed funds rate was 5.25 percent during January, market participants didn't expect any rate change at the January 31 meeting of the FOMC. And since there was no meeting of the Fed scheduled for February, market participants expected the fed funds rate to remain unchanged at 5.25 percent during the entire month of February as well.

Estimating the probability of a change in the fed funds rate is a little more difficult than simply subtracting a price index from 100, and requires some elementary knowledge of probability and statistics.

Let's assume that today is March 27, 2007, and you want to know the likelihood of a 25-basis-point rate cut at the upcoming May 9 meeting of the FOMC. First we look in the newspaper and get an implied yield for the May 2007 fed funds contract:

Contract month	Settle	Implied yield
May	94.80	5.20%

We proceed by plugging the data into a standard probability equation to find the probability, p, of a 25-basis-point rate cut, and $1 - p$, the probability of the Fed leaving its benchmark rate unchanged:

$$\left(5.25\% \times \frac{9}{31}\right) + [(5.00\% \times p) + (5.25\% \times (1 - p))] \times \frac{22}{31} = 5.20\%,$$

where 5.25 percent is the fed funds rate on March 27 and 9/31 is the proportion of the month that the target rate will be 5.25% (May 1 through May 9). The rate for the remaining portion of the month, 22/31 (May 10 through May 31), is unknown, but we are assuming that the rate will either be unchanged at 5.25 percent or be lowered by 25 basis points to 5.00 percent.

The step-by-step solution to computing the value of p and $1 - p$ is

$$5.25 \times 0.29032 + [5.00p + 5.25(1 - p)] \times 0.70968 = 5.20$$
$$5.25 \times 0.29032 + [5.00p - 5.25p + 5.25] \times 0.70968 = 5.20$$
$$1.52418 + 3.5484p - 3.7258p + 3.7258 = 5.20\%$$
$$3.5484p - 3.7258p = 5.20 - 1.52418 - 3.7258$$
$$-0.17740p = 3.67582 - 3.7258$$
$$-0.17740p = -0.05000$$
$$p = -0.05000 \div -0.17740$$
$$p = 0.2818, \text{ or } 28.2\% \text{ probability.}$$

We can therefore say that according to the current value of the May fed funds futures contract, the market is pricing in a 28 percent chance of a 25-basis-point reduction in the fed funds rate to 5.0 percent at the May 9 meeting of the FOMC. To get a more detailed presentation of this process, review the Chicago Board of Trade's reference guide on CBOT fed funds futures.

As we just saw, there are many reasons to include fixed-income-market indicators in the examination of economic conditions and subsequent market activity. Readily available, and free, data help investors understand what fixed-income-market participants are doing, and why, which can greatly enhance an investor's ability to make sound trading decisions. We showed how the bond market provides information about inflation expectations, the state of affairs in the equity markets, the underlying level of risk in the financial markets, potential changes in the business cycle, and the probability of a change in the Federal Reserve's target overnight borrowing rate. These insights are critical in the determination of any investment.

The most desirable quality of these indicators is that they are determined by the financial markets, backed by actual investments. These are the proverbial "putting your money where your mouth is" indicators. That places them heads and shoulders above traditional surveys or polls, and atop the list of key economic indicators.

Commodities 14

THE NOTION OF COMMODITIES as economic indicators may be the simplest, most elementary economic concept there is. It makes sense that as the economy accelerates, so will the demand for commodities and related materials. This increase in demand generally results in price appreciation, itself a useful economic indicator. Conversely, as economic activity cools, so too will the demand for most materials, lowering their respective prices. There are plenty of reasons for investors to include commodities in their arsenal of economic indicators. In addition to being a distinct and important asset class, commodities and their respective prices reveal a great deal about underlying economic conditions and provide insight into the outlook for inflation. Every serious investor should know about the latest trends and events in the commodities markets.

Eighty to ninety years ago, when the economy was much more dependent on natural resources, the link between economic performance and commodities prices was considerably stronger. Back then, macroeconomic performance was directly measured by tallying the amounts of metal, glass, textiles, chemicals, food, paper, and rubber being produced. Today, services industries dominate the economic landscape. Yet they too are dependent on commodities, if less directly. A simple example is transportation, a large services industry that is heavily dependent on materials. Airline services require aluminum for frames and fuselages, copper for wiring and components, oil for fuel, rubber for tires, and of course foodstuffs for that delicious airline cuisine.

Trends in several commodity indexes, including the individual commodity series such as gold, crude oil, lead, lumber, cotton, gasoline, and copper, are an excellent barometer of the business cycle. As long as materials are needed in the creation of goods and the provision of services, commodities will have a reserved spot on Wall Street economists' dashboards. The fact that commodities indicators are determined by trading in the financial markets adds to their allure.

There are thousands of indicators representing the price movements of raw materials and other commodities. The most popular aggregates are the Reuters/Jefferies Commodity Research Bureau (CRB) commodity price index, the Goldman Sachs commodity index (GSCI), the Journal of Commerce–Economic Cycle Research Institute industrial price index, and the *Economist*'s commodity price index. In this chapter we explore several of these indexes and compare them with changes in several key macroeconomic variables.

Of all the individual commodities that have been analyzed over the years, crude oil and its derivatives—gasoline, home heating oil, and jet fuel—have received the most attention. The interest focused on these commodities has intensified as conflict and war in the Middle East have escalated in recent years. The promise of ethanol as a fuel source has added a new dimension to the analysis, with ethanol influencing the prices of other commodities and consumer prices generally.

Two more economically significant products, copper and lumber, are near the top of the list of indicators watched closely by investors. Trends in these materials tell us a great deal about the housing industry, which is one of the largest consumers of copper and lumber. Other basic materials prices help investors understand the activities in particular industries and even individual companies. Palladium, a material used in catalytic converters, is closely watched by analysts in the automobile industry. Nickel, used to make stainless steel, is tracked by those in the home hardware business.

The price of gold has been in the economist's toolbox for centuries. This precious metal has been a safe haven during periods of crises and has provided investors with a widely accepted "store of value." Perhaps the most interesting trait of gold is its function as a hedge against inflation. As inflation erodes the value of other investments, gold prices rise. Gold is a reasonably good indicator of inflationary expectations.

Because commodity prices are determined by supply and demand, any unforeseen interruptions to either of those economic determinants can greatly influence the overall price picture. It is important to observe the individual commodities markets because noneconomic developments may be driving supply and demand in some of them, causing fluctuations in prices. For example, commodities prices can be greatly influenced by climate, so it is always a good idea to know the weather conditions, which will help differentiate short-term temporary movements from longer-term structural changes. Newly enacted laws or regulations can influence the supply and demand of particular crops. Tax credits may boost supplies of cotton, corn, or soybeans, and tariffs can reduce demand from abroad. Environmental pollution controls placed on automobiles can influence the price of palladium used in catalytic converters.

EVOLUTION OF AN INDICATOR

Commodities and commodities prices have the distinction of being among the oldest of economic indicators. The practice of following the trends in commodities and materials predates the modern use of the word *economics*. The monitoring of commodities production and prices had been carried out centuries before that—probably as long as trade and commerce have existed. Prior to the creation of the national income and product accounts (see Chapters 1 and 4), economists used the industrial production index of commodities as a gauge of economic activity.

As far as the first recorded use of commodities as indicators of economic wealth, it's fairly safe to assume that the mercantilists, who hoarded gold bullion and other precious commodities and banned their export during a phase called *bullionism* from the Middle Ages through the seventeenth century, were the first to observe commodity activity. More recently, in the early twentieth century, several economists and traders were making economic and market

Figure 14.1   Reuters/Jefferies CRB Index Versus OECD GDP Index

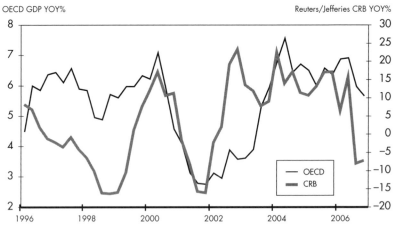

forecasts based on activity in the commodities markets. Noted investor Roger Babson wrote in his celebrated book *Business Barometers for Profits, Security, Income,* "the price of commodities is one of the best business barometers."

Because the United States has morphed into a services-dominated economy, the once-strong correlation between commodities prices and U.S. economic growth has relaxed a bit. More than 80 percent of U.S. workers are employed in service jobs and over 55 percent of total consumption is on services. Americans have greatly reduced their domestic manufacturing presence, sending workers and facilities offshore to nations that are more efficient at producing hard goods and products. The United States, with its highly educated workforce, excels in innovation—designing, creating, and developing new types of goods and services—whereas nations with supplies of cheaper labor concentrate on manufacturing processes. For that reason, commodity activity is more closely linked to world economic growth than growth in the United States alone.

The year-over-year change in the quarterly average of the Reuters/Jefferies CRB index shows a reasonably strong correlation with the year-over-year change in the Organization for Economic

Cooperation and Development's (OECD's) gross domestic product (GDP) index of the economic growth of its thirty member states (see **FIGURE 14.1**). The OECD index includes such commodity-dominant nations as Canada and Australia. The United States is also included in this statistic.

Nevertheless, a services-based economy remains dependent on basic materials and commodities. Airplanes, buses, trucks, trains, tractors, and other types of transportation wouldn't operate without fuel, and homes and office buildings couldn't be constructed without lumber, steel, and cement. The restaurant and dining industry couldn't serve food and beverages without corn, wheat, coffee, and sugar. And what would the fashion and apparel industry be without cotton, wool, and leather hides? These commodities all contribute to the pace of macroeconomic activity, so the direction of their prices is a good gauge of what the economy is doing and where it might be headed.

COMMODITY PRICE INDEXES

The oldest and most widely followed index of commodities prices is the Reuters/Jefferies CRB commodity price index that was used in Figure 14.1. This Wall Street standard was created in 1957 and has undergone at least ten revisions. Its first appearance was in the 1958 *CRB Commodity Year Book*. In 1986 the index began trading on the New York Futures Exchange, which is now the New York Board of Trade.

The *Journal of Commerce* dates back to 1827 and reported on the nation's shipping, trade, and commerce, including daily prices of commodities like wheat, burlap, wool, sugar, and linseed oil. It was only natural that this distinguished newspaper would eventually develop a measure of commodities prices. The *Journal of Commerce*'s industrial price index was created in the mid-1980s under the review of the pioneering business-cycle economist Geoffrey H. Moore, and later updated in the late 1990s by his staff at the New York–based Economic Cycle Research Institute (ECRI). Its composition was most recently readjusted in early 2000.

The Goldman Sachs commodity index (GSCI) was created in 1991, using historical data dating back to 1970. It is a production-weighted index, which means its components' weights are based on the average value of production over the previous five years. The index is adjusted annually. In early 2007, the GSCI was acquired by Standard & Poor's and rechristened the S&P GSCI.

DIGGING FOR THE DATA

Essentially all of the foregoing individual and composite commodity data—as well as their histories and detail—are available for download on the Bloomberg Professional service. For the smaller investor without such a service, commodities data are harder to come by. The composite indexes, such as the Reuters/ Jefferies CRB index and the S&P GSCI, are not available in a historical context as the government or Institute for Supply Management data are—though the daily closing prices are usually printed in the business sections of the larger newspapers. Many financial websites provide the latest readings, and some actually chart a brief history. Unfortunately, a complete historical download is available only on a fee basis. The *Economist* magazine also charges for historical data for its commodity price index.

The website http://www.CRBtrader.com presents a complete history of the revisions to and other information regarding the Reuters/Jefferies CRB index. This site also offers data products, publications, and a section on the calculations of the CRB.

The price of the S&P GSCI appears in most of the business newspapers like the *Wall Street Journal*, the *Financial Times*, and *Investor's Business Daily* on a daily basis. The Chicago Mercantile Exchange's CME DataMine offers a history of this series for a fee. The details of its composition, weighting scheme, and trading specifications, along with a complete overview, may be found at http://www2.goldmansachs.com/gsci/. The latest press releases and the associated *GSCI Manual* are also available on this site.

Of all the composite commodity indexes, the Journal of Com-

Figure 14.2   The JOC-ECRI Industrial Price Index

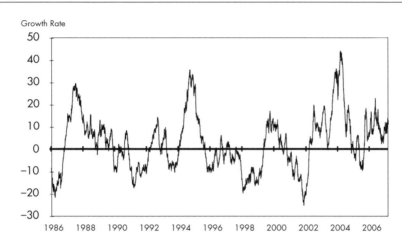

Source: Economic Cycle Research Institute

merce–Economic Cycle Research Institute (JOC-ECRI) industrial price index is the most respected on the Street. Although the index's components and their respective weights are proprietary secrets, the index differs from the other top composite indexes because it doesn't rely entirely on exchange-traded components but includes other commodities as well, such as burlap. And since the JOC-ECRI industrial price index actually has predictive power—an impressively accurate history of forecasting turns in the inflation cycle—it has become a much-relied-on reference for Wall Street investors. If you follow only one commodity index, make sure it's this one (see **FIGURE 14.2**). Check out the information at http://www.businesscycle.com.

The Economist magazine has one of the more respected commodity price measures. It is updated and provided to subscribers each week on the second to last page of each issue and on the magazine's website, http://www.economist.com.

ENERGY

The U.S. Department of Energy's (DOE's) Energy Information Administration (EIA) is the generally accepted home for all data and related information on the energy market. In addition to the closely watched weekly crude-oil, gasoline, and natural-gas inventory numbers, the DOE's EIA publishes in-depth commentary and analysis, as well as a deep historical database on all energy matters, including petroleum, natural gas, electricity, coal, nuclear, and renewable and alternative fuels, and offers international statistical reports. Most Wall Street traders and economists get their data and information—free—from the EIA's website at http://eia.doe.gov.

Each Monday, the EIA releases the weekly U.S. Retail Gasoline Price Report, which includes a breakdown of prices by regions, states, and major cities. Highlights from the Weekly Petroleum Status Report are released every Wednesday at 10:30 a.m. (ET) and include weekly stocks for crude oil, motor gasoline, and distillate fuel oil, as well as prices for many of the principal petroleum products like no. 2 heating oil, kerosene-type jet fuel, and propane. Some insight on refinery activity is also presented. The complete Weekly Petroleum Status Report is available every Thursday and contains information on the supply and prices of crude oil and its related products. This report is a must-have.

Natural gas is an important economic indicator, and the EIA releases the closely watched Weekly Natural Gas Storage Report every Thursday at 10:30 a.m. (ET). This release is followed up by a useful summary entitled Natural Gas Weekly Update.

Some additional information, like the latest news and production schedules from the Organization of the Petroleum Exporting Countries (OPEC), can be found on its website at http://www.opec.org. Reserves and capacity data are reported there, and the site posts the latest press releases from their meetings. These statements have been known to move the financial markets. In addition to other OPEC facts and figures, the OPEC site posts several publications. No serious trader should be without the OPEC Monthly Oil Market Report or the equally informative OPEC Bulletin.

There are other notable resources for oil and energy market statistics. However, most come at a cost. The American Petroleum Institute (http://www.api.org) and the International Energy Agency (http://www.iea.org) are two of the premier sources of critical information for the analysis and study of the oil markets. Serious traders should also consider subscribing to the industry's top trade publications, the *Oil & Gas Journal* and the *Oil and Gas Investor*.

AGRICULTURAL PRODUCTS

The U.S. Department of Agriculture (USDA) provides just about all the information on agriculture that an investor could ever ask for on its website (http://www.usda.gov). There are data sources detailing farm income and costs, agricultural markets and trade, food markets, prices, and consumption, as well as commodity outlook reports.

The USDA has several agencies that provide a plethora of data and information about the nation's farm economy. One of these is the Agricultural Research Service (ARS). This group conducts research and analysis on U.S. agricultural problems and publishes its findings in thousands of economically relevant research reports. All are available on its website, at http://www.ars.usda.gov. Another source for information and data is the USDA's Economic Research Service (ERS) website (http://www.ers.usda.gov), which provides information on the farm economy, the food sector, and the commodity outlook. There are countless publications and data sets that are helpful for analyzing anything related to agriculture. Some of the more popular reports include Outlook for U.S. Agricultural Trade, and the individual Outlook reports on cotton and wool; livestock, dairy, and poultry; tobacco; and wheat. The ERS also provides the USDA Long-Term Macroeconomic Outlook, which includes a detailed summary of projections and macroeconomic assumptions.

Another source of economic information at the USDA worth mentioning is the Office of the Chief Economist (http://www.usda .gov/oce). Papers, speeches, and the World Agricultural Supply and Demand Estimates (WASDE) report are also available on its website.

MINING

An excellent source for information and data on minerals, mining, and quarrying is the U.S. Geological Survey website (http://www.usgs.gov). In addition to lengthy historical databases, this site contains mountains of free publications regarding the production, stockpiling, and prices of key economic indicators like cement, tungsten, titanium, nickel, aluminum, copper, clay, lime, salt, zinc, tin, sulfur, potash, mercury, lead, gypsum, cobalt, and titanium dioxide pigment. The Mineral Commodity Summaries, the Mineral Industry Surveys, the *Minerals Yearbook*, the individual commodity data sheets, and the monthly Metal Industry Indicators are informative, and make for interesting reading. If you want to know the quantity of aluminum stocks used in U.S. automobiles or the most recent price trend for lithium, this site will give it to you.

JOURNALS AND ASSOCIATIONS

Trade publications are an ideal source for information for specific commodities. Many of these magazines and journals provide pricing of individual commodities. Related trade publications like *Chemical Week*, *Packaging Today*, *Packaging World*, *Paint & Coatings Industry*, *Plastics News*, *Pulp & Paper*, *Metal World*, *Copper Monitor*, *Random Lengths* (which covers lumber), *Cement Products*, and *Concrete Monthly* are also usual desktop references for equity analysts that deal with those respective industries.

Trade associations and groups such as the Portland Cement Association, the American Copper Council, the American Iron and Steel Institute, the World Gold Council, the American Forest and Paper Organization, the American Zinc Association, and the Copper Development Association often provide an insightful look into their respective industries.

WHAT DOES IT ALL MEAN?

The broad-based composite commodities indexes are attempts to aggregate economically relevant materials into a single, and often tradable, index. With a composite of the most meaningful commodities in the economy, investors are given an alternative asset class. In recent years, the arrival of exchange-traded funds (ETFs) has made investing in individual commodities or commodities baskets as simple as investing in an individual stock. These too are wonderful economic indicators, but they do not have a very long history. Both the Reuters/Jefferies CRB index and the S&P GSCI are traded on an exchange. The JOC-ECRI industrial price index is designed not as a trading vehicle but as an economic indicator and benchmark.

THE REUTERS/JEFFERIES CRB INDEX

The Reuters/Jefferies CRB index may be the most popular commodity price index. It is composed of nineteen commodities futures prices. The current (2005) makeup seen in **FIGURE 14.3** is a far cry from that of the 1957 index, which contained twenty-eight components.

Gone are the commodities like barley, onions, potatoes, flaxseed, eggs, and lard, as these materials are no longer a useful representation of the twenty-first-century commodity picture.

The Reuters/Jefferies CRB index uses a four-tier weighting approach, with group I limited to petroleum products; group II, the seven most liquid commodities; group III, four liquid commodities;

Figure 14.3 Composition of the Reuters/Jefferies CRB Commodity Price Index

Group I		Group II		Group III		Group IV	
Petroleum		**Highly Liquid**		**Liquid**		**Diversified**	
WTI Crude Oil	23%	Natural Gas	6%	Sugar	5%	Nickel	1%
Heating Oil	5%	Corn	6%	Cotton	5%	Wheat	1%
Unleaded Gas	5%	Soybeans	6%	Cocoa	5%	Lean Hogs	1%
		Live Cattle	6%	Coffee	5%	Orange Juice	1%
		Gold	6%			Silver	1%
		Aluminum	6%				
		Copper	6%				
Group Total:	33%		42%		20%		5%
						Index Total:	100%

Source: Reuters/Jefferies Commodity Research Bureau

and group IV, a diverse grouping of softs (which include goods like sugar, coffee, and cocoa), grains, industrial metals, meats, and precious metals.

From a sector perspective, the index is predominantly weighted in energy and agriculture: WTI crude oil, heating oil, unleaded gas, and natural gas make up 39 percent of the index; and corn, soybeans, sugar, cotton, cocoa, coffee, wheat, and orange juice make up 34 percent. Industrial metals (aluminum, copper, and nickel) make up 13 percent of the index, and precious metals (gold and silver) and livestock (live cattle and lean hogs) each account for 7 percent.

THE GOLDMAN SACHS COMMODITY INDEX

Like the Reuters/Jefferies CRB index, the S&P GSCI is composed entirely of commodity futures (see **FIGURE 14.4**). The weights are based on global production of each commodity in the index. There are currently twenty-four commodities in the S&P GSCI, which is divided into five categories: energy (74.55 percent), industrial metals (8.46 percent), precious metals (2.07 percent), agriculture (10.16 percent), and livestock (4.76 percent). The largest individual commodity in the index is crude oil, with a weight of 36.86 percent.

THE JOC-ECRI INDUSTRIAL PRICE INDEX

The JOC-ECRI industrial price index is everything an economist would want in an indicator (see **FIGURE 14.5**). Rather than getting bogged down in an attempt to have a tradable group of commodities, the JOC-ECRI tracks materials that drive industry. Only commodities that fuel commerce are included in this eighteen-commodity index. Just looking at the components, you get the feeling of the production process at work: machines and turbines pumping, massive heavy-construction trucks unearthing mineral deposits, hot-rolled steel moving out of mills, and lumberyards filling with the scents of plywood and oak. An economist can almost smell the economy cranking out goods.

Figure 14.4 Composition of the Goldman Sachs Commodity Index

Energy	Industrial Metals	Precious Metals	Agriculture	Livestock
Crude				Live
Oil 36.86%	Aluminum 3.05%	Gold 1.84%	Wheat 2.21%	Cattle 2.61%
Brent	Copper 3.41%	Silver 0.23%	Red	Cattle 0.66%
Crude	Lead 0.28%		Wheat 0.92%	Lean
Oil 14.98%	Nickel 0.80%		Corn 2.12%	Hogs 1.49%
RBOB	Zinc 0.92%		Soybeans 1.44%	
Gas 1.46%			Cotton 0.87%	
Heating			Sugar 1.77%	
Oil 6.09%			Coffee 0.65%	
Gas Oil 5.27%			Cocoa 0.18%	
Natural				
Gas 9.89%				
Group				
Total: 74.55%	8.46%	2.07%	10.16%	4.76%
			Index Total:	100%

Source: Goldman Sachs

The JOC-ECRI index does a better job than the Reuters/Jefferies CRB index and the S&P GSCI of predicting changes in the economy and turning points in the inflation cycle because it contains non-exchange-traded commodities. Because the Reuters/Jefferies CRB index and the S&P GSCI use futures prices, they include a speculative component. Many times, investors—particularly hedge funds—will buy a commodity future in anticipation of a change in the movement of a particular commodity. This has been known to

Figure 14.5 Components of the JOC-ECRI Industrial Price Index

Cotton	Steel	Hides	Crude Oil
Burlap	Copper	Rubber	Benzene
Polyester	Aluminum	Tallow	Ethylene
	Zinc	Plywood	
	Lead	Red Oak	
	Tin		
	Nickel		

Source: Economic Cycle Research Institute

inject a great deal of added volatility into commodities markets and mask the true underlying trend in commodities prices. Furthermore, farmers often hedge against poor crop yields by purchasing commodities futures. Because some of the components in the JOC-ECRI are not futures, there isn't a concern about speculative influences.

THE NEED FOR REVISION

Composite commodities indexes like those previously examined have experienced several revisions throughout their histories, making historical comparison difficult. Unfortunately, this necessary evil must occur in order for the indexes to accurately depict the commodities markets. As the economy changes, so does the demand for raw materials. It makes you wonder what will be in the Reuters/Jefferies CRB index, the S&P GSCI, and the JOC-ECRI industrial price index in another fifty years.

Individual Commodities

Study of commodities prices in the aggregate is quick and relatively easy, but some investors might want to take a more micro approach and understand the latest trends in individual materials. The following dozen commodities are among the most economically important. Although a detailed up-to-the moment appreciation isn't necessary, it would behoove an investor to know the primary use of each commodity and how each commodity affects the macroeconomy and interacts with other economic indicators.

Copper. It is said that copper is the economic indicator with a PhD because it is so good at predicting trends in global macroeconomic activity (see **FIGURE 14.6**). It is frequently referred to as "Dr. Copper" or "red gold." This makes sense because copper is one of the most widely used commodities; it is used in home construction (plumbing, piping, fittings, tubing, wiring, roofing, and flashing), electronics, and industrial, automotive, and marine applications. Like the composite commodities indexes, it shows a strong relationship with overall economic activity.

Figure 14.6   Copper Prices Versus GDP

Sources: Bloomberg; U.S. Department of Commerce, Bureau of Economic Analysis

Nickel. The biggest single use of nickel (about 48 percent) is in stainless and alloy steel production. Stainless steel, because it resists corrosion, is a highly desired ferrous metal. Nickel also has applications with many end uses in transportation, household appliances, electrical equipment, machinery, and the production of nickel metal hydride (NiMH) batteries. This is a commodity to watch because automakers plan to use NiMH batteries in their hybrid vehicles in coming years.

Crude Oil. Oil, of course, is the basis of other fuels like gasoline, diesel fuel, residual fuel (tankers), and jet fuel. It is also the source for many plastics and other petrochemicals. In the United States, two-thirds of the petroleum consumed is used for transportation purposes. According to the EIA, a barrel of crude oil (42 gallons) yields—on average—the following: gasoline (19.4 gallons), distillate fuel (10.5 gallons), jet fuel (4.1 gallons), heavy or residual fuel oil (1.7 gallons), liquefied petroleum gas (1.5 gallons), and other products (4.8 gallons).

Natural Gas. Natural gas is an extremely important indicator because roughly 17 percent of the nation's electricity is generated by burning it. If natural-gas prices are rising in the summer months, you can bet consumers are going to feel pinched when they run their air conditioners and fans. In the winter months, economists like to observe natural-gas trends because 50 percent of the homes in the United States are heated with it. In the Midwest, almost 80 percent of the 25.1 million households heat their homes with natural gas. Higher prices crimp spending and ultimately economic growth.

Aluminum. Aluminum is one of the most important commodities to the economy. It is used in the production of countless consumer goods, from appliances, automobiles, and CDs to food and beverage packaging, closures, and medicines. The aerospace and defense industries buy substantial amounts of aluminum each year. Commercial and industrial applications include buildings (stadiums, girders, and facades), machinery, and antennas. In 2006, transportation accounted for about 40 percent of domestic consumption of aluminum, followed by packaging (28 percent), building (13 percent), and consumer durables (7 percent).

Lumber and Containerboard. Not surprisingly, lumber is the single biggest resource used in building a new home. Typically, a new moderate-sized wood-framed house requires anywhere from 12,000 to 16,000 board feet of lumber. In 2006, even with the housing market slumping, there were still about 14 million (seasonally adjusted annual rate) new privately owned one-unit structures started during the year. That's a lot of lumber. Add to this the renovation, remodeling, and additions that require framing lumber, flooring, molding, and related wood products. Economists also like to look at containerboard production and corrugated box shipments. As long as the economy produces goods, there will be a need for packages. Watching the trends in packaging, cardboard, paper, or container production will yield a good estimate of economic activity.

Gold. For centuries, gold has been recognized as a form of wealth, a means of commerce, and a thing of beauty and luxury. It has adorned furniture, frames, and architecture and has actually been an ingredient in food and beverages. It is soft, heavy, and malleable—three qualities that are desired by manufacturers and jewelry makers. In addition to serving as a hedge against inflation, gold is used in dentistry, in coins, and in electrical and electronic components like cellular phones and computers. It does not corrode and is

Figure 14.7   Cement Production Versus Construction Activity

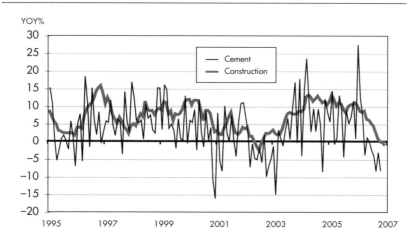

Sources: U.S. Department of Commerce, U.S. Geological Survey

an excellent conductor of heat and electricity. Most of the U.S. gold production in 2006 was used in jewelry making (almost 84 percent), followed by electrical and electronics manufacture (6 percent) and dentistry and other uses (10 percent).

Cement. Cement, fittingly, has a solid relationship with total construction activity. Think of all the structures that call for it, usually as a constituent of concrete: highways, buildings, home foundations, dormitories, bridges, offices, schools, apartment buildings, sporting arenas, churches. Such projects are constantly under construction. As **FIGURE 14.7** suggests, cement production is a strong economic indicator.

Palladium. Palladium is an important metal for certain manufacturing processes. It is used chiefly by automakers for use in catalytic converters. Dentists also use it, as do pharmaceutical makers—it is an ingredient in such notable medications as Tylenol and Viagra.

Titanium, Titanium Dioxide, and Titanium Mineral Concentrates. Titanium and its derivatives have a multitude of uses. The U.S. Geological Survey reports that during 2006, nearly 72 percent of all titanium metal was used in aerospace, and the balance was used for other applications and products like chemical processing, medical equipment, sports equipment, and power generation. Titanium dioxide pigment is used in paints, varnishes, and lacquers, as well as plastics, paper, and ceramics.

Gypsum. Think of gypsum, and you think of wallboard. But gypsum is also used in the manufacturing of concrete, which we just saw is a pretty powerful indicator in its own right. The U.S. Geological Survey said that roughly 91 percent (about 37.2 million tons) of all gypsum consumed in 2006 was used for wallboard and plaster products, and 3 million tons were used for concrete. A little more than a million tons went to agricultural purposes. As hurricanes and other natural disasters destroy homes and infrastructure, gypsum production rises.

Zinc. Of all the metals produced in the world today, zinc ranks fourth by tonnage. About 75 percent of all zinc is used in the galvanization process, protecting iron and steel from corrosion. A good portion is used in brass and bronze. Zinc, zinc compounds, and zinc dust are used in the chemical, rubber, medical, and paint industries. Zinc is also used in dry-cell batteries, television screens, household appliances, and fluorescent lights, as well as in agriculture.

HOW TO USE WHAT YOU SEE

The general idea of this section is to show how commodities prices interact with the financial markets and the economy. Composite commodities indexes, as well as the individual series, can be extremely volatile. Most of the indexes have components that can be influenced by the weather, making those indexes overall subject to unforeseen disturbances. Therefore, it is best to observe them over time. The following three examples compare the year-over-year change in the Reuters/Jefferies CRB index with the stock market, the economy, and the benchmark 10-year Treasury note.

Commodities are used in the process of goods' production, as well as in the service sector. And because corporate performance may be measured by trends in the S&P 500, we see a relatively solid relationship between the S&P 500 and the Reuters/Jefferies CRB Index, as shown in **FIGURE 14.8**.

The association between the U.S. economic growth, as measured by the year-over-year change in the Conference Board's index

Figure 14.8   Reuters/Jefferies CRB Commodity Price Index Versus S&P 500

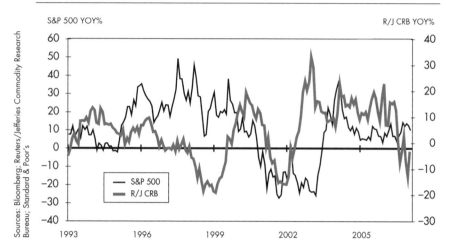

Sources: Bloomberg; Reuters/Jefferies Commodity Research Bureau; Standard & Poor's

of coincident indicators, and the year-over-year change in the Reuters/Jefferies CRB index is not as strong as the economy's association with the other economic indicators. Nonetheless, we see a telling relationship between the coincident index and the price level of commodities (see **FIGURE 14.9**).

Inflation and commodities prices tend to move in the same direction. Because commodities prices are a measure of inflation at the most basic level, they in turn have a relatively close relationship with interest rates. **FIGURE 14.10** depicts the strong correlation between the year-over-year change in the benchmark 10-year Treasury note and the year-over-year change in the Reuters/Jefferies CRB index. This is easily explained. Increases in the rate of commodity price inflation erode the value of fixed-income securities and send yields higher.

BASIC MATERIAL AND COMMODITY COMPANIES

One of the greatest sources of insight into the commodities markets has been the quarterly earnings conference calls conducted by basic material and commodities companies. These publicly traded businesses often reveal a surprising amount of information and perspective on the production, pricing, and consump-

Figure 14.9   Reuters/Jefferies CRB Commodity Price Index Versus
Coincident Index

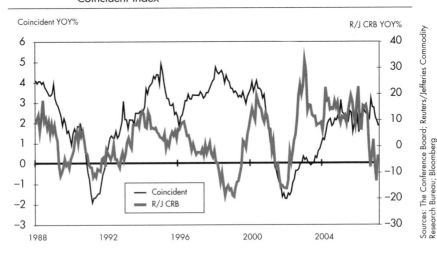

Figure 14.10   Reuters/Jefferies CRB Commodity Price Index Versus 10-Year
Treasury Note

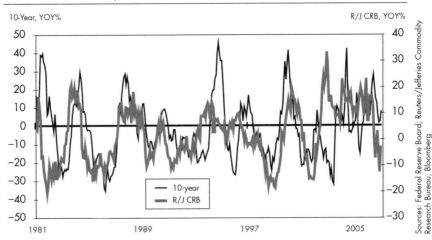

tion of raw materials and commodities. Who could know more
about aluminum than Alcoa Inc.? Steel giants United States
Steel Corporation and Nucor Corporation are undoubtedly the
best references for the latest developments and trends in the
steel industry, and Exxon Mobil Corporation, Chevron Corpo-

ration, and ConocoPhillips should be able to provide investors with much of what they need to know about the oil market. One company, International Flavors & Fragrances Inc., utilizes upward of five thousand commodities. There may not be another company on the planet that can tell you more about the price of Madagascar cinnamon or the supply of Sri Lankan sandalwood. Although the price trends in cinnamon and sandalwood may not be meaningful to the macroeconomist, some, like food and beverage analysts, might find it worthy for their study.

THE AGRICULTURE PRICES SUMMARY REPORT

Another way to see price activity at the earliest stage of production, without getting too granular, is the USDA's Agriculture Prices report, released at the end of every month. In each report there are dozens of tables, charts, and diagrams describing price activity in essentially all crop types and livestock. With all of this information, the reports are usually more than sixty pages.

See **FIGURE 14.11** for the most popular series in the report, the index of prices received by farmers. Economists like to watch this index because it gives an early reading on food price trends about two weeks before the producer or consumer price indexes are released. If farmers are receiving higher prices for their crops or livestock, you'll see it here first. Furthermore, the report allows economists to determine whether prices are trending in a particular direction and whether price increases will be short-lived or sustained. The in-depth commentary in each report is worth wading through.

THE CRUDE-OIL MARKET

The price level of crude oil is usually broadcast every thirty seconds on business stations like CNBC and Bloomberg Television. Most Wall Streeters make it their business to know where oil is trading at every moment. Why? Spikes in the price of crude oil usually precede economic downturns.

Other than the obvious—that exorbitant energy prices can send

Figure 14.11   Index of Prices Received by Farmers

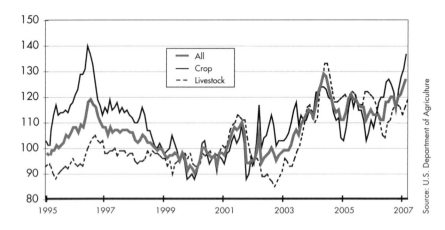

Source: U.S. Department of Agriculture

the economy into recession and cripple consumer spending—why do investors find it so important to keep abreast of developments in the crude-oil market? Well, as **FIGURE 14.12** implies, because the Federal Reserve Board evidently finds the latest trends in West Texas Intermediate crude oil quite interesting. Although we seriously doubt that the Fed conducts monetary policy solely with respect to the price of crude oil, we do believe it is on the Fed's radar screen. Anything that is powerful enough to cause a widespread inflation threat throughout the economy is an attention-getter for the central bank. And if the Fed watches it, Wall Street watches it.

All economic recessions since 1973 have been preceded by a spike in the price of crude oil, and each of those price spikes has been accompanied by an increase in the Federal Reserve's target overnight borrowing rate. Although there isn't much an increase in the overnight borrowing rate can do directly to influence energy prices, the Fed might just believe that if it can cool down the economy with higher interest rates, then demand for oil will in turn weaken and bring down oil prices.

Prices of refined products—gasoline, home heating fuel, jet kerosene, and so on—can move in different directions from the price of crude oil. The primary cause of this deviation is supply disruptions. Since new refineries have not been built in the United

Figure 14.12 West Texas Intermediate (WTI) Oil Versus Fed Funds Rate

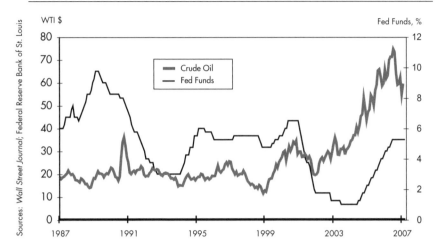

States for over thirty years, this infrastructure is prone to break-downs, outages, and fires. When outages are reported, the price of the distillates produced at those refineries will trade independently of the price of oil, even though crude is an ingredient in the refining process. These outages are usually short-term, isolated events. However, when widespread disaster strikes, like the Atlantic hurricanes of 2005 that knocked out about 25 percent of America's energy-producing capabilities, there's a good chance that prices of all related energy resources will escalate.

GOLD

Investors have long used commodities, particularly precious metals like gold, as a hedge against inflation. Because the price of gold moves in concert with the general price level, traders, portfolio managers, and hedge fund managers purchase gold to protect their assets in a rising-price environment. Inflation erodes the value of fixed-income securities and hurts the valuation of other investments like stocks. Gold has also served as a safe haven against uncertain times or periods of intense geopolitical strife.

The gold-inflation relationship isn't exactly the strongest of all

Figure 14.13   Gold Prices Versus Consumer Price Index

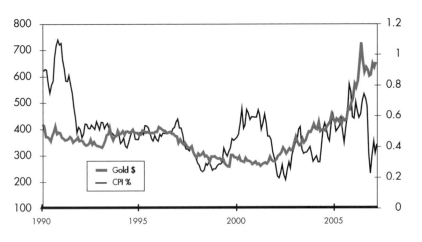

Sources: Bloomberg; U.S. Department of Labor, Bureau of Labor Statistics

commodity-economy indicators. One of the problems with using gold as a measure of inflation expectations is that you cannot separate "inflation expectations" from the value of gold's "safe haven" status. Notice in **FIGURE 14.13** how the consumer price index slumped to some relatively low readings in 1998 and then again in 2002. Gold prices dipped during those periods, as fears of a deflationary environment were prevalent among market participants. But in early 2003, the price of gold started to surge as the United States and other nations engaged in war with Iraq and geopolitical uncertainty escalated. In addition, rising crude-oil prices also contributed to the fear of widespread global inflation. But as the consumer price index clearly suggests, inflation never really developed in the United States.

TRICKS FROM THE TRENCHES

Sometimes economic trends aren't readily apparent, and it might take a little investigation to unearth possible meaningful developments. This chapter's offering is essentially an instruction to think outside the box, because economic indicators don't always follow a linear path. For example, a commodity like corn, an unlikely macroeconomic indicator, may have the power to influence monetary policy.

Recent activity in the energy markets and the demand for alternative biofuels have placed upward pressure on food and grain prices, as well as the general price level. The U.S. Congress has passed a number of laws supporting the pursuit of greener energy, providing incentives to those that create and adopt environmentally friendly methods of energy production and use. Unfortunately, a possible nationwide inflation problem may be brewing, and the clues to this situation can be found in the commodities market.

Demand for corn-based fuels like ethanol and for cellulose materials (corn stalks, fibers, saw grass, and other feedstock) has surged, sending corn prices to record highs. The more lucrative corn crops become, the more land farmers will dedicate toward growing it. The amount of arable land is relatively fixed, so when farmers dedicate a larger portion of their land to the cultivation of corn, they reduce the amount of land available for other grains like wheat, barley, or soybeans. Naturally, as the supply of those crops diminishes, prices rise, resulting in higher prices not only for corn but for other grains and crops as well.

There's more to corn than our consumption of it on the Fourth of July or at a summer weekend clambake. Corn is used as feed for livestock. So when the price of feed rises, so too does the price of poultry, pork, and beef. Furthermore, corn derivatives are used as sweeteners in processed foods and beverages. The most universal of these sweeteners is high-fructose corn syrup. As seen in **FIGURE 14.14**, the USDA reports the monthly price of high-fructose corn syrup, and it has been rising in recent years. Barley is used in the production of beer and other foodstuffs, so costs of alcoholic beverages rise. According to a recent article in the *Financial Times*, the land area dedicated to barley cultivation in 2006 was around 2.95 million acres, which was the lowest since records started being kept in 1866.

All of this isn't even a worst-case scenario. What would happen to prices if a drought or a flood, for example, damaged farmers'

Figure 14.14 High-Fructose Corn Syrup Prices

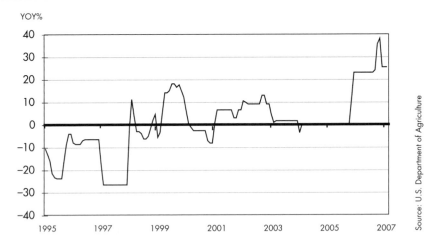

corn—an already pressured commodity—and other crops?

Higher grocery bills would be the most obvious expense incurred by the consumer. Should the pressure on food prices be sustained, supermarkets and restaurants might be inclined to pass along their higher costs. Perhaps other food-service facilities like catering halls, amusements parks, sporting arenas, and similar eating establishments would raise their prices because of higher input costs. Eventually, inflation would surface on the retail level, which might cause some economic imbalances. If these gains were strong enough and prolonged, the Federal Reserve might have to temper things with a rate increase. In light of all this, it pays to watch trends in all commodities prices, even those that are not widely accepted as economic indicators.

The activity driven by new markets for ethanol and high-fructose corn syrup, incidentally, hasn't been for naught. The economy and many businesses have benefited immensely. Farmland values have surged in recent years, injecting new life into the nation's agricultural sector, which had been stagnant for decades. Archer Daniels Midland Company—the largest ethanol producer in the country—has experienced solid appreciation in its stock price. Sales of combines, tractors, and other agricultural equipment have boosted the income of companies like John Deere. This equipment must be transported, helping the truck and rail industries. All of this has transpired in an attempt to make the U.S. economy less dependent on fossil fuels, and more reliant on cleaner, renewable energy sources.

It is clear from this chapter that commodities play an integral role in the direction of the global economy and are an important influence on such economic variables as construction, industrial production, inflation, employment, and aggregate demand. The industries that are influenced by commodity trends include everything from transportation to agriculture to energy to food and beverages. Even many services industries like airlines, railroads, communications, oil drilling, and equipment rental are greatly affected by the trends in the commodity markets. Because of these strong associations, most Wall Street trading desks have no fewer than a dozen commodities indicators flashing on their screens at any given moment. Industry analysts have their own specific sets of closely watched commodities indicators that are used in the analysis of their respective industries, and trading-floor economists are frequently asked about developments in several of the broad commodity indexes.

Because prices and economic trends are so important to the investment process, commodities of all types deserve a notable place on every investor's dashboard.

References

Introduction

Burns, Arthur F., and Wesley Clair Mitchell. 1946. *Measuring Business Cycles*. New York: National Bureau of Economic Research.

Cottle, Sidney, Roger F. Murray, and Frank E. Block. 1988. *Graham and Dodd's Security Analysis*. New York: McGraw-Hill.

Crescenzi, Anthony. 2002. *The Strategic Bond Investor*. New York: McGraw-Hill.

Goldberg, Linda, and Deborah Leonard. 2003. "What Moves Sovereign Bond Markets? The Effects of Economic News on U.S. and German Yields." *Federal Reserve Bank of New York Current Issues in Economics and Finance* 9, no. 9 (September).

Graham, Benjamin, and David Dodd. 1934. *Security Analysis*. New York: McGraw-Hill.

Hagenbaugh, Barbara. 2003. "Hints of Optimism Point to Rebound." *USA Today*, August 21.

Hager, George. 2001. "Economists Seek Clues in Daily Life." *USA Today*, February 12.

Mitchell, Wesley Clair. 1927. *Business Cycles: The Problem and Its Setting*. New York: National Bureau of Economic Research.

National Bureau of Economic Research. 2003. "U.S. Business Cycle Expansions and Contractions." http://www.nber.org/cycles/cyclesmain.html.

Vance, Julia. 2001. "Titanium Dioxide's Message." *The Dismal Scientist, Economy.com*, April 12. http://www.dismal.com/todays_econ/te_041201_2.asp.

Yamarone, Richard. 1999. "The Business Economist at Work: Argus Research Corporation." *Business Economics*, July, 65–70.

Chapter 1: Gross Domestic Product

Baumol, William J., and Alan S. Blinder. 1991. *Macroeconomics Principles and Policy*. 5th ed. New York: Harcourt Brace Jovanovich.

Bernanke, Ben S., and Andrew B. Abel. 1998. *Macroeconomics*. 3rd ed. New York: Addison-Wesley.

Congressional Budget Office. 2000. *The Budget and Economic Outlook: An Update.* Washington, DC. Also available online at http://www.cbo.gov/ftpdoc .cfm?index=2241&type=1.

———. 2001. *CBO's Method for Estimating Potential Output: An Update.* Washington, DC. Also available online at http://www.cbo.gov/ftpdoc .cfm?index=3020&type=1.

Jones, Charles I. 2002. "Using Chain-Weighted NIPA Data." *Federal Reserve Bank of San Francisco Economic Letter*, August 2.

Landefeld, J. Steven. 1995. "BEA's Featured Measure of Output and Prices." *National Association for Business Economics: NABE News*, no. 113 (September): 3–6, 26.

Mankiw, N. Gregory. 1998. *Principles of Macroeconomics.* Fort Worth, TX: Dryden Press.

Mitchell, Wesley C., ed. 1921. *Income in the United States: Its Amount and Distribution 1909–1919.* New York: Harcourt, Brace and Company.

Okun, Arthur M. 1962. "Potential GNP: Its Measurement and Significance." *Proceedings of the Business and Economic Statistics Section of the American Statistical Association*, 98–104.

Popkin, Joel. 2000. "The U.S. National Income and Product Accounts." *Journal of Economic Perspectives* 14, no. 2 (Spring): 214–224.

Prakken, Joel L., and Lisa T. Guirl. 1995. "Macro Modeling & Forecasting with Chain-Type Measures of GDP." *National Association for Business Economics: NABE News*, September, 7–13.

Ruggles, Nancy D., and Richard Ruggles. 1999. *National Accounting and Economic Policy.* Cheltenham, UK: Edward Elgar.

Steindel, Charles. 1995. "Chain-Weighting: The New Approach to Measuring GDP." *Federal Reserve Bank of New York Current Issues in Economics and Finance* 1, no. 9 (December).

U.S. Department of Commerce, Bureau of Economic Analysis. 1985. *An Introduction to National Economic Accounting.* Methodology Paper Series MP-1. Washington, DC: Government Printing Office. Also available online at http://www.bea.gov/methodologies/index.htm.

———. 1998. *National Income and Product Accounts of the United States*, 1929–94. 2 vols. Washington, DC: Government Printing Office.

———. 2000. "GDP: One of the Great Inventions of the 20th Century." *Survey of Current Business*, January, 6–14. Also available online at http://www .bea.gov/scb/toc/0100cont.htm.

———. 2002. *Corporate Profits: Profits Before Tax, Profits Tax Liability and Dividends.* Methodology Paper Series. Washington, DC: Government Printing Office. Also available online at http://www.bea.gov/methodologies/index.htm.

———. "Gross Domestic Product" (various releases). Also available online at http://www.bea.gov/newsreleases/relsarchivegdp.htm.

———. *Survey of Current Business* (various issues). Also available online at http:// www.bea.gov/scb/date_guide.asp.

Whelan, Karl. 2000. *A Guide to the Use of Chain Aggregated NIPA Data*. Finance and Economics Discussion Series 2000-35. Washington, DC: Federal Reserve Board of Governors.

Chapter 2: Indexes of Leading, Lagging, and Coincident Indicators

Anderson, Gerald H., and John J. Erceg. 1989. "Forecasting Turning Points with Leading Indicators." *Federal Reserve Bank of Cleveland Economic Commentary*, October 1.

Burns, Arthur F., and Wesley Clair Mitchell. 1938. "Statistical Indicators of Cyclical Revivals." *NBER Bulletin 69*.

———. 1946. *Measuring Business Cycles*. New York: National Bureau of Economic Research.

Conference Board. *Business Cycle Indicators*, New York: Conference Board (various issues).

———. *U.S. Leading Economic Indicators and Related Composite Indexes*. New York: Conference Board (various issues).

Diebold, Francis X., and Glenn D. Rudebusch. 1991. "Forecasting Output with the Composite Leading Index: A Real-Time Analysis." *Journal of the American Statistical Association* 86 (September): 603–610.

Dueker, Michael J. 1997. "Strengthening the Case for the Yield Curve as a Predictor of U.S. Recessions." *Federal Reserve Bank of St. Louis Review* 79, no. 2 (March/April): 41–51.

Duesenberry, James S. 1958. *Business Cycles and Economic Growth*. New York: McGraw-Hill.

Estrella, Arturo, and Frederic S. Mishkin. 1996. "The Yield Curve as a Predictor of U.S. Recessions." *Federal Reserve Bank of New York Current Issues in Economics and Finance* 2, no. 7 (June).

Gordon, Robert J., ed. 1986. *The American Business Cycle*. Chicago: University of Chicago Press.

Haubrich, Joseph G., and Ann M. Dombrosky. 1996. "Predicting Real Growth Using the Yield Curve." *Federal Reserve Bank of Cleveland Economic Review* 32, no. 1 (1st Quarter): 26–35.

Kozicki, Sharon. 1997. "Predicting Real Growth and Inflation with the Yield Spread." *Federal Reserve Bank of Kansas City Economic Review* (4th Quarter): 39–57.

Lee, Dara, and Ataman Ozyildirim. 2005. "Forthcoming Revisions to the Index of Leading Economic Indicators." Conference Board. http://www.conference-board.org/economics/bci/methodology.cfm.

Mankiw, N. Gregory. 1998. *Principles of Economics*. Fort Worth, TX: Dryden Press.

Mitchell, Wesley C. 1954. *Business Cycles, the Problem and Its Setting*. New York: National Bureau of Economic Research.

Moore, Geoffrey H. 1983. *Business Cycles, Inflation and Forecasting*. 2nd ed. Cambridge, MA: Ballinger Publishing.

———. 1990. *Leading Indicators for the 1990s*. Homewood, IL: Dow Jones-Irwin.

National Bureau of Economic Research. 1951. *Conference on Business Cycles*. New York: National Bureau of Economic Research.

———. 2003. "U.S. Business Cycle Expansions and Contractions." http://www .nber.org/cycles.html.

Sherman, Howard J. 1991. *The Business Cycle: Growth and Crisis Under Capitalism*. Princeton, NJ: Princeton University Press.

Stock, James H., and Mark W. Watson. 1993. *Business Cycles, Indicators, and Forecasting*. Chicago: University of Chicago Press.

Zarnowitz, Victor. 1992. *Business Cycles*. Chicago: University of Chicago Press.

Chapter 3: The Employment Situation

Baumol, William J., and Alan S. Blinder. 1991. *Macroeconomics Principles and Policy*. 5th ed. New York: Harcourt Brace Jovanovich.

Dwyer, Gerald P., Jr., and R. W. Hafer. 1989. "Interest Rates and Economic Announcements." *Federal Reserve Bank of St. Louis Review* 71, no.2 (March/April): 34–46.

Fleming, Michael J., and Eli M. Remolona. 1997. "What Moves the Bond Market?" Federal Reserve Bank of New York Research Paper 9706.

Getz, Patricia M., and Mark G. Ulmer. 1990. "Diffusion Indexes: A Barometer of the Economy." *Monthly Labor Review* 113, no. 4 (April): 13–21.

Hagenbaugh, Barbara. 2003. "Part-Time Workforce Grows, Which Is Good and Bad." *USA Today*, June 17.

Hager, George. 2001. "Why Hasn't Today's Jobless Rate Skyrocketed?" *USA Today*, August 20.

Jossi, Frank. 2003. "Temporary Canary." *Federal Reserve Bank of Minneapolis fedgazette*, March.

Leonhardt, David. 2001. "A Tale of 2 Totals in the Jobs Report." *New York Times*, January 28.

Mankiw, N. Gregory. 1998. *Principles of Macroeconomics*. Fort Worth, TX: Dryden Press.

Miller, Rich. 1999. "The Labor Pool: Why Greenspan Is Worried." *BusinessWeek*, December 6.

Schweitzer, Mark, and Jennifer Ransom. 1999. "Measuring Total Employment: Are a Few Million Workers Important?" *Federal Reserve Bank of Cleveland Economic Commentary*, June.

U.S. Department of Labor, Bureau of Labor Statistics. 1997. *BLS Handbook of Methods*. Washington, DC: Government Printing Office. See chap. 1 "Labor

Force Data Derived from the Current Population Survey," and chap. 2 "Employment, Hours, and Earnings from the Establishment Survey." Also available online at http://www.bls.gov/opub/hom/homtoc_pdf.htm.

————. 2001. "How the Government Measures Unemployment." http://www.bls.gov/cps/cps_htgm.htm.

————. "Employment Situation" (various releases). Also available online at http://www.bls.gov/schedule/archives/empsit_nr.htm.

Chapter 4: Industrial Production and Capacity Utilization

Board of Governors of the Federal Reserve System. 1986. *Industrial Production: 1986 Edition with a Description of the Methodology*. Washington, DC.

————. Federal Reserve Statistical Release G.17. "Industrial Production and Capacity Utilization" (various releases). Also available online at http://www.federalreserve.gov/releases/G17/.

Corrado, Carol, Charles Gilbert, and Norman Morin. 2002. "Industrial Production and Capacity Utilization: The 2001 Annual Revision." *Federal Reserve Bulletin*, March, 173–187.

Corrado, Carol, and Kristen Hamden. 2003. "Industrial Production and Capacity Utilization: The 2002 Historical and Annual Revision." *Federal Reserve Bulletin*, April, 151–176.

Emery, Kenneth M., and Chih-Ping Chang. 1997. "Is There a Stable Relationship Between Capacity Utilization and Inflation?" *Federal Reserve Bank of Dallas Economic Review* (1st Quarter): 14–20.

Finn, Mary G. 1995. "Is 'High' Capacity Utilization Inflationary?" *Federal Reserve Bank of Richmond Economic Quarterly* 81, no. 1 (Winter): 1–16.

————. 1996. "A Theory of the Capacity Utilization/Inflation Relationship." *Federal Reserve Bank of Richmond Economic Quarterly* 82, no. 3 (Summer): 67–86.

Garner, C. Alan. 1994. "Capacity Utilization and U.S. Inflation." *Federal Reserve Bank of Kansas City Economic Review* 79, no. 4 (4th Quarter): 5–21.

Gittings, Thomas A. 1989. "Capacity Utilization and Inflation." *Federal Reserve Bank of Chicago Economic Perspectives* 13, no. 3 (May/June): 2–9.

Hall, Robert E. 2001. *Recessions*. Cambridge, MA: National Bureau of Economic Research. Also available online at http://www.ber.org.

Koenig, Evan F. 1996. "Capacity Utilization as a Real-Time Predictor of Manufacturing Output." *Federal Reserve Bank of Dallas Economic Review* (3rd Quarter): 16–23.

Rogers, R. Mark. 1992. "Forecasting Industrial Production: Purchasing Managers' versus Production-Worker Hours Data." *Federal Reserve Bank of Atlanta Economic Review*, January/February, 25–36.

Shapiro, Matthew D. 1989. "Assessing the Federal Reserve's Measures of Capacity and Utilization." *Brookings Papers on Economic Activity* 1:181–225.

Chapter 5: Institute for Supply Management Indexes

Economic Cycle Research Institute. http://www.businesscycle.com.

Harris, Ethan S. 1991. "Tracking the Economy with the Purchasing Managers' Index." *Federal Reserve Bank of New York Quarterly Review* 16, no. 3 (Fall): 61–69.

Institute for Supply Management. 2002. *Institute for Supply Management's Manufacturing Report on Business Information Kit* (as of September 2002).

———. *Manufacturing ISM Report on Business* (various issues). Also available online at http://www.ism.ws/ISMReport/.

———. *Non-Manufacturing ISM Report on Business* (various issues). Also available online at http://www.ism.ws/ISMReport/.

Klein, Philip A., and Geoffrey H. Moore. 1988. "NAPM Business Survey Data: Their Value as a Leading Indicator." *Journal of Purchasing and Materials Management* 24 (Winter): 32–40.

Raedels, Alan. 1990. "Forecasting the NAPM Purchasing Managers' Index." *Journal of Purchasing and Materials Management* 26 (Fall): 34–39.

Chapter 6: Manufacturers' Shipments, Inventories, and Orders

Gordon, Robert J. 1990. *The Measurement of Durable Goods Prices*. Chicago: University of Chicago Press, for the National Bureau of Economic Research.

Harberger, Arnold C., ed. 1960. *The Demand for Durable Goods*. Chicago: University of Chicago Press.

Klein, Lawrence R. 1951. "Studies in Investment Behavior." In *Conference on Business Cycles*, 233–303. New York: National Bureau of Economic Research.

Mayer, Thomas, and S. Sonenblum. 1955. "Lead Times for Fixed Investment." *Review of Economics and Statistics* 37, no. 3 (August): 300–304.

Roos, C. F. 1948. "The Demand for Investment Goods." *American Economic Review* 38, no. 2 (May): 311–320.

Stone, J. R. N., and D. A. Rowe. 1957. "The Market Demand for Durable Goods." *Econometrica* 25, no. 3 (July): 423–443.

U.S. Department of Commerce, Bureau of the Census. 1963. *Manufacturers' Shipments, Inventories, and Orders: 1947–1963 Revised*. Series M3-1. Washington, DC: Government Printing Office.

———. 2002. *Manufacturers' Shipments, Inventories, and Orders: 1992–2001*. Series M3-1 (01). Washington, DC: Government Printing Office. Also available online at http://www.census.gov/indicator/www/m3/bench/m3-01.pdf.

———. 2007. *Instruction Manual for Reporting in Monthly Survey M3*, M3-SD(I). Washington, DC: Government Printing Office. Also available online at http://bhs.econ.census.gov/BHS/M3/index.html.

———. "Advance Report on Durable Goods Manufacturers' Shipments, Inventories, and Orders" (various releases). Also available online at http://www.census.gov/indicator/www/m3/priorrel.htm.

————. "Manufacturers' Shipments, Inventories, and Orders" (various releases). Also available online at http://www.census.gov/indicator/www/m3/priorrel.htm.

Zarnowitz, Victor. 1973. *Orders, Production, and Investment*. New York: Columbia University Press, for the National Bureau of Economic Research.

Chapter 7: Manufacturing and Trade Inventories and Sales

Abramovitz, Moses. 1950. *Inventories and Business Cycles: With Special Reference to Manufacturers' Inventories*. New York: National Bureau of Economic Research.

Allen, Donald S. 1995. "Changes in Inventory Management and the Business Cycle." *Federal Reserve Bank of St. Louis Review* 77, no. 4 (July/August): 17–26.

Bils, Mark, and James A. Kahn. 1996. "What Inventory Behavior Tells Us about Business Cycles." Rochester Center for Economic Research Working Paper 428, University of Rochester.

Blanchard, Oliver J. 1983. "The Production and Inventory Behavior of the American Automobile Industry." *Journal of Political Economy* 91 (June): 365–400.

Blinder, Alan S. 1981. "Retail Inventory Behavior and Business Fluctuations." *Brookings Papers on Economic Activity* 2: 443–505.

Blinder, Alan S., and Louis J. Maccini. 1991. "Taking Stock: A Critical Assessment of Recent Research on Inventories." *Journal of Economic Perspectives* 5, no. 1 (Winter): 73–96.

Fair, Ray C. 1989. "Production Smoothing Model Is Alive and Well." *Journal of Monetary Economics* 24: 353–370.

Fitzgerald, Terry J. 1997. "Inventories and the Business Cycle: An Overview." *Federal Reserve Bank of Cleveland Economic Review* 33, no. 3 (3rd Quarter): 11–22.

Fitzgerald, Terry J., and Jennifer K. Ransom. 1998. "What Happened to the Inventory Overhang?" *Federal Reserve Bank of Cleveland Economic Commentary*, March 15.

Holmes, Thomas J. 1999. "Bar Codes Lead to Frequent Deliveries and Superstores." Federal Reserve Bank of Minneapolis Research Department Staff Report 261.

Holt, Charles C., Franco Modigliani, John F. Muth, and Herbert A. Simon. 1960. *Planning Production, Inventories and Work Force*, Englewood Cliffs, NJ: Prentice-Hall.

Huh, Chan. 1994. "Just-in-Time Inventory Management: Has It Made a Difference?" *Federal Reserve Bank of San Francisco Weekly Letter*, May 6.

Kahn, James A. 1987. "Inventories and the Volatility of Production." *American Economic Review* 77, no. 4 (September): 667–679.

Little, Jane Sneddon. 1992. "Changes in Inventory Management: Implications for the U.S. Recovery." *Federal Reserve Bank of Boston New England Economic Review*, November/December, 37–65.

McConnell, Margaret M., and Gabriel Perez Quiros. 1998. "Output Fluctuations in the United States: What Has Changed Since the Early 1980s?" Federal Reserve Bank of New York Staff Report 41.

Metzler, Lloyd A. 1941. "The Nature and Stability of Inventory Cycles." *Review of Economics and Statistics* 23, no. 3 (August): 113–129.

Morgan, Donald P. 1991. "Will Just-in-Time Inventory Techniques Dampen Recessions?" *Federal Reserve Bank of Kansas City Economic Review* 76, no. 2 (March/April): 21–33.

Ramey, Valerie A. 1989. "Inventories as Factors of Production and Economic Fluctuations." *American Economic Review* 79, no. 3 (June): 338–354.

U.S. Department of Commerce, Bureau of the Census. "Economic Census: Retail Trade" (various reports). Also available online at http://www.census.gov/econ/census02/.

———. 2002. *Annual Benchmark Report for Wholesale Trade: January 1992 Through February 2002*. Current Business Reports, Series BW/01-A. Washington, DC. Also available online at http://www.census.gov/prod/www/abs/bw_month.html.

———. *Monthly Wholesale Trade Survey* (various releases). Also available online at http://www.census.gov/mwts/www/mwtshist.html.

———. "Manufacturing and Trade Inventories and Sales" (various releases). Also available online at http://www.census.gov/mtis/www/mtishist.html.

West, Kenneth D. 1990. "The Sources of Fluctuations in Aggregate Inventories and GNP." *Quarterly Journal of Economics* 105, no. 4 (November): 939–971.

Worthington, Paula R. 1998. "The Increasing Importance of Retailers' Inventories." *Federal Reserve Bank of Chicago Economic Perspectives* 22, no. 3 (3rd Quarter): 2–12.

Zarnowitz, Victor. 1973. *Orders, Production, and Investment*. New York: Columbia University Press, for the National Bureau of Economic Research.

Chapter 8: New Residential Construction

Hagenbaugh, Barbara. 2002. "More People Refinance to Wring Cash Out of Their Homes." *USA Today*, Money Section, October 28.

Hancock, Jay. 2002. "Amazing Housing Market Bound to Help the Economy." *Baltimore Sun*, February 27.

Mortgage Bankers Association. http://www.mbaa.org.

National Association of Home Builders. 2002. "Housing: The Key to Economic Recovery." Washington, DC. Also available online at http://www.novoco.com/low_income_housing/resource_files/research_center/recoverkey.pdf.

National Association of Realtors. http://www.realtor.org.

Smart, Tim. 1998. "The Housing Boom Gives the Economy a Boost." Washington Post, December 9.

U.S. Department of Commerce, Bureau of the Census. 2001. *Expenditures for Improvements and Repairs of Residential Properties* (3rd Quarter). Also available online at http://www.census.gov/prod/www/abs/c50.html.

―――. "New Residential Construction" (various releases). Also available online at http://www.census.gov/const/www/newresconsthist.html.

―――. *New Residential Construction Survey Documentation.* www.census.gov/const/www/newresconstdoc.html.

Chapter 9: Conference Board Consumer Confidence and University of Michigan Consumer Sentiment Indexes

Bram, Jason, and Sydney Ludvigson. 1998. "Does Consumer Confidence Forecast Household Expenditure? A Sentiment Index Horse Race." *Federal Reserve Bank of New York Economic Policy Review* 4, no. 2 (June): 59–78.

Carroll, Christopher D., Jeffrey C. Fuhrer, and David W. Wilcox. 1994. "Does Consumer Sentiment Forecast Household Spending? If So, Why?" *American Economic Review* 84, no. 5 (December): 1397–1408.

Conference Board. *Consumer Confidence Survey.* New York (various issues).

Curtin, Richard T. 1982. "Indicators of Consumer Behavior: The University of Michigan Surveys of Consumers." *Public Opinion Quarterly* 46: 340–352.

―――. "Index Calculations." University of Michigan. Mimeo.

―――. "Surveys of Consumers." University of Michigan. Mimeo.

Friend, Irvin, and F. Gerald Adams. 1964. "The Predictive Ability of Consumer Attitudes, Stock Prices, and Non-Attitudinal Variables." *Journal of the American Statistical Association* 89 (December): 987–1005.

Fuhrer, Jeffrey C. 1993. "What Role Does Consumer Sentiment Play in the U.S. Macroeconomy?" *Federal Reserve Bank of Boston New England Economic Review* (January/February): 32–44.

Garner, C. Alan. 1991. "Forecasting Consumer Spending: Should Economists Pay Attention to Consumer Confidence Surveys?" *Federal Reserve Bank of Kansas City Economic Review* 76, no. 3 (May/June): 57–71.

Graber, Doris A. 1982. "Reading Between the Lines of Consumer Confidence Measures." *Public Opinion Quarterly* 46: 336–339.

Katona, George. 1960. *The Powerful Consumer.* New York: McGraw-Hill.

Katona, George, and Eva Mueller. 1968. *Consumer Response to Income Increases.* Washington, DC: Brookings Institution.

Keynes, John Maynard. 1936. *The General Theory of Employment, Interest, and Money.* New York: Harcourt, Brace and Company.

Kulish, Nicholas. 2001. "Michigan's Consumer Sentiment Index for January Fell More Than Expected." *Wall Street Journal*, January 22.

Lansing, John B., and James N. Morgan. 1980. *Economic Survey Methods.* Ann Arbor, MI: University of Michigan Press.

Leeper, Eric M. 1991. "Consumer Attitudes and Business Cycles." Federal Reserve Bank of Atlanta Working Paper 91-11.

———. 1992. "Consumer Attitudes: King for a Day." *Federal Reserve Bank of Atlanta Economic Review* 77, no. 4. (July): 1–15.

Linden, Fabian. 1982. "The Consumer as Forecaster." *Public Opinion Quarterly* 46: 353–360.

Matsusaka, John G., and Argia M. Sbordone. 1993. "Consumer Confidence and Economic Fluctuations." Federal Reserve Bank of Chicago Working Paper 93-13.

Mehra, Yash P., and Elliot W. Martin. 2003. "Why Does Consumer Sentiment Predict Household Spending?" *Federal Reserve Bank of Richmond Economic Quarterly* 89, no. 4 (Fall): 51–67.

Mishkin, Frederic S. 1978. "Consumer Sentiment and Spending on Durable Goods." *Brookings Papers on Economic Activity* 1: 217–232.

Roper, Burns S. 1982. "The Predictive Value of Consumer Confidence Measures." *Public Opinion Quarterly* 46: 361–367.

Throop, Adrian W. 1991. "Consumer Confidence and the Outlook for Consumer Spending." *Federal Reserve Bank of San Francisco Economic Letter*, July 19.

Tobin, James. 1959. "On the Predictive Value of Consumer Intentions and Attitudes." *Review of Economics and Statistics* 41, no. 1 (February): 1–11.

University of Michigan. "Surveys of Consumers." Ann Arbor, MI: University of Michigan Survey Research Center (various issues).

Chapter 10: Advance Monthly Sales for Retail and Food Services

Coleman, Calmetta. 2001. "Retailers Suffer Sales Slowdown for December." *Wall Street Journal*, January 5.

Driscoll, Marie. 2001. "Monthly Retail Review." *Argus Research Investment Analysis* 68, no. 284 (November).

Harris, Ethan S., and Clara Vega. 1996. "What Do Chain Store Sales Tell Us about Consumer Spending?" Federal Reserve Bank of New York Research Paper 9614.

Lazear, Edward P. 1986. "Retail Pricing and Clearance Sales." *American Economic Review* 76, no. 1 (March): 14–32.

Mencke, Claire. 2000. "Hot Retail Seems to Cinch Rate Hike Even as Producer Prices Stay Tame." *Investor's Business Daily*, April 14.

Nakamura, Leonard I. 1998. "The Retail Revolution and Food-Price Mismeasurement." *Federal Reserve Bank of Philadelphia Business Review*, May/June, 3–14.

U.S. Department of Commerce, Bureau of the Census. 2001. *Home Computers and Internet Use in the United States: August 2000*. Current Population Reports, P23-207, by Eric C. Newburger. Washington, DC. Also available online at http://www.census.gov/prod/2001pubs/p23-207.pdf.

———. 2002. *Annual Benchmark Report for Retail Trade and Food Services: January 1992 Through March 2002*. Current Business Reports, Series BR/01-A. Washington, DC. Also available online at http://www.census.gov/prod/2002pubs/br01-a.pdf.

———. Retail E-Commerce Reports (various issues 1999–2002). Also available online at http://www.census.gov/eos/www/ebusiness614.htm.

———. "E-Commerce Frequently Asked Questions (FAQs)." http://www.census.gov/mrts/www/efaq.html.

Chapter 11: Personal Income and Outlays

Chow, G. C. 1957. *Demand for Automobiles in the United States*. Contributions to Economic Analysis 13. Amsterdam: North-Holland Publishing Co.

Larkins, Daniel. 1999. "Note on the Personal Saving Rate." *Survey of Current Business*, February, 8–9. Also available online at http://www.bea.gov/scb/toc/0299cont.htm.

Leonhardt, David. 2001. "Belt Tightening Is Called Threat to the Economy." *New York Times*, July 15.

Madigan, Kathleen, and David Lindorff. 1998. "Consumers Have Money to Burn." *BusinessWeek*, April 20.

Mitchell, Wesley C., ed. 1921. *Income in the United States: Its Amount and Distribution, 1909–1919*. New York: Harcourt, Brace and Company.

Moran, Larry R., and Clinton P. McCully. 2001. "Trends in Consumer Spending, 1959–2000." *Survey of Current Business*, March, 15–21. Also available online at http://www.bea.gov/scb/toc/0301cont.htm.

U.S. Department of Commerce, Bureau of Economic Analysis. 1990. *Personal Consumption Expenditures*. Methodology Paper Series MP-6. Washington, DC: Government Printing Office. Also available online at http://www.bea.gov/methodologies/index.htm.

———. 1998. *National Income and Product Accounts of the United States, 1929–94*. 2 vols. Washington, DC: Government Printing Office.

———. "Personal Income and Outlays" (various releases). Also available online at http://www.bea.gov/newsreleases/relsarchivepi.htm.

Chapter 12: Consumer and Producer Price Indexes

Advisory Commission to Study the Consumer Price Index. 1996. *Toward a More Accurate Measure of the Cost of Living: Final Report to the Senate Finance Committee*. Washington, DC. Also available online at http://www.ssa.gov/history/reports/boskinrpt.html.

Aluminum Association Inc. "Industry Overview: From Alumina to Automobiles." http://www.aluminum.org/template.cfm?Section=The_Industry.

Bryan, Michael F., and Stephen G. Cecchetti. 1993. "The Consumer Price Index as a Measure of Inflation." *Federal Reserve Bank of Cleveland Economic Review* 29, no. 4 (4th Quarter): 15–24.

Bryan, Michael F., Stephen G. Cecchetti, and Rodney L. Wiggins II. 1997. "Efficient Inflation Estimation." National Bureau of Economic Research Working Paper 6183. Cambridge, MA.

Bullard, James B., and Charles M. Hokayem. 2003. "Deflation, Corrosive and Otherwise." *Federal Reserve Bank of St. Louis National Economic Trends*, July.

Cagan, Phillip, and Geoffrey H. Moore. 1981. *The Consumer Price Index, Issues and Alternatives*. Washington, DC: American Enterprise Institute for Public Policy Research.

Clark, Todd E. 1997. "Do Producer Prices Help Predict Consumer Prices?" Federal Reserve Bank of Kansas City Research Working Paper 97-09.

Copper Development Association. "Copper Facts." Also available online at http://www.copper.org/education/c-facts/homepage.html.

Fair, Ray C. 1996. "Econometrics and Presidential Elections." *Journal of Economic Perspectives* 10, no. 3 (Summer): 89–102.

———. 2002. *Predicting Presidential Elections and Other Things*. Stanford, CA: Stanford University Press.

Fuerbringer, Jonathan. 2003. "Commodity Costs Soar, but Factories Don't Bustle." *New York Times*, July 31.

Groshen, Erica L., and Mark E. Schweitzer. 1997. "Identifying Inflation's Grease and Sand Effects in the Labor Market," Federal Reserve Bank of Cleveland Working Paper 9705.

Hagenbaugh, Barbara. 2003. "Fuel Prices 'Cream' Firms." *USA Today*, August 6.

Hess, Gregory D., and Mark E. Schweitzer. 2000. "Does Wage Inflation Cause Price Inflation?" Federal Reserve Bank of Cleveland Policy Discussion Paper 1.

Madrick, Jeff. 2001. "Economic Scene." *New York Times*, December 27.

Platt, Gordon. 1998. "No Pickup in Inflationary Pressures." *Journal of Commerce*, July 30.

Solomon, Jolie. 2001. "An Economic Speedometer Gets an Overhaul." *New York Times*, December 23.

U.S. Department of Labor, Bureau of Labor Statistics. 1997. *BLS Handbook of Methods*. Washington, DC: Government Printing Office. See chap. 16, "The Producer Price Index," and chap. 17, "The Consumer Price Index." Also available online at http://www.bls.gov/opub/hom/homtoc_pdf.htm.

———. 1997. "Measurement Issues in the Consumer Price Index." http://www.bls.gov/cpi/cpigm697.htm.

———. 1998. "How Does the Producer Price Index Differ from the Consumer Price Index?" *PPI Program Spotlight* 98-3. Also available online at http://stats.bls.gov/ppi/ppivcpi.pdf.

Wallace, Allison, and Brian Motley. 1999. "A Better CPI." *Federal Reserve Bank of San Francisco Economic Letter*, February 5.

Wu, Tao. 2003. "Improving the Way We Measure Consumer Prices." *Federal Reserve Bank of San Francisco Economic Letter*, August 22.

Chapter 13: The Fixed-Income Market

Board of Governors of the Federal Reserve System. Federal Reserve Statistical Release, H.15. *Selected Interest Rates* (various issues).

Carlson, John B., William R. Melick, and Erkin Y. Sahinoz. 2003. "An Option for Anticipating Fed Action." *Federal Reserve Bank of Cleveland Economic Commentary*, September 1.

Carlstrom, Charles L., and Timothy S. Fuerst. 2004. "Expected Inflation and TIPS." *Federal Reserve Bank of Cleveland Economic Commentary*, November.

Chicago Board of Trade. 2003. *Reference Guide: CBOT Fed Funds Futures*. Chicago, IL: Board of Trade of the City of Chicago, Inc.

_____. *Practical Applications Using CBOT Fed Funds Futures*. 1997. Chicago, IL: Board of Trade of the City of Chicago, Inc.

_____. *Insights into Pricing the CBOT Fed Funds Futures*. 1997. Chicago, IL: Board of Trade of the City of Chicago, Inc.

Craig, Ben. 2003. "Why Are TIIS Yields So High? The Case of the Missing Inflation-Risk Premium." *Federal Reserve Bank of Cleveland Economic Commentary*, March 15.

Crescenzi, Anthony. 2002. *The Strategic Bond Investor*. New York: McGraw-Hill.

Duca, John V. 1999. "What Credit Market Indicators Tell Us." *Federal Reserve Bank of Dallas Economic and Financial Review* (Third Quarter): 2–13.

Estrella, A., and F.S. Mishkin. 1996. "The Yield Curve as a Predictor of U.S. Recessions." *Federal Reserve Bank of New York, Current Issues in Economics and Finance* 2, no. 7 (June).

Fernald, John and Bharat Trehan. 2006. "Is a Recession Imminent?" *Federal Reserve Bank of San Francisco Economic Letter*, no. 32 (November 24).

Graja, Christopher. 1997."Yield to the Curve." *Bloomberg Personal Finance* (December): 21–23.

Gurkaynak, Refet S., Brian Sack, and Jonathan H. Wright. 2006. "The U.S. Treasury Yield Curve: 1961 to the Present." *Finance and Economic Discussion Series*, no. 28. Washington, DC: Federal Reserve Board of Governors.

Haubrich, Joseph G. 2006. "Does the Yield Curve Signal Recession?" *Federal Reserve Bank of Cleveland Economic Commentary*, April 15.

_____. 2004. "Interest Rates, Yield Curves, and the Monetary Regime." *Federal Reserve Bank of Cleveland Economic Commentary*, June.

Homer, Sidney. 1963. *A History of Interest Rates*. New Brunswick, New Jersey: Rutgers University Press.

Jones, David M. 2002. *Unlocking the Secrets of the Fed*. Hoboken, New Jersey: John Wiley & Sons, Inc.

Kitter, Gregory V. 1999. *Investment Mathematics for Finance and Treasury Professionals: A Practical Approach*, New York: John Wiley & Sons, Inc.

Krainer, John. 2004. "What Determines the Credit Spread?" *Federal Reserve Bank of San Francisco Economic Letter*, no. 36 (December 10).

Robertson, John C. and Daniel L. Thorton. 1997. "Using Federal Funds Futures Rates to Predict Federal Reserve Actions." *Federal Reserve Bank of St. Louis Economic Review* 79, no. 6 (November/December): 45–53.

Sack, Brian. 2000. "Deriving Inflation Expectations from Nominal and Inflation-Indexed Treasury Yields." *Journal of Fixed Income* 10 (September): 1–12.

Securities Industry and Financial Markets Association (SIFMA). 2006. *Research Quarterly*, November.

Stigum, Marcia. 1983. *The Money Market*. New York: McGraw-Hill.

Stojanovic, Dusan and Mark D. Vaughan. 1997. "Yielding Clues About Recessions: The Yield Curve as a Forecasting Tool." *Federal Reserve Bank of St. Louis Regional Economist* (October): 10–11.

Wright, Jonathan H. 2006. "The Yield Curve and Predicting Recessions." *Finance and Economic Discussion Series 2006–07*. Washington, DC: Federal Reserve Board of Governors.

Wu, Tao. 2005. "The Long-Term Interest Rate Conundrum: Not Unraveled Yet?" *Federal Reserve Bank of San Francisco Economic Letter*, no. 8 (April 29).

_____. 2006. "Globalization's Effect on Interest Rates and the Yield Curve." *Federal Reserve Bank of Dallas Economic Letter* 1, no. 9 (September).

Zipf, Robert. 1988. *How the Bond Market Works*. New York: New York Institute of Finance.

Chapter 14: Commodities

Armesto, Michelle T. and William T. Gavin. 2005. "Monetary Policy and Commodity Futures." *Federal Reserve Bank of St. Louis Review* (May/June): 395–405.

Babson, Roger W. 1958. *Business Barometers for Profits, Security, Income*. 8th ed. New York: Harper & Brothers Publishers.

Barrionuevo, Alexei. 2007. "Rise in Ethanol Raises Concerns About Corn as a Food." *New York Times*, January 5.

Barsky, Robert B. and Lutz Kilian. 2004. "Oil and the Macroeconomy Since the 1970s." *Journal of Economic Perspectives* 18, no. 4 (Fall): 115–134.

Bernstein, Peter L. 2000. *The Power of Gold: The History of an Obsession*. New York: John Wiley & Sons, Inc.

Bouchentouf, Amine. 2006. *Commodities for Dummies*. Hoboken, New Jersey: John Wiley & Sons, Inc.

Bray, E. Lee. *Mineral Commodity Summaries*. Reston, Virginia: U.S. Geological Survey (various issues).

Brown, Stephen P. A. 2000. "Do Rising Oil Prices Threaten Economic Prosperity?" *Federal Reserve Bank of Dallas Southwest Economy*, no. 6 (November/December): 1–5.

Brown, Stephen P. A. and Mine K. Yucel. 2000. "Oil Prices and the Economy" *Federal Reserve Bank of Dallas Southwest Economy*, no. 4 (July/August): 1–6.

Carey, John and Adrienne Carter. 2007. "Food vs. Fuel." *BusinessWeek*, February 5.

Carlstrom, Charles T. and Timothy S. Fuerst. 2005. "Oil Prices, Monetary Policy, and the Macroeconomy." *Federal Reserve Bank of Cleveland Economic Commentary*, July.

Commodity Research Bureau. 2007. *Reuters/Jefferies CRB Indexes*. http://www.crbtrader.com/crbindex.

Dhawan, Rajeev and Karsten Jeske. 2006. "How Resilient Is the Modern Economy to Energy Price Shocks?" *Federal Reserve Bank of Atlanta Economic Review*. (Third Quarter): 21–32.

Economic Cycle Research Institute. *U.S. Cyclical Outlook* (various issues).

Edlestein, Daniel L. *Mineral Commodity Summaries*. Reston, Virginia: U.S. Geological Survey (various issues).

Einhorn, Cheryl Strauss. 2000. "Russian Roulette, Palladium Spike on Export Halt." *Barron's*, August 7.

Eugeni, Francesca, Charles Evans, and Steven Strongin. 1993. "Commodity-Based Indicators: Separating the Wheat from the Chaff." Federal Reserve Bank of Chicago, *Chicago Fed Letter*, no. 75 (November).

Eugeni, Francesca, and Joel Krueger. 1994. "The Ups and Downs of Commodity Price Indexes." Federal Reserve Bank of Chicago, *Chicago Fed Letter*, no. 88 (December).

Fernald, John and Bharat Trehan. 2005. "Why Hasn't the Jump in Oil Prices Led to a Recession?" *Federal Reserve Bank of San Francisco Economic Letter*, no. 31 (November 18).

Fisher, Douglas Alan. 1963. *The Epic of Steel*. New York: Harper & Row Publishers.

Founie, Alan. *Mineral Commodity Summaries*, Reston, Virginia: U.S. Geological Survey (various issues).

Furlong, Fred and Robert Ingenito. 1996. "Commodity Prices and Inflation." *Federal Reserve Bank of San Francisco Economic Review*, no. 2: 27–47.

Gamborgi, Joseph. *Mineral Commodity Summaries*, Reston, Virginia: U.S. Geological Survey (various issues).

George, Micheal W. *Mineral Commodity Summaries*, Reston, Virginia: U.S. Geological Survey (various issues).

Goldman Sachs. 2007. *The GSCI Manual: A Guide to the Goldman Sachs Commodity Index—2007 Edition*, January.

Gould, Bruce G. 1981. *The Dow Jones-Irwin Guide to Commodities Trading*, Homewood, Illinois: Dow Jones-Irwin.

Hagenbaugh, Barbara. 2006. "Commodity Prices on a Roll as Demand Rises." *USA Today*, March 30.

_____. 2004. "Cement Weighs on Construction." *USA Today*, August 9.

Hunt, E.K. 1979. *History of Economic Thought: A Critical Perspective*. Belmont, California: Wadsworth Publishing Company.

Jefferies & Co. *Reuters/Jefferies CRB Index Materials*. http://www.jefferies.com/ cositemgr.pl/html/ProductsServices/SalesTrading/Commodities/Reuters JefferiesCRB/index.shtml.

Mehra, Yash P. and Jon D. Petersen. 2005. "Oil Prices and Consumer Spending." *Federal Reserve Bank of Richmond Economic Quarterly* 91, no. 3 (Summer).

Moore, Geoffrey H. 1990. *Leading Indicators for the 1990s*. Homewood, Illinois: Dow Jones-Irwin.

Morrison, Kevin. 2007. "Blow for Beer as Biofuels Edge Out Barley." *Financial Times*, February 26.

Rogers, Jim. 2004. *Hot Commodities: How Anyone Can Invest Profitably in the World's Best Market*. New York: Random House.

Simons, Howard. 2004. "Commodities: Barometer or Broken Clock?" *Futures*, July.

Simmons, Matthew R. 2005. *Twilight in the Desert: The Coming Saudi Oil Shock and the World Economy*. Hoboken, New Jersey: John Wiley & Sons, Inc.

Tolcin, Amy C. *Mineral Commodity Summaries*, Reston, Virginia: U.S. Geological Survey (various issues).

Van Oss, Hendrik G. *Mineral Commodity Summaries*, Reston, Virginia: U.S. Geological Survey (various issues).

Yergin, Daniel. 1992. *The Prize: The Epic Quest for Oil, Money & Power*. New York: Free Press.

Index

About Bloomberg

Bloomberg L.P., founded in 1981, is a global information services, news, and media company. Headquartered in New York, the company has sales and news operations worldwide.

Bloomberg, serving customers on six continents, holds a unique position within the financial services industry by providing an unparalleled range of features in a single package known as the BLOOMBERG PROFESSIONAL® service. By addressing the demand for investment performance and efficiency through an exceptional combination of information, analytic, electronic trading, and Straight Through Processing tools, Bloomberg has built a worldwide customer base of corporations, issuers, financial intermediaries, and institutional investors.

BLOOMBERG NEWS®, founded in 1990, provides stories and columns on business, general news, politics, and sports to leading newspapers and magazines throughout the world. BLOOMBERG TELEVISION®, a 24-hour business and financial news network, is produced and distributed globally in seven languages. BLOOMBERG RADIO^{SM} is an international radio network anchored by flagship station BLOOMBERG® 1130 (WBBR-AM) in New York. BLOOMBERG.COM® delivers in-depth market information and news.

In addition to the BLOOMBERG PRESS® line of books, Bloomberg publishes *BLOOMBERG MARKETS*® magazine. To learn more about Bloomberg, call a sales representative at:

London: +44-20-7330-7500
New York: +1-212-318-2000
Tokyo: +81-3-3201-8900

About the Author

Richard Yamarone, senior vice president and director of economic research at Argus Research Corporation, has more than two decades of experience on Wall Street, analyzing and researching domestic and international economic trends, monitoring monetary and fiscal policy developments, and forecasting the U.S. macroeconomy. He has consulted monetary and fiscal policymakers, and he serves as an economic adviser to several major U.S. corporations. He has worked for international and domestic money center and investment banks in a variety of senior positions. In addition, he has taught numerous courses on macroeconomics and economic indicators at several colleges and institutions. He has served as president of the prestigious Downtown Economists Club of New York City and is a member of the National Association for Business Economists, the American Economic Association, the New York State Economics Association, and the Money Marketeers of New York University.

At Argus Research, Yamarone is a member of the Investment Policy Committee and is responsible for establishing the firm's top-down economic and interest-rate forecasts, as well as its estimates for monthly economic indicators. He makes frequent appearances on business television and radio shows, and is one of the most quoted economists on the Street today. In early 2007, *USA Today* highlighted Yamarone as one of the top ten economists in the nation.

Continuing Education Exam
for CFP Continuing Education Credit

Certified Financial Planners (CFPs) can earn ten hours of continuing-education credit by taking an exam based on the book *The Trader's Guide to Key Economic Indicators* on our website, http://www.bloomberg.com/ce. The material covered has been previewed by the CFP Board of Standards.